WAYSIDE SCHOOL
BENEATH THE CLOUD OF DOOM

LOUIS SACHAR
ILLUSTRATED BY TIM HEITZ

Wayside School Beneath the Cloud of Doom
Text copyright © 2020 by Louis Sachar
Illustrations copyright © 2020 by Tim Heitz
All rights reserved.

This English edition was published by Longtail Books in 2023 by arrangement with
Louis Sachar c/o Trident Media Group, LLC, New York through KCC(Korea Copyright
Center Inc.), Seoul.

ISBN 979-11-91343-04-5

Longtail Books

For Ruth

1. THE BELLS OF WAYSIDE

It is very important that the children at Wayside School know the bell system.

The first bell in the morning sounds like this: *WHOOP-WHOOP! WHOOP-WHOOP! WHOOP-WHOOP!*

When they hear it, they know they have sixteen minutes to get to class. That's not too difficult for those in Mr. Hardgroves's class on the third floor.

But Wayside School is a thirty-**story** building, with one room on each floor. So for those who happen to be in Mrs. Jewls's class, way up on the thirtieth floor, they must be ready on first *whoop*.

Todd was in Mrs. Jewls's class. He was **stuck** behind a mass of kids outside the building waiting for the doors to open. He jumped up and down, trying to see over the heads of those in front of him. If he was late, Mrs. Jewls would put his name on the **blackboard**, under the word DISCIPLINE.

The kids who went to class on the lower floors often **dillydallied**. If Todd got stuck behind a large group of dilly-dalliers, he'd have no chance.

Inside the **principal**'s office, Mr. Kidswatter sat behind his **enormous** desk as he watched the clock. At the moment the second hand[1] reached the number twelve, he **shriek**ed into his microphone. *"WHOOP-WHOOP! WHOOP-WHOOP! WHOOP-WHOOP!"*

The doors un**lock**ed, and the children **stamped**ed into the building and up the stairs. Todd tried his best to **weave** his way to the front, but there wasn't a lot of room.

🍎 🍎 🍎

Eight minutes later, Mr. Kidswatter **tug**ged on the rope hanging through the hole in the **ceiling**, and the second bell rang. *CLANG! CLANG! CLANG! CLANG! CLANG! CLANG! CLANG! CLANG!*

Todd **count**ed the clangs. Eight. That meant he now had

---

1 second hand 시계의 초침.

eight minutes to get to class. Seven or nine clangs would have meant something completely different. Seven meant a helicopter was **land**ing on the **roof**. Nine clangs meant a porcupine[2] had entered the building.

So far, he had only **made it** to the seventh floor, but he had finally managed to weave his way past all the dilly-dalliers. There was nothing to slow him down now.

When he reached the eighteenth floor, he heard this sound: *ching-a-ling, ching-a-ling, ching-a-ling.*

Nothing to worry about there. That just meant they were out of doughnuts in the teachers' **lounge**.

The **scary** bell was the late bell. It didn't matter where he was. It always sounded like an angry driver was **slam**ming on a car **horn**, right behind him. It made Todd jump every time.

He quickly **dash**ed from the eighteenth to the twentieth floor. There was no nineteenth floor.

His legs were **sore**, and he was breathing hard as he reached the top. Just ahead, he could see Joy entering the classroom.

"Don't shut the—" Todd shouted.

Joy shut the door behind her.

"Goozack,[3]" said Todd.

He was just opening it when the horn **blare**d, as if right

---

2 porcupine 호저. 고슴도치와 비슷한 동물로, 몸과 꼬리 윗면에 부드러운 털과 뻣뻣한 가시털이 빽빽이 나 있다.

3 goozack 3권에서 교장 선생님 Mr. Kidswatter가 문(door) 대신 사용 도록 만들어 낸 단어.

behind him.

"You're late, Todd," said Mrs. Jewls as he entered the classroom. "Write your—"

"I know," he said. He wrote his name on the blackboard, under the word DISCIPLINE.

Other bells rang throughout the day. At noon, the lunch bell kaboinked[4] three times. Three kaboinks meant macaroons[5] and cheese.

The bell for **recess** was just a single *ding*, but nobody ever missed it.

At the end of each day, Mr. Kidswatter would **bang** a **giant** gong[6] with a large **iron** mallet.[7] It was his favorite thing about being principal.

Todd sat at his desk, **glum**ly looking at the blackboard. The day had started off badly for him and had only gotten worse.

There was now a check **mark** next to his name, under the word DISCIPLINE.

Next to that, Mrs. Jewls kept adding new homework

---

4 **kaboink** 웨이사이드 스쿨(Wayside School)의 점심시간을 알리는 종소리로, 여기에서는 '점심시간 종이 울리다'라는 의미의 동사로 쓰였다. 이 종소리가 나는 횟수로 그날 제공되는 점심 메뉴를 알 수 있다.

5 **macaroon** 마카롱. 아몬드나 코코넛, 밀가루, 달걀 흰자위, 설탕 등을 넣어 만든 고급 과자.

6 **gong** 공. 청동이나 놋쇠로 만든 원반 모양의 타악기. 그것의 소리를 따서 지어진 이름으로, 우리나라에서는 징이라고 부른다.

7 **mallet** 나무로 만든 망치. 본문의 징처럼 쇠망치로 두드리면 깨지거나 우그러지기 쉬운 물건을 두드릴 때에 쓴다.

assignments.

> READ A BOOK. WRITE A BOOK REPORT. DRAW A PICTURE.
> (DON'T FORGET YOUR PAPER CLIP!!![8])
> HISTORY—READ PAGES 55-59 AND ANSWER QUESTIONS ON
> PAGES 61 AND 62.
> MATH WORKSHEET—DO EVEN- AND ODD-NUMBERED
> PROBLEMS.
> SCIENCE—READ PAGES 29-34, AND DO EXPERIMENT ON 37.

Todd had a sick feeling in his **stomach**, and it wasn't just the mac and cheese.[9] In big letters, across the top of the blackboard, Mrs. Jewls had written:

ULTIMATE TEST STARTS TOMORROW!

Mrs. Jewls had been **warn**ing the class about the Ultimate Test all year. The test would **last** for three days. If he failed, Todd would be sent back to **kindergarten**.

And then he heard it—the most magical bell of all!

Ping . . . PONG!

This bell had only rung once in the history of Wayside School, and nobody knew who rang it. But everyone knew what it meant.

---

8 clip 클립. 철사 조각으로 만든 문구의 한 종류로, 소량의 종이나 색인 카드를 철하는 데 사용하는 도구.

9 mac and cheese 맥앤드치즈. 마카로니 앤드 치즈(macaroni and cheese)를 줄인 말로, 글자 그대로 마카로니와 치즈를 버무린 짭짤한 맛의 음식이다. 미국에서 간식으로 인기가 많다.

All around, kids began cheering and **clap**ping their hands. Shouts of joy could be heard coming from every floor of Wayside School.

Todd just sat there, in **stun**ned **disbelief.**

It rang again.

Ping . . . PONG!

It was the **Erase**-the-Blackboard bell.

Mrs. Jewls had no choice. She picked up the eraser. Up and down Wayside School, teachers were doing the same thing.

Todd smiled as the homework assignments were **wiped** away. The Ultimate Test was canceled. His name was **removed** from the discipline list, and even the word DISCIPLINE soon disappeared.

Deep in the **basement**, a man with a black **mustache snap**ped open a black **attaché case**. Another man, also with a black mustache, placed a small silver ball into the case. A third man, who was **bald**, put in a **solid** gold Ping-Pong[10] paddle.[11]

---

10 **Ping-Pong** 핑퐁 또는 탁구. 직사각형의 나무로 만든 대(臺)의 가운데에 그물을 치고 라켓으로 플라스틱 공을 상대방 쪽으로 쳐 넘겨 승부를 겨루는 구기(球技) 경기.

11 **paddle** 라켓. 탁구 등의 종목에서 공을 칠 때 사용하는 장비로, 짧은 손잡이와 넓고 평평한 둥근 날로 이루어져 있다.

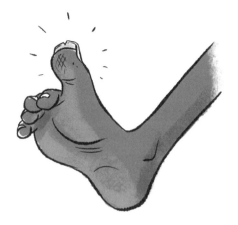

2. A MILLION

By the time Terrence got to school, he had already kicked ninety-nine different things.

It started the moment he woke up. He kicked his bed. He kicked Rocky, his favorite **stuff**ed animal. When he left his bedroom, he kicked the door shut.

He kicked the wall as he sat at the kitchen **counter** and ate cereal. He kicked a table. He kicked three chairs. He kicked rocks on the way to school. He kicked the **flagpole**.

Still, as much as Terrence liked to kick things, it would take him his whole life to kick a million things.

"How much is a million?" Mrs. Jewls asked her class.

"Ooh! Ooh! I know, I know!" said Mac, **stretch**ing his hand high.

Mrs. Jewls **called on** Mac.

"A million," Mac answered proudly.

"Well, yes, I suppose that's **correct**," said Mrs. Jewls. "A million is a million. Anyone else? John."

John lowered his hand. "Nine hundred and ninety-nine thousand, nine hundred and ninety-nine . . ." He **paused**, then added, "Plus one." He smiled.

"Ooh, that's good, John," said Dana, very **impress**ed.

"John's really smart," Joe agreed.

Terrence wasn't **paying attention**. His big toe hurt from all that kicking. His toe**nail** was too long.

Sharie, who had been sleeping at her desk, suddenly **awoke** and said, "Ten **times** ten, times ten, times ten, times ten, times ten." She **rest**ed her head on her red-and-blue **overcoat** and went back to sleep.

"Is that right, Mrs. Jewls?" asked Jason.

"Um . . ." said Mrs. Jewls as she tried to **multiply** all of Sharie's tens. "Well, if Sharie said it, it must be right!"

"**Arithmetic** makes my brain **numb**," said Dameon.

"That's why they're called 'numb-ers,'" said D.J.

Terrence's big toe **throb**bed in pain. He couldn't think about anything else.

"There's really one way to understand just how big a million is," said Mrs. Jewls. "And it's not by using arithmetic. We need to collect a million *somethings*."

"Dollars!" **exclaim**ed Joy.

Everyone cheered. They liked that idea.

"Then we could have the biggest party ever," said Deedee.

"We're not collecting a million dollars," said Mrs. Jewls. "Any other ideas?"

"**Pumpkin**s!" suggested Dana.

Everyone cheered Dana's idea too, but not as loudly as Joy's.

"I don't think a million pumpkins would **fit** in the school," said Mrs. Jewls. "We need something small, and not too expensive."

Stephen suggested, "Little pieces of paper."

Nobody cheered.

"Bo-ring," sang Kathy.

Stephen felt hurt, but deep down, he had to admit that collecting bits of paper wouldn't have been a whole lot of fun.

Ron suggested mud, but that too was **reject**ed. "It's a good idea, Ron," said Mrs. Jewls, "but you can't **count** mud."

"Why not?" he asked.

"There's no such thing as one mud, or two muds," explained Mrs. Jewls.

"Why not?" Ron asked again.

"I don't know," Mrs. Jewls had to admit.

Terrence couldn't **take it** any longer. He took off his shoe, then his sock.

One desk over, Rondi **stare**d at him, **horrified**.

Terrence's toenail was **bent out of shape**, and it had turned black and blue.

He opened his desk and took out his pair of safety **scissors**.[1] Then, crossing one leg over the other, he started **snip**ping.

"You can't cut your toenail in class," said Rondi. "It's against the rules."

"Who says?" said Terrence.

It was one tough toenail, and the scissors weren't all that sharp.

"Mrs. Jewls!" called Rondi. "Terrence is cutting his toenail, right in class!"

Some kids laughed. Some said, "**Gross!**"

Terrence pushed hard on the scissors. At last, a piece of his toenail fell free. His toe **instant**ly felt better.

"Terrence! Come up here now!" **demand**ed Mrs. Jewls. "And bring your toenail with you!"

Terrence picked up the **clipping** off the floor. One shoe off, one shoe on, he **hobble**d to the front of the room.

"Give me that!" Mrs. Jewls demanded.

---

1 **safety scissors** 안전 가위. 가윗날에 다치는 것을 막기 위해, 날을 플라스틱으로 만들거나 날 끝을 둥글게 처리한 가위.

14

Terrence dropped the nail clipping into his teacher's **outstretch**ed hand.

"You're a **genius**, Terrence," said Mrs. Jewls.

She held his nail clipping high in the air. "That's one!" she **announce**d. "Nine hundred and ninety-nine thousand, nine hundred and ninety-nine . . . to go!"

3. UP AND DOWN

"Up!" said D.J.

"Down!" replied Kathy, who sat next to him.

"Up!" D.J. repeated.

"Down!" Kathy **insist**ed.

In truth, Kathy didn't know what D.J. was talking about. She just liked to argue. No matter what D.J. said, she always said the **opposite**.

"Up!" D.J. said again.

"Down!" Kathy **instant**ly replied.

"Shh!" said Dana, who sat behind Kathy. "I'm trying to read."

Kathy turned around. Dana's face was **streak**ed with tears.

"Why are you crying?" asked Kathy.

Dana showed her the book she'd been reading. *The Lost Giraffe.*

"So?" asked Kathy.

"The giraffe is lost," Dana **sob**bed.

"Well, what did you expect, stupid?" asked Kathy.

She didn't like Dana any more than she liked D.J.

"Up!" said D.J.

"Down!" **snap**ped Kathy.

"Dana, Kathy, D.J.," said Mrs. Jewls. "You are making a lot of noise for silent reading."

"Sorry," said D.J. "I can't—up!—help it. I have the—up!—**hiccup**s."

Kathy turned red. She had been arguing with a hiccup.

"Has this ever happened before?" Mrs. Jewls asked him.

"I've had the—up!—hiccups before," said D.J., "but they—up!—always went—up!—away."

"**Stand on your head** and drink a glass of water," Myron suggested.

"Eat a lemon," said Jenny.

"Hold your **tongue** while you say the **Pledge of Allegiance**,[1]" said Joy.

---

1 Pledge of Allegiance 미국의 국기에 대한 맹세. 우리나라에서 하듯이 오른손을 왼쪽 가슴 위에 얹고, 애국심을 고취하는 내용의 정해진 구절을 암송한다.

D.J. tried their **suggestions**. When he finished, his mouth was **pucker**ed, his shirt was wet, and he still had the hiccups.

He felt very **patriotic**, however.

"I think you better go see Dr. Pickle," said Mrs. Jewls. "Kathy will take you."

Kathy **hop**ped out of her seat, glad she wouldn't have to read. "C'mon, **dummy**," she said, and led D.J. out the door.

"Up!" hiccuped D.J.

"Down!" said Kathy.

She couldn't help herself.

Dr. Pickle's real name was Dr. Pickell. His office was on the fourth floor. Kathy **knock**ed on the door.

Dr. Pickle opened it. He had a **pointy beard** and wore glasses. "Yes?" he said.

"Stupid here got the hiccups," said Kathy.

"Up!" hiccuped D.J.

"Down," said Kathy.

Dr. Pickle **rub**bed his **chin**. "Very interesting," he **mutter**ed, although he was looking at Kathy, not at D.J. "Very, very interesting."

He told Kathy to wait, and invited D.J. inside.

"And he smiles too much too!" Kathy called, just before the door shut.

D.J. sat down on a **couch**.

Dr. Pickle sat across from him. He held a long gold chain. On one end hung a green stone shaped like a pickle.[2]

Dr. Pickle gently **swung** the stone, **back and forth**. "Watch the pickle," he said. His voice was warm and **soothing**.

D.J.'s eyes moved back and forth with the stone.

"I will count to five. And then you will fall into a deep, deep sleep." Dr. Pickle slowly counted. "One . . . two . . . BOO!"

D.J. fell off the couch.

"Well?" asked Dr. Pickle.

D.J. got up. He waited a moment. "I think they're gone," he said.

Dr. Pickle led him to the door. "First thing we learned in **psychiatrist** school," he said, **pat**ting D.J. on the head.

"My hiccups are all gone!" D.J. told Kathy.

"Who cares," said Kathy.

"Wait," said Dr. Pickle. "Would you mind stepping inside my office, young lady?"

"Me?" asked Kathy.

"Please," said Dr. Pickle.

"But he's the sicko![3]" said Kathy, pointing at D.J.

---

2 pickle 피클. 오이와 양파 등의 채소를 식초, 설탕, 소금, 향신료를 섞어 만든 액체에 담아 절여서 만든 음식.

3 sicko 정신 질환이 있는 사람을 비하하듯 지칭하는 속어.

"Please," Dr. Pickle repeated.

Kathy **shrug**ged, then entered the **counselor**'s office. "That beard is really ugly," she said. "I guess your face must be even worse, huh?"

D.J. sat on the floor in the **hallway**, with his back against the wall, waiting for Kathy. He smiled, happy that his hiccups were gone. Although he missed them a little bit too. Hiccups are **annoy**ing, but kind of fun.

Some time later, the counselor's door opened.

"Thank you, Dr. Pickell," said Kathy, calling him by his **proper** name. "You are very **wise**. And I like your beard."

"That's very nice of you to say, Kathy," said the school counselor.

She stepped out the door. "Hi, D.J.," she **greet**ed him. "Thanks for waiting. You're a good friend."

The smile left D.J.'s face. Something was **definite**ly wrong with Kathy.

"Let's go up," said D.J.

"Yes, up," Kathy agreed.

Now he was really worried.

4. CONSIDER THE PAPER CLIP

Read a book. Write a book report. Draw a picture.

That was the **assign**ment Mrs. Jewls put up on the board.

Dana's picture showed a giraffe studying a map. She had drawn a large question **mark** over the giraffe's head.

Her book report only had to be one page, but she had written two whole pages. *The Lost Giraffe* was her favorite book ever!

Now all she needed was a paper clip.

She searched her desk.

She found quite a few pencils, mostly broken. There were lots of **eraser** bits and **crayon nubs**. There was also a **crumb**-

covered pink piece of paper that had come off the bottom of a cupcake.

"Oh no, oh no, oh no," she **moan**ed as she continued to search.

She raised her hand.

"Yes, Dana," said Mrs. Jewls.

"I need a new paper clip."

"But I gave you one at the beginning of the year," said Mrs. Jewls.

"I know, Mrs. Jewls. I'm sorry. I just can't find it!"

Mrs. Jewls **sigh**ed. "I'm very disappointed in you, Dana."

"I need a paper clip too," said Joe.

Mrs. Jewls **glare**d at him. "What did you do with the one I gave you?" she **demand**ed.

"I think I used it on my science homework," said Joe.

"I handed that back yesterday," Mrs. Jewls **remind**ed him. "Didn't you save the paper clip?"

"I guess not," Joe admitted.

Bebe was finishing up the last part of her picture. "Paper clip, please," she said, without looking up from her work.

"One for me too," said Calvin.

Mrs. Jewls **slam**med her hand on her desk. "Do you think paper clips grow on trees?" she asked.

"I don't know," said Calvin.

"I gave each one of you a paper clip at the beginning of the year. It was your **responsibility** to take care of it." She opened her desk **drawer**, took out her paper clip box, and opened it. "There are only six left," she said, shaking her head in **dismay**.

"Ooh, can I have one?" asked Joy. "I can't find mine."

Mrs. Jewls was too angry to reply. She moved to the front of the room. "You children are so **spoil**ed," she said. "Do you have any idea what it takes to make just one paper clip?"

She held up one of her last remaining paper clips. "Look at the perfect double **loop**. And the way it **gleam**s in the light, almost like a mirror."

Her anger seemed to **melt** away as she **marvel**ed at the **magnificent** metal **masterpiece**.

"It takes a lot of very **talent**ed people, and years of training and hard work," she explained. "First, there's the **wire** maker. Paper clip wire has to be just right, not too **stiff**, but not too **wiggly** either.

"Then there's the wire **polish**er," she continued. "That's who gives the paper clip its special gleam. And the wire cutter, who cuts each wire to the **precise** length.

"And finally, and most important, the master **bend**er. The bender carefully bends the wire into the perfect double loop." She put her hand over her heart. "Sadly, in these **rush**-rush, hurry-hurry days, not too many young people study the art of paper clip bending. There are only a **handful** of master benders left in the whole world. And who knows, in ten or twenty years there might not be any. Everyone will have to **switch** to staples.[1]"

"That is so sad," said Dana.

Mrs. Jewls gave the paper clip to Dana. "Now don't lose it!"

"I won't!" Dana promised.

"Let me see," said Bebe.

Dana proudly showed Bebe her new paper clip.

"It's so beautiful!" said Bebe, **admiring** the double loops. "I never **notice**d before."

"I'm going to be a paper clip bender when I grow up," said Calvin.

Mrs. Jewls smiled at Calvin. She had never been more proud of a student.

---

1 **staple** 서류 등을 철할 때 사용하는 도구인 스테이플러(stapler)에 사용되는 철사 침으로, 'ㄷ'자 모양으로 생겼다.

5. ERIC, ERIC,
AND *WHAT'S-HIS-NAME?*

Oh, that's right—Eric.

There are three Erics in Mrs. Jewls's class: Eric Fry, Eric Bacon, and the other one—who everyone always forgets—Eric Ovens.

Eric Fry is strong and fast. He is usually the first one chosen when picking teams.

Eric Bacon is funny, clever, and just a little bit **sneaky.** Everyone in Mrs. Jewls's class likes him, but no one completely trusts him.

Eric Ovens is kind, quiet, and 100 percent **trustworthy.**

Sadly, that kind of person is often **overlook**ed.

But not today, he thought as he sat at his desk, **patient**ly waiting for Mrs. Jewls to finish taking **attendance**. Today would be his day of **glory**!

In his pocket was a plastic bag[1] with eighty-three **nail clipping**s!

Two numbers had been written on the **blackboard**: 71 and 2,677.

So far, the class had collected a total of 2,677 nail clippings. Seventy-one were the most brought in by any one kid.

They didn't just have to be toenails. Fingernails counted too.

Eric Ovens took his bag out of his pocket and placed it on his desk.

"How many you got?" **whisper**ed Kathy, who sat next to him.

Eric didn't want to **jinx** his big day by saying the number aloud. **Besides**, he knew Kathy would only say something mean, or **mock** him.

Mrs. Jewls closed her attendance book. "Anyone have any nail clippings this morning?"

Eric Ovens raised his hand.

"Yes, Eric," said Mrs. Jewls.

---

1   plastic bag 비닐봉지.

Eric Ovens quietly pushed his chair back, but before he could get up, he saw Eric Fry already **making his way** to the front of the room.

"Forty!" Eric Fry **declare**d proudly.

Eric Fry had kept his hand in a **fist** all morning. Everyone thought he was just trying to be tough. Now he opened his fist and let forty nail clippings fall into the collection **bucket**.

"Well done, Eric!" said Mrs. Jewls.

Everyone **clap**ped their hands.

Eric Ovens smiled as he clapped his hands too. Eighty-three was more than double forty.

Eric Fry did the math on the board.

$$\begin{array}{r} 2677 \\ + \ 40 \\ \hline 2717 \end{array}$$

"**Halfway** to a **million**!" cheered Stephen.

"Not quite," Allison told him.

"Anyone else?" asked Mrs. Jewls.

Again Eric Ovens raised his hand, but Eric Bacon had already **hop**ped out of his seat and was headed toward the front of the room.

He handed Mrs. Jewls a plastic bag full of nail clippings. "Three hundred and forty-nine!" he declared **triumphant**ly.

The class **went wild**. Sharie **gasp**ed. Stephen fell out of his chair.

Eric Bacon danced around Mrs. Jewls's desk, like a football player who had scored a touchdown.[2]

Mrs. Jewls was **skeptical** of the **spectacle**. "I could count them," she **warn**ed.

Eric stopped dancing. "Go ahead," he **challenge**d her.

Mrs. Jewls **stare**d Eric Bacon in the eye. Eric Bacon stared right back.

Mrs. Jewls **dump**ed the bag on her desk, and **divide**d the clippings into four **pile**s. She asked Dameon, Allison, and John to help. They each took a pile, and then Mrs. Jewls added their totals together.

"Three hundred and forty-nine," she **announce**d, "just as Eric said."

Again, everyone cheered, and Eric Bacon continued his victory dance.

"How did you get so many?" Mrs. Jewls asked him.

Eric B. stopped dancing. "I went door-to-door, asking my neighbors," he said.

Everyone laughed.

Leslie had sold **wrap**ping paper door-to-door, but she couldn't imagine asking people for their toenails!

---

2 **touchdown** 터치다운. 럭비나 미식축구 등에서 공을 가지고 상대편의 골라인을 넘는 일 또는 거기서 얻은 득점.

"It's easier than asking for money," said Eric. "Everyone was happy to **donate**."

He **erased** the number 71 and put 349 in its place. Then he did the math.

$$2717$$
$$+ \, 349$$
$$3066$$

"Almost a million!" Stephen called out.

"Not even close," **muttered** Allison.

Mrs. Jewls told Eric Bacon to take a Tootsie Roll Pop[3] from her coffee can.

He took one. Then, when she wasn't looking, he took another.

"Anyone else?" asked Mrs. Jewls.

Eric Ovens sat **glum**ly at his desk.

"Raise your hand," **urge**d Kathy.

"Why **bother**?" he muttered.

Kathy got up from her seat and stood next to him. She **grab**bed Eric's arm and raised it for him. "Eric Ovens brought a whole lot!" she announced.

"Bring them on up," said Mrs. Jewls.

---

3   Tootsie Roll Pop 툿시 롤 팝. 초콜릿 캔디의 이름.

He had no choice. "It's just eighty-three," he said, and then emptied his bag into the nail bucket.

"That's the second most ever!" shouted Kathy. She started clapping.

Amazingly, everyone else clapped too.

They were still clapping as he did the math on the board.

$$3066$$
$$+\ 83$$
$$3149$$

"That's closer to a million!" **exclaim**ed Stephen.

Everyone cheered.

Even Allison couldn't argue with that.

6. OPPOSITOSIS[1]

Eric Ovens wasn't the only one who had **notice**d that Kathy had become nice. Others, too, began to notice her **odd** behavior.

"I like your picture," Kathy told Bebe.

"What's wrong with it?" Bebe asked.

"Nothing," said Kathy. "It's perfect. You are very **talent**ed."

It took Bebe a moment to realize that Kathy hadn't **insult**ed her.

Mrs. Jewls also noticed the change. "Kathy, will you come here, please?" she asked.

---

1 **oppositosis** 'opposite(반대)'라는 단어와 '-osis(병)'이라는 접미사를 더해 '반대로 말하는 병'이라는 의미로 쓰였다.

Kathy approached her teacher's desk. "Yes, Mrs. Jewls?" she asked.

Mrs. Jewls smiled. "You have been doing very well, Kathy," she said. "I've noticed a real **improve**ment in your work, *and* in your **attitude**."

"That must be because you're such a good teacher," said Kathy.

"Well, thank you," said Mrs. Jewls. "But there's a tiny little problem. I'm having a hard time reading your homework."

"What do you mean?"

"Look at it," said Mrs. Jewls, showing Kathy her most recent homework assignment.

"What's wrong with it?" asked Kathy.

ⓔ ⓔ ⓔ

"First thing we learned in **psychiatrist** school," Dr. Pickle said as he **pat**ted D.J. on the head.

"My **hiccup**s are all gone!" D.J. told Kathy.

"Who cares," Kathy grumpled.[2]

"Would you mind stepping inside my office, young lady?" asked Dr. Pickle.

"But he's the sicko!" said Kathy, pointing at D.J.

"Please," said Dr. Pickle.

---

2 **grumple** '심술궂게 투덜거리다'라는 의미로 'grumpy(성격이 나쁜)'와 'grumble(투덜거리다)'을 합쳐 만들어 낸 말.

She entered the **counselor**'s office. "That **beard** is really ugly. I guess your face must be even worse, huh?"

Dr. Pickle didn't get angry. He just **stroke**d his beard and said, "Very interesting."

Kathy **sniff**ed. "Smells like pickles," she **comment**ed.

"Very interesting, indeed," the counselor said, and then asked her to sit down.

Kathy sat on the **couch**. "**Lumpy**," she **complain**ed.

"I'm going to try a little **experiment**," said Dr. Pickle. "I'm going to say a word, and then I want you to say the first word that **pop**s into your head."

"Stupid!" said Kathy.

"I haven't started yet," said Dr. Pickle.

"**Sloppy**!" said Kathy.

Dr. Pickle realized he had better hurry up and get started. "Cold," he began.

"Hot," Kathy replied.

"Hard."

"Soft."

"**Skinny**."

"Fat."

"This is kind of fun, isn't it, Kathy?" asked Dr. Pickle.

"No, it's **boring**," said Kathy.

"Worse than I thought," said Dr. Pickle. "I studied your condition in psychiatrist school. "I'm afraid you have a bad case of oppositosis."

"No, I don't. You do!"

Dr. Pickle stroked his beard.

Unfortunately, there was no known **cure** for oppositosis. Other psychiatrists had tried to help their **patients** learn to be kind and think **positively**.

Dr. Pickle knew that would never work on Kathy. He had his own **theory**, however. He could try to turn her opposites into double opposites.

He opened his desk **drawer** and took out his pickle-stone and chain.

Kathy watched the green stone as it gently **swung back and forth**. She fell asleep on the **count** of five.

"Can you hear me, Kathy?" he asked.

"And I can smell you too," she replied.

"You are looking into a mirror," he told her.

"I'm looking into a mirror," Kathy repeated, eyes closed.

"Tell me what you see."

"I see a beautiful girl with black hair," she said. "And I see a funny-looking man with a **pointy** beard."

"Very good," said Dr. Pickle. "Now I want you to **reach out** and touch the mirror."

Kathy slowly moved her arm.

"But as you try to touch it," said Dr. Pickle, "you'll discover the mirror isn't **solid**. Your hand will go right through it."

Kathy **stuck** her hand **out** farther. "That's **weird**," she said.

"Now stand up, and walk through the mirror."

Kathy stood up. She took one step, then another. She **hesitate**d for a moment, and then took one last step.

"**Amazing**!" she exclaimed.

"You are on the other side of the mirror," said Dr. Pickle. "What do you see?"

Kathy looked around. "Nice office," she said. She sniffed. "Smells nice too."

"I'm glad you like it," said Dr. Pickle. "Would you like to sit on the couch?"

Kathy sat back down. "Very comfortable," she **note**d.

"When I count to three, you will wake up. But you will still be on the other side of the mirror. One . . . two . . . three."

Kathy opened her eyes.

"How do you feel?" he asked her.

"Fine, thanks," said Kathy. "How are you?"

"Very well, thank you," said Dr. Pickle. "Do you mind if we continue with our little experiment?"

"Sounds like fun," said Kathy.

"Happy," said Dr. Pickle.

"Smile," said Kathy.

"Smart," said Dr. Pickle.

"Mrs. Jewls," said Kathy.

"Friend," said Dr. Pickle.

"D.J.," said Kathy.

Dr. Pickle led her to the door.

"Thank you, Dr. Pickell," she said, shaking his hand. "You are very **wise**. And I like your beard."

☙ ☙ ☙

"What's wrong with my homework?" asked Kathy.

"It's written backward!" said Mrs. Jewls. "Every sentence. Every word. Every letter. Even the numbers are backward."

"Looks normal to me," said Kathy. "Do you want me to do it over?"

Mrs. Jewls **sigh**ed. "No, that's all right, Kathy. I'm just happy to see you doing so well. I'll **figure** it **out**."

Kathy smiled, and then returned to her seat.

7. THE CLOSET
THAT WASN'T THERE

Mac was a **curious** kid.

When Miss Mush **served** chicken fingers,[1] he asked her how many fingers a chicken had on each hand.

After lunch, he played basketball. **Besides** playing, he was also the self-**appoint**ed announcer,[2] **describing** every shot,[3] every

---

1 **chicken fingers** 치킨 핑거. 닭의 안심이나 가슴살을 손가락 크기로 길게 자른 뒤 반죽을 입혀 튀겨 낸 음식.

2 **announcer** 아나운서. 뉴스 보도, 사회, 실황 중계의 방송을 맡아 하는 사람.

3 **shot** 숏. 축구나 농구 등의 구기 경기에서, 골대나 바스켓 쪽을 향하여 공을 차거나 던지는 일.

pass,[4] and every dribble.[5]

Jenny finally told him to put a sock in it.[6]

Only then, when he stopped talking, did Mac remember that he'd left his catcher's[7] mask in the **cafeteria**. Mac liked to wear his catcher's mask for all sports, **including** basketball.

He was a curious kid.

The cafeteria was on the fifteenth floor. Mac found his mask right where he'd left it, but by then, it **hardly** seemed **worth** it to go **all the way** back down to the **playground**. So he continued on up to the thirtieth **story**.

And there, just outside his classroom door, was the most curious thing that Mac had ever seen. Next to the wall was some sort of **giant** closet. It hadn't been there before lunch.

But that wasn't what made it curious. The closet was **wrap**ped up in heavy chains, and **lock**ed with a giant padlock.[8]

Mac moved closer. Behind the chains, he could see double doors, with a **steel** bar **clamp**ed across them. Several **sign**s were taped to the doors.

"KEEP BACK!"

---

4 **pass** 패스. 구기 종목에서 같은 편끼리 서로 공을 주거나 받는 일.

5 **dribble** 드리블. 구기 종목에서 발이나 손 등을 이용하여 공을 몰아가는 일.

6 **put a sock in it** 시끄러워서 방해가 되는 상대에게 사용하는 구어적인 표현으로 '조용히 해라', '입 좀 다물어라'라는 뜻이다.

7 **catcher** 포수. 야구에서 본루를 지키며 투수가 던지는 공을 받는 선수로, 날아오는 공으로부터 몸을 보호하기 위해 철망이 달린 마스크와 같은 보호구를 항상 착용한다.

8 **padlock** 맹꽁이자물쇠. 반타원형의 고리와 몸통 부분으로 이루어져 있으며, 열쇠로 열면 고리의 한쪽 다리가 몸통에서 떨어져 나오게 되어 있는 자물쇠.

"DO NOT OPEN DOORS!"

"DANGER!"

"CALL THE **FIRE DEPARTMENT** IF YOU SMELL SOMETHING UNUSUAL!"

Mac **sniff**ed, but all he could smell were chicken fingers.

Behind the chains, and the steel bar, each door had its own lock. He could see two keyholes, one red and the other green.

He put on his catcher's mask, just to be safe, and tried to open one door, then the other. They wouldn't **budge**.

He tried to **peer** through the keyholes, but they were too tiny.

He **knock**ed on one of the doors. It seemed to be made of thick wood. "Anyone in there?" he called.

There was no answer. He knocked again, and then **press**ed his ear against the side of the closet.

Still nothing.

"What's that?" asked Deedee, coming up the stairs.

Mac **shrug**ged.

Deedee read the signs aloud. "Keep back. Do not open doors. Danger."

She tried one of the doors.

"I think it's locked," said Mac.

More kids **made it** up the stairs. Each one stopped at the closet, read the signs, and then tried to open the doors.

Terrence kicked the doors.

Jason **rattle**d the chains. "Look, it's one long chain," he **determine**d, "wrapped around four times."

"What do you think is inside?" asked Leslie.

"Snakes," said Paul. He was afraid of snakes.

"Spiders," said Rondi. She was afraid of spiders.

"Monsters," said Allison.

She loved monsters.

"What if it's Mrs. Gorf?" guessed Calvin.

Everyone **shudder**ed.

Mrs. Gorf was the worst teacher they'd ever had.

"Give me a **boost**," said Mac.

Jenny **cup**ped her hands, and Mac stepped up, first onto Jenny's hands, then onto the steel bar. He **grip**ped the top edge of the closet and tried to **shimmy** up.

"**Get away** from there!" shouted Mrs. Jewls. "All of you!"

She had returned from the teachers' **lounge** only to see the children hanging all over the closet, like monkeys.

"Mac, get down, now!"

Mac tried to **hop** down, but his foot got **tangle**d in the chains, and he fell onto his back.

"Ooh, I think I broke my tailbone,⁹" he **complain**ed.

"You're lucky that's all you broke!" said Mrs. Jewls.

"What's inside?" asked Terrence.

---

9 tailbone 꼬리뼈. 척추의 가장 아랫부분에 있는 작고 뾰족한 뼈.

"Never you mind!" said Mrs. Jewls. "Don't you children know the meaning of DANGER? You are not to go anywhere near my closet! Don't look at it. Don't even think about it. It's not there!"

"But I can see it," said Mac, still lying on the floor.

"It's Not There!" Mrs. Jewls insisted.

"But—"

"No Ifs, Ands, or Buts![10]" said Mrs. Jewls.

Everyone shuffled inside the classroom.

Mac was still on the floor. He stood up and adjusted his catcher's mask, which had become cockeyed when he fell. He took one last look at the closet that wasn't there, then walked into the classroom, more curious than ever.

---

10 no ifs, ands, buts '토 달지 마라', '잔말 마라'라는 의미로, 자신의 말에 대한 어떠한 가정이나 부가 설명 혹은 반대 의견을 허용하지 않을 때 쓰는 표현.

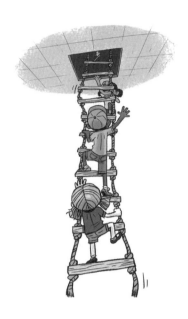

8. SCIENCE

Twenty-nine hands were raised.

There were only twenty-eight kids in Mrs. Jewls's class, but Joy **stretch**ed both her arms high in the air. She **figure**d it **double**d her chances of being chosen. She **wave**d them back and forth, and around in circles.

"Pick me, pick me!" **beg**ged Bebe.

"Pick me, Mrs. Jewls," **urge**d Calvin, sitting next to Bebe.

"Sorry, Calvin, you're too heavy," Mrs. Jewls told him. "And your toes are too tiny, Bebe."

Todd sat behind Joy but Mrs. Jewls couldn't see him behind Joy's helicopter arms.

"Okay, Joy!" said Mrs. Jewls.

Everyone else **groan**ed.

Joy was all smiles. "You lose, losers!" she said as she headed toward the door.

This week, for science, they would be studying clouds. Luckily, Mrs. Jewls's class was on the thirtieth floor. It was the classroom closest to the sky.

Last week, they studied **dirt**. That wasn't so lucky. By the time they made it down to the ground, science was over, and they had to turn around and **trudge** back up.

Everyone brought their science notebooks and **gather**ed just outside the door, by the **closet** that wasn't there.

Mrs. Jewls put her hands around Joy's **waist**. "Alley-oopsy!¹" she called out, and lifted Joy straight up.

Joy **giggle**d.

This was why Mrs. Jewls hadn't chosen Calvin. He was too heavy for her to lift.

Mrs. Jewls set Joy on top of the closet. Just above her, a **trapdoor** led to the **roof**. Joy stood on her **tiptoe**s and pushed it open. This was why Mrs. Jewls hadn't chosen Bebe. Her toes weren't long enough.

A rope **ladder tumble**d down.

One by one, the children climbed the rope ladder to the roof.

---

1 alley-oopsy 영차. 무거운 물건을 들어 올리거나 몸을 힘겹게 일으킬 때 내는 소리.

"Be sure to stay away from the edge," Mrs. Jewls called up to them.

There was a safety **railing** around the edge, but it was for taller people. Mrs. Jewls was afraid her students could **slip** right under it.

She was the last one up through the trapdoor. When she reached the roof, she saw everyone standing at the edge.

"What did I just say?" she **demand**ed.

Everyone stared **blank**ly at her.

"Alley-oopsy?" asked Dameon.

"Well, at least somebody was **paying attention**," said Mrs. Jewls. She told everyone to take two steps back, and to sit on their bottoms.

"But then we'll be farther away from the clouds," Mac complained.

"Sometimes, safety is more important," said Mrs. Jewls.

She pointed out the clouds to her class. "That one there is a cumulus cloud.²"

Some of the students wrote it down in their notebooks. Bebe drew a picture of a sleeping **giant**. The cumulus cloud was his **pillow**.

"And that's a cirrus cloud³ over there," said Mrs. Jewls.

---

2 cumulus cloud 뭉게구름 또는 적운. 수직으로 발달한 구름으로, 밑은 평평하고 꼭대기는 솜을 쌓아 놓은 것처럼 뭉실뭉실한 모양이며 햇빛을 받으면 하얗게 빛난다.

3 cirrus cloud 새털구름 또는 권운. 푸른 하늘에 높이 떠 있는 하얀 섬유 모양의 구름. 미세한 얼음 결정으로 이루어져 있으며 해나 달 주위에서 무리로 나타나기도 한다.

Bebe drew a picture of flying angels. Hundreds of white feathers had fallen from their wings and had **swirl**ed into a cloud.

Bebe could draw really fast.

"What kind of cloud is that one, Mrs. Jewls?" asked Benjamin.

He was pointing at a **dull**, dark cloud way off in the **distance**.

Mrs. Jewls **gasp**ed.

If Bebe were to draw it, her picture would look **exact**ly like the inside of a **vacuum** cleaner bag, while the vacuum was still on.

But Bebe had never seen the inside of a vacuum cleaner bag while the vacuum was still on. So she couldn't draw it.

"Everyone back to the classroom!" Mrs. Jewls shouted. "Double quick!"

The children **scrambl**ed to the trapdoor.

"Hurry!" ordered Mrs. Jewls.

Some fell right through. Others got rope burns.[4]

Mrs. Jewls didn't worry about little things like that.

She was the last one through the **hatch**. Sitting **atop** the closet that wasn't there, she **toss**ed the ladder back on the roof and locked the trapdoor.

---

4 rope burn 밧줄을 타고 너무 빠르게 내려오다 그 마찰열로 손에 입게 되는 화상.

She climbed down, stepping onto the chains and **steel** bar.

The children were waiting quietly inside the classroom, hands folded on their desks.

Mrs. Jewls walked to the side of the room and looked out the window. Either the cloud was moving closer, or it was getting bigger.

Or both.

"What kind of cloud is it, Mrs. Jewls?" asked Leslie.

There are times when adults hide the truth from children, so as not to worry them. But Mrs. Jewls was a teacher. And this was science.

"Take a good look, boys and girls," she said, pointing out the window. Then, with a **slight tremble** in her voice, she said, "That is a Cloud of **Doom**."

The room **darken**ed.

9. THE GONNNNNG

Louis, the **yard** teacher, was filling a green ball with air when the Cloud of **Doom cast** its **gloomy** shadow over the schoolyard. He felt an **eerie chill** as he pushed down on his air pump.

Suddenly there was a loud *BANG*, and the next thing Louis knew, he was lying on the **blacktop**.

He slowly sat up. He **wiggle**d his fingers. He **stuck out** his **tongue** and moved it from side to side. He seemed to be okay. He stood up, still a little **wobbly**.

Bits of green **rubber** were **scatter**ed across the **playground**. His air pump was on the other side of the dodgeball[1] circle.

The ball must have **explode**d from too much air, he realized.

He always tried to put the maximum amount of air into each ball. The kids liked them **bouncy**. The bouncier the better.

He picked up a piece of green rubber. Then another. And another.

There already weren't enough balls to go around. The school couldn't **afford** to lose another one. He'd have to **sew** it back together.

In the end he found seventy-three pieces. It was unusually dark for this time of day. He hoped he hadn't missed any.

"The gong!" he remembered. He hurried to the **principal**'s office, **stuff**ing **cotton** balls into his ears as he ran.

"You're late, Louis," said Mr. Kidswatter, but Louis couldn't hear him.

He **wheel**ed the giant gong out of the office to the bottom of the stairs.

At one time, the gong had been bright and shiny, but that was before Louis's time. Now it was **dull** and heavily **dent**ed. A large mallet, also made of **iron**, hung from a **hook** bolted[2] to

---

1 dodgeball 도지볼. 흔히 '피구'로 많이 알려져 있으며, 일정한 구획 안에서 두 팀으로 갈라져 공격 팀이 수비 팀 선수에게 공을 던져 맞히는 운동 경기.
2 bolt 볼트. 두 물체를 고정하는 데 사용하는 육각형 또는 사각형 모양의 머리를 가진 나사. 여기서는 '볼트로 고정하다'라는 뜻의 동사로 쓰였다.

the gong's wood **frame**.

Louis unhooked it, and then took a couple of steps backward to **steady** himself. The mallet was heavy, even for someone as strong as the yard teacher.

He handed it to Mr. Kidswatter, who easily raised it over his shoulder. Mr. Kidswatter had thick arms, a thick neck, and a thick head.

Louis started the **countdown**. "Ten . . . nine . . . eight . . ."

There was a red **dot** in the center of the gong. On the count of "One!" Mr. Kidswatter swung the mallet and hit it **dead** center.

GONNNNN-nnnnn-NNNNN-nnnnn-NNNNN-nnnnn-NNNNN . . .

Despite the cotton balls, the sound **rattle**d inside Louis's head, and **echo**ed up and down the stairs.

. . . nnnnn-NNNNN-nnnnn-NNNNN-nnnnn . . .

Louis took the mallet from Mr. Kidswatter and hung it back on its hook. He wheeled the gong off to the side, just before a river of children **flood**ed down the stairs.

"Hi, Louis!" "Bye, Louis! "See you tomorrow, Louis!" they called to him as they ran by.

He smiled and **wave**d, but all he heard was "Gonnnnnng!"

"Why don't they ever say those things to me?" Mr. Kidswatter asked a little while later, as they were leaving the school together.

"Maybe if you did something nice?" Louis suggested.

"Like what?" asked the principal.

"Maybe let a kid ring the gong?"

"**No way**," **snap**ped Mr. Kidswatter. "That's the best part about being principal."

"Or how about getting some more balls for **recess**?" Louis suggested.

"Too expensive," said Mr. Kidswatter.

"What if I pay for them?" asked Louis.

Mr. Kidswatter laughed. "You? Where would you get that kind of money? Did you **rob** a bank?"

"I have money," said Louis. "I've written some books about Wayside School."

"And you got paid for that?" Mr. Kidswatter asked.

Louis shrugged.

Mr. Kidswatter **frown**ed.

Louis hoped he hadn't broken a law.

"Do you mention me in the books?" asked Mr. Kidswatter.

"Maybe once or twice," Louis admitted.

"You don't say anything bad about me, do you?"

"Ummm . . ." said Louis.

"You should write a chapter about me!" **declare**d Mr. Kidswatter. "Call it 'The Best Principal Ever!!!' with three **exclamation** points."

"First, you would have to do something that makes you the

best principal ever," Louis explained.

"Like what?"

"Let a kid ring the gong."

This time, Mr. Kidswatter didn't snap at Louis. He was thinking about it.

Louis looked up at the gloomy cloud. He hadn't paid much attention to science, back when he was going to school. He didn't know it was a Cloud of Doom.

Had he known, he never would have made such a dangerous **suggestion** to Mr. Kidswatter.

10. STUCK

Everybody has a special **talent**. Bebe can draw. Joe can **stand on his head** and sing "**Jingle Bells.**[1]"

But this story isn't about Bebe or Joe. It's about Dana.

Dana can make funny faces.

Just by **puff**ing **out** one **cheek** and raising the **opposite eyebrow**, she can make Jenny and Leslie **crack up** every time.

Or there's the one she calls her **goofball** face. She puts her glasses on **upside down**. Then she pulls down one corner of her mouth with her **pinky** finger, while with her other hand, she

---

1 Jingle Bells 징글 벨. 세계적으로 가장 널리 알려진 크리스마스 캐럴의 하나로, 눈썰매가
   질주하며 울려 퍼지는 경쾌한 종소리에 대한 묘사가 가사의 주된 내용이다.

tugs her **earlobe**.

When Dameon and Myron saw that one, they laughed so hard they **bump**ed heads.

Even Mrs. Jewls laughs at Dana's funny faces. "But you need to be careful, Dana," she **warn**ed. "You don't want your face to get stuck that way."

Dana wasn't worried about that. No matter how **weird**ly she stretched it, her face always **bounce**d **back**.

But that was before the Cloud of Doom **settle**d over the school. It had been there a week now, even as other clouds **drift**ed past. Each day, it seemed to grow a little bit larger.

Dana and Leslie were on the playground, waiting for Jenny. It was recess, and Jenny went to get "**Patch**es" from Louis.

"Patches" was the ball that Louis had **blow**n **up**, in more ways than one.

Louis never found all the pieces, and had to cut up an old yellow **raincoat** to fill in the **gap**s. Jenny, Leslie, and Dana liked Patches the best, because it was impossible to **predict** which way it would **bounce**.

"Hey, Dana, there's a giant **worm** on your foot!" said John.

Dana looked down at her **sneaker**.

"Made you look!" John exclaimed. He and Joe laughed.

"So she looked at her foot?" asked Leslie. "What's wrong with that?"

"There wasn't even a worm!" explained Joe.

Dana felt like a big **doofus**. Why did she always **fall for** John's **trick**s?

She made her Doofus Face.

She closed her right eye, raised her left eyebrow, puffed out her right cheek, and stuck out her tongue.

When John looked at it, he suddenly felt like a big doofus. "Sorry," he **mutter**ed. "It was just a **dumb** joke."

He **hung his head** and walked away. Joe followed.

Dana felt sad for John. She hadn't meant to call him a doofus. She had just wanted to make him laugh. She liked it when John **tease**d her.

Jenny returned with Patches.

"You missed it!" said Leslie. "Dana **got back at** John good!"

Jenny turned to Dana. "Why are you calling me a doofus?" she asked.

Dana didn't realize she was still wearing her Doofus Face. She tried to pull her tongue back in but it wouldn't **budge**. Her cheek wouldn't unpuff. Her right eye remained shut, and her left eyebrow stayed up.

"That's not nice," said Jenny.

"Uhhhhh . . ." said Dana.

"Oh my gosh!²" exclaimed Leslie. "Is your face stuck?"

---

2 **oh my gosh** (= oh my god) '맙소사!', '세상에!'라는 뜻으로 놀람이나 기쁨을 나타내는 감탄사.

Dana **nod**ded. Her Doofus Face moved up and down.

"So you're not doing it **on purpose**?" asked Jenny.

Her Doofus Face turned right, then left.

"It's the Cloud of Doom!" exclaimed Jenny.

Leslie covered her mouth with her hand.

The three girls looked up at the dark and **swirl**ing cloud.

"I'll get Louis," Leslie said, and hurried away.

She returned with the **yard** teacher a short while later.

Louis laughed when he saw Dana.

"It's her Doofus Face," said Jenny.

"It's a good one," said Louis. "I think I like it even better than your Goofball Face."

"But now her face is stuck that way!" said Leslie.

Louis thought a moment, and then **blew** his **whistle** real loud. Jenny and Leslie covered their ears.

Dana's face remained stuck.

Louis didn't really expect it to work. He just liked blowing his whistle.

Kids from all over the playground came running at the sound of it.

"What's up, Louis?" asked Todd.

"Dana's face is stuck," Jenny explained.

"Really?" asked Todd. He **poke**d Dana's puffed-out cheek. It was like poking a rock.

Mr. Kidswatter also heard the whistle. "Out of my way, let me through," he ordered as he **made his way** to Louis and Dana. "What's going on here?" he demanded.

He looked at Dana.

Dana looked back at Mr. Kidswatter.

Their eyes **lock**ed.

It became a **staring** contest.[3] Everyone wondered who would **blink** first.

But Dana couldn't blink.

Finally, Mr. Kidswatter turned away. "Cute kid," he said, and **pat**ted Dana on the head. He headed back to the building.

Dana's face **instant**ly **pop**ped back into place.

"Your face is fixed!" exclaimed Jenny.

Dana smiled, but then she made her face return to just **plain** normal. She didn't want her smile to get stuck. Even that could be un**pleasant**. As long as they were under the Cloud of Doom, she would have to be very careful with her facial **expression**s.

Mr. Kidswatter walked quickly back to his office. He shut the door behind him.

He was sticking out his tongue. His left eye was shut tight, his right eyebrow was raised, and his left cheek was all puffed out.

---

3 staring contest 눈싸움. 서로 눈을 마주하여 깜박이지 않고 오래 견디기를 겨루는 일.

11. WHAT'S THE POINT?

In some classrooms, teachers choose the weekly **spell**ing words. Not so in Mrs. Jewls's class. She lets her students pick.

Nearly everyone had a hand raised. Mrs. Jewls **call**ed **on** Rondi.

"Pistachios,[1]" said Rondi.

This is why other teachers don't let their students choose the words. Mrs. Jewls couldn't spell *pistachios*.

So she did what every teacher everywhere does in such situations. "That's an excellent word, Rondi," she said. "Would

---

1 pistachio 피스타치오. 견과류의 한 종류로 그린아몬드라고도 하며, 아몬드와 비슷한 풍미를 가지고 있다. 열매는 녹색으로 타원형이고 과자와 아이스크림 등을 만드는 데 사용한다.

you like to come up and write it on the board?"

Rondi came to the front of the room. Mrs. Jewls **paid** close **attention** as Rondi wrote *pistachios* on the **blackboard**.

"I love pistachios," said Kathy when Rondi returned to her seat.

"Me too," said Allison. "They're my third-favorite nut."

Mrs. Jewls called on D.J.

"Grumple," he said.

"I don't think 'grumple' is a word," Mrs. Jewls **pointed out**.

"So?" asked D.J. "We should still know how to spell it."

"It might become a word someday," Kathy agreed.

Mrs. Jewls wrote *grumple* under *pistachios*.

Joy raised her hand. "A," she suggested.

"*A what?*" asked Mrs. Jewls.

"Just a," said Joy.

"Don't you think that's a little too easy?" said Mrs. Jewls.

"It's a very common word," said Kathy. "It's important that we all know how to spell it."

Mrs. Jewls couldn't argue with that. She added *a* to the list.

Myron had his hand raised.

"Yes, Myron," said Mrs. Jewls.

"What's the point?" Myron asked.

"That's three words," said Mrs. Jewls.

"And all good ones too," **chirp**ed Kathy.

"The Cloud of Doom is getting bigger every day!" Myron

exclaimed. "What does it matter if we can spell?"

"So we can read and write," Mrs. Jewls replied.

"What's the point of reading?" asked Leslie.

"What's the point of writing?" asked Jason.

"What's the point of **arithmetic**?" asked Benjamin.

"There is no point!" Myron grumpled. He **slam**med his pencil down hard on his desk. The point broke off of it.

"I understand you're **scare**d and upset," said Mrs. Jewls. "But *what's the point* of quitting? We can all just sit around and grumple, or we can try to do our best, cloud or no cloud.

"And it hasn't been all bad," Mrs. Jewls continued. "We've been getting a whole lot more **nail clipping**s."

That was true. Ever since the Cloud of Doom appeared, everyone's fingernails and toenails had been growing a lot faster. They had to be **clip**ped three or four times a week.

The number on the board was now 19,457.

"Someday, the Cloud of Doom will be gone," said Mrs. Jewls. "And the world will be a much better place, even better than before the cloud. Colors will be more colorful. Music will be more musical. Even Miss Mush's food will taste good. The bigger the **storm**, the brighter the rainbow."

At that moment, a **crack** of **thunder** shook the classroom, and then the lights went out.

The children screamed. They weren't scared. They just liked screaming in the dark.

Mrs. Jewls **lit** a candle, and everyone **settled down**. "Now, shall we continue with our spelling?"

Jenny raised her hand and suggested, "Hope."

"Excellent word," said Mrs. Jewls.

She held her candle in one hand, and the **chalk** in the other. She said the letters out loud as she wrote them on the blackboard.

"H-o-p-e."

12. MRS. SURLAW

The library was on the seventh floor. Mrs. Surlaw was the **librarian**.

A **giant** stuffed walrus[1] sat next to her desk. The walrus was bigger than most of the kids in the school, and a couple of the teachers too.

Kindergarteners often got **scare**d the first time they saw Mrs. Surlaw's walrus. When they **dare**d touch one of its giant **tusk**s, however, they discovered it was soft as a **pillow**.

---

1 **walrus** 바다코끼리. 코끼리의 상아와 비슷한 송곳니 한 쌍을 가지고 있으며, 바다에서 생활하는 포유류. 두껍고 주름이 많은 피부를 가졌으며 지느러미 모양의 네 다리로 걸을 수 있다.

There were lots of rules in the library. No eating, no drinking, no **yell**ing, no **somersault**s, and no hugging the walrus until after you **check**ed **out** a book.

Mrs. Surlaw **wheel**ed her book cart along a **row** of bookcases. She picked up a book, turned to the last page, and then put it on the shelf where it **belong**ed. She took another book, checked its last page, and put that one in its **proper** place as well.

She heard the **rumble** of feet on the stairs, and the **chirp**s and **shriek**s of young voices. This was followed by **shush**ing sounds.

Mrs. Jewls's class **polite**ly entered the library. They were scared of Mrs. Surlaw.

While the two adults **greet**ed each other, the children **scurried** to different parts of the library. They had only fifteen minutes to choose and check out a book.

"Have you read *The Pig, the Princess, and the Potato*?" Leslie asked Jenny.

"Is it good?"

"Only the best book ever!"

Mrs. Surlaw smiled when she heard that. The only thing she loved more than books were children who loved books. She may have seemed **severe** on the outside, but inside, her heart was soft as a pillow.

Some libraries have **separate** areas for fiction[2] and nonfiction.[3] Mrs. Surlaw didn't believe in that sort of thing. After all, who was she to decide what was true and what wasn't?

She also didn't believe in **alphabetical order**.

Her books were organized by number of pages. **Skinny** books were at one end of the library, and the fat ones were at the opposite end.

Along the shelves were number **mark**ers: 10, 20, 30 . . . **all the way** to 1,000. If someone in Mrs. Jewls's class wanted to read this book, he or she could find it between the 180 and 190 markers.

Joy was looking through the books between the 40 and 50 markers. She had already read every book in the library with fewer than forty pages.

Allison liked long novels. She was looking through the ones that were between 230 and 240 pages.

Jason stood behind her, watching.

At last, Allison chose her book. It had 232 pages.

Jason took the one next to it, with 233 pages.

Allison **scowl**ed at him. She put her book back, and then chose one farther down the shelf, with 238 pages.

Jason put his book back too. He took one with 239 pages.

Allison **pretend**ed not to **notice**, even though she was burning inside. She looked at her book. "I think I already read this," she said aloud. She returned it to the shelf. "La-di-da," she said. "What book do I want to read?"

---

2 fiction 픽션 또는 소설. 실제로는 없는 사건을 작가의 상상력으로 재창조해 낸 이야기.

3 nonfiction 논픽션 또는 비소설. 상상으로 꾸민 이야기가 아닌 사실에 근거하여 쓴 작품으로 수기, 자서전, 기행문 등이 여기에 속한다.

Suddenly she **dash**ed to the end of the **aisle**, and around a corner.

Jason had trouble **squeezing** his book back into place. By the time he did, he couldn't see Allison anywhere.

He went from one end of the library to the other, searching between the aisles. When he finally saw her, she was hugging the walrus. That meant she had already checked out her book.

He went to her. "Hey, Allison," he said. "Can I see your book?"

"No," she replied.

"How many pages?" he asked.

"I'm not telling you."

"More than three hundred?"

"Maybe."

"**No way**," he said. "Even you wouldn't read a book with more than three hundred pages."

Allison **shrug**ged.

"More than three hundred and fifty?" he asked.

"Maybe."

"Five hundred?"

"Maybe."

"Just tell me the title."

"No!"

"I'm just trying to help you," he explained. "Maybe I've already read it. I could tell you if it's any good. You don't want to read a five-hundred-page book if it's **boring**, or has a **bunch** of kissing in it."

Rondi finished checking out her book, and then hugged the walrus too.

"Let's go, Rondi," said Allison.

Jason watched the two girls leave the library.

He went to Mrs. Surlaw. "How many pages in Allison's book?" he asked.

"I'm sorry, Jason," the librarian told him. "That is **confidential** information."

Jason **sigh**ed.

He returned to the bookshelves, wondering if Allison really chose a book with five hundred pages. It seemed impossible. Nobody could read a book that long, even if it had big print and short chapters.

Still he couldn't be sure. Just to be safe, he chose a book with 510 pages. There was no way Allison chose a longer book than that! He started to bring it to Mrs. Surlaw.

But what if she did?

He put the book back, then found one with 573 pages. She couldn't have chosen a book with more pages than that!

Again, he started to Mrs. Surlaw's desk.

But what if she did?

He returned the book to its place on the shelf, and then chose one with 611 pages. A moment later he returned it.

No matter which book he chose, the same question kept returning.

But what if she did?

Finally, Jason chose the last book, on the last shelf, at the very end of the library. He had to hold it with both hands as he **lug**ged it to the checkout desk.

The number on its last page was 999. The book made a loud **thud** as he **plop**ped it down on the desk.

"Excellent choice, Jason!" Mrs. Surlaw said when she saw the book. "I know you will enjoy reading it."

Reading it? He couldn't even carry it.

Jason hugged the walrus.

13. UMBRELLA

Sharie liked walking in the rain. She liked **stomp**ing through **puddle**s in her yellow rain **boot**s. Most of all, she loved her umbrella, even if it did get heavy after a while.

Her umbrella was purple with green **stripe**s. Or maybe it was green with purple stripes. She couldn't be sure. The whole thing was covered with yellow **polka dot**s of various sizes.

She liked listening to the **raindrop**s **bounce** off of it. The harder it rained, the better the sound. She liked the feel of the **smooth**, **curve**d wooden handle.

She was still a **block** away from the school when she heard the *whoop-whoop*. Now she was going to be late! She had done too much puddle stomping, and not enough straight-ahead walking.

She tried to hurry, but it was difficult to run while carrying her umbrella, especially in her yellow boots.

By the time she reached the outer edges of the school, the eight-minute warning bell was already **clang**ing.

She **count**ed the clangs and was disappointed when they stopped at eight. She was hoping for a porcupine.

Glancing down, she noticed the **sidewalk** around the school was dry. She **stuck out** one hand. The rain seemed to have stopped.

She **tilt**ed the umbrella a little to the side and looked up.

The Cloud of **Doom** had kept all the other clouds away, **including** the rain clouds. Sharie **glared** at the **horrible** cloud. It almost seemed alive as it turned and **churn**ed inside itself.

Suddenly a **gust** of wind **tore** the umbrella from her hand.

Horrified, she watched it bounce across the **blacktop** toward the school. She **chased** after it.

The umbrella hit the bike **rack** and stuck there for a moment. But just as Sharie got there, it **swoop**ed upward.

She jumped and managed to **grab** the curved handle.

The umbrella continued to rise.

She thought about **let**ting **go**, but she didn't want to lose her umbrella. She held on with both hands.

When she passed the second-floor window, she realized she

probably should have let go sooner.

When she rose past the third floor, she wished she had let go at the second floor.

When she reached the fourth floor, she wished she had let go when she was back at the third floor.

By the time she reached the sixth floor, it was **definite**ly too late.

Her left rain boot **slip**ped off when she passed the ninth floor. She watched it fall the long way down.

Higher and higher, **scarier** and scarier. She passed the seventeenth floor, the eighteenth, the twentieth.

(There was no nineteenth floor.)

She could see inside the classroom windows as she went past them. Some of the kids **wave**d at her.

She couldn't wave back. She couldn't **risk** falling.

Although the **alternative** wasn't much better. If she continued to **hang on**, she realized, she'd be **suck**ed into the Cloud of Doom.

She passed the twenty-fifth floor, then the twenty-sixth, and the twenty-seventh. She knew the floor numbers by the teachers she saw through the windows.

At the thirtieth floor, she could see her own desk, next to the window.

The window was open.

She closed her eyes, then jumped.

A **horn blar**ed.

When Sharie opened her eyes, she lay **sprawl**ed across the top of her desk.

"Oh, you *are* here, Sharie," said Mrs. Jewls. "Funny, I didn't see you. I was just about to mark you **absent**. Were you sleeping?"

Maybe it was a dream. She hoped so. If not, her favorite umbrella was lost forever!

Her left foot felt cold.

On her right foot she wore a yellow rain boot, but on the left, just a thin red sock.

14. MR. K AND DR. P

*(Author's note: Due to **strict** rules about **confidentiality**, and to avoid unnecessary **embarrassment** for those **involved**, the names of the characters have been **omitted** from this story. Please don't try to guess.)*

Mr. K headed up the stairs. He wore a paper bag over his head. It was ten o'clock in the morning. All the little **brats**—as he liked to call them—should be in class, but he wore the paper bag **just in case** he **encounter**ed a **stray** one.

When he reached the third floor, he **trip**ped over the top step and fell onto the **landing**.

"I knew I should have cut out some eyeholes," he said to himself. His knee hurt, but that was the least of his worries. He **got** back **to his feet** and **limp**ed up the stairs.

Actually, only one eyehole would have helped. His left eye was shut tight. His other eye was wide open. The **eyebrow** was raised in a **constant expression** of surprise.

By counting his steps, he knew when he reached the fourth floor. He felt his way to the door, then **knock**ed.

"Yes, who's there?" asked Dr. P from the other side.

Mr. K did not want to say his name aloud in case anyone was listening. He opened the door and entered.

If Dr. P was surprised to see a person with a bag over his head, he didn't show it. He had been trained to keep a **straight face**, *no matter what*! Whenever someone came to see him, it was part of his job to act like everything was perfectly normal.

"Yes, what seems to be the problem?" he asked, **stroking** his **beard**.

Mr. K **remove**d the bag.

"Yikes!¹" screamed Dr. P, throwing both his hands up in the air.

He quickly **regain**ed his **composure**. "So, why did you come see me?" he asked as he **rub**bed his beard.

Mr. K made an "uhhhh" noise as he pointed to his face.

---

1 yikes 이크. 갑자기 놀라거나 겁을 먹었을 때 내뱉는 감탄사.

"Your face is **stuck**?" said Dr. P.

Mr. K **nod**ded.

"Please, have a seat."

Mr. K sat on the **couch**.

Dr. P came closer to get a better look. He **poke**d a **puffed-out cheek**. "Does this hurt?" he asked.

Mr. K shook his head.

"How about this?" He **tug**ged on the **tip** of Mr. K's **tongue**.

Again, Mr. K shook his head.

"Very interesting," said Dr. P.

He walked to the bookshelf. "Hmm . . ." he **mutter**ed as he tried to find the book he needed. "This should do it!" he **declare**d, removing a very fat book.

He **bonk**ed Mr. K on the top of the head with it.

"Uhh!" **exclaim**ed Mr. K.

"Any better?"

"I **bit** my tongue," Mr. K said without moving his lips.

"Hmm, this will be more difficult than I thought," said Dr. P. He returned to the bookshelf, chose a different book, and brought it to his desk. He **thumb**ed **through** the pages. "Cold feet . . . **sticky** fingers . . . ah, here we are, stuck face!"

He silently read to himself for a minute or two, then looked up and asked, "Did you have a **pet** when you were a child?"

Mr. K nodded.

Dr. P looked back at his book and read some more.

"A cat?"

Mr. K shook his head.

"A dog?"

He nodded.

"Did you love your dog?"

Mr. K's head didn't move at all. A tear **trickle**d out of his eye and **drip**ped down his face.

"Excellent!" declared Dr. P. "I think we're making real **progress**."

He shut the book, **scoot**ed his chair up close, and **lean**ed toward Mr. K. "Look into my eyes," he said.

With his one eye, Mr. K **stared** at Dr. P.

Dr. P stared back.

He held up a gold chain with a green stone **attach**ed. He let the stone **swing** gently **back and forth** between them. Their faces were so close, the stone kept **barely** missing their noses.

"I'm going to take you back to another time and place," said Dr. P. "You are just a young boy, playing with your dog in your back**yard**. Your grandmother smiles from the kitchen window. A pie is **baking** in the oven. You can smell cinnamon.[2]"

Mr. K's nose **twitch**ed.

"Now your grandmother is outside, holding the pie. She asks if you want some."

Mr. K's tongue remained sticking out. However, it slowly

---

2   cinnamon 시나몬. 육계나무의 껍질을 말려서 만든 향신료의 일종으로 계피와 유사한 독특한 향기가 있는 것이 특징이다.

moved from one side of his mouth to the other.

Dr. P **note**d the **breakthrough**.

"But instead of giving you a piece of pie," he said, "she **smash**es it in your face!"

Mr. K's mouth **pop**ped open. Then his face **snap**ped back into place.

His eyebrow lowered. His eye opened. His cheek unpuffed. His tongue went back inside where it **belong**ed.

"Why did she do that to me?" he cried.

Dr. P handed him a **tissue**.

Mr. K **wipe**d his eyes, and then cleaned the **imaginary** pie off his face. He stood and **straighten**ed his **suit**.

"You won't tell anybody anything about this, will you?" he asked.

"Everything that happens inside this office is strictly confidential," Dr. P **assure**d him.

Mr. K left the office feeling as **dignified** as ever.

Dr. P leaned back in his chair, with his hands behind his head. He felt very **satisfied**. It's not every day that he gets to help someone as important as Mr. K.

Dr. P's tongue was sticking out.

His left eyebrow was raised. His right eye was shut tight. And it looked like he was trying to **swallow** a tennis ball.

15. THE UNBREAKABLES

It's bad enough when two friends fight. It's even worse when three friends **pick on** a fourth.

Joe and John were best friends.

"Shut up!" said Joe.

"You shut up!" said John.

Rondi and Allison were best friends.

"May I borrow a pencil?" asked Allison.

"Here, stick it up your nose!" said Rondi.

Maybe it was because they were worried and **anxious** about the Cloud of Doom **loom**ing above them. Maybe it was because their finger**nail**s and toenails were growing too fast. For whatever reason, the longer everyone spent beneath the Cloud, the **crabbier** they got.

Maurecia, Joy, Deedee, and Ron were more than just best friends forever. Their friendship was so strong, they called themselves the "Unbreakables."

Every morning, they met before school by the **flagpole**. They had a special four-handed handshake. Each would hold out one hand, and they'd **lock thumb**s to **pinkies**. Then they'd raise and lower their hands three times and shout, "Unbreakable!"

The lunch bell kaboinked four times, and the Unbreakables headed down the stairs together.

"I wonder what we're having today," Deedee said.

"Didn't you count the kaboinks?" asked Maurecia.

"Spaghetti and feetballs,[1]" said Joy.

"Ooh, I like those," said Deedee.

"You would," said Ron. "They smell as bad as your feet."

---

1 feetball 'feet(발)'과 'meatball(미트볼)'을 합쳐서 만들어 낸 단어로 '발 모양의 미트볼'이 라는 의미로 쓰였다. 미트볼은 다진 고기에 각종 재료를 섞어 만든 반죽을 동그랗게 빚은 다음 튀겨 낸 서양 요리의 하나이다.

He **held his nose.**

"My feet don't **stink**," said Deedee.

Joy held her nose too, and said, "Not to you, but to everyone else!"

Maurecia and Ron laughed.

They entered the **cafeteria**. Deedee took a **tray** and pushed it to Miss Mush. The lunch teacher handed her a **plate** of spaghetti **top**ped with a foot-shaped meat patty.[2]

Deedee set the plate on her tray, next to her history book. She was careful not to **spill** any feetsauce.[3] Her half-finished homework was folded inside the book. It was **due** after lunch.

She sat down with the others at one of the long tables. She cut off a piece of a feetball, **swish**ed it around in the sauce, and ate it.

"You eat the **heel** first?" asked Maurecia.

"So, what's wrong with that?" asked Deedee.

"It's **gross**!" said Ron. "You're supposed to start with the toes!"

"Who says?"

"It's just how it's done," said Joy. "Ask anyone."

"You don't know everything!" Deedee said angrily as she shook her fork at her friends.

---

2 patty 패티. 육류를 다져 양념한 뒤 쟁반 모양으로 동글납작하게 빚어 구운 음식으로, 보통 빵 사이에 넣어 먹는다.

3 feetsauce '발(feet)'과 '소스(sauce)'를 합쳐서 만들어 낸 단어로 '발처럼 지독한 냄새가 나는 소스'라는 의미로 쓰였다.

A bit of sauce dropped on her paper.

"Now look what you did!" she **accused** them.

"You did it to yourself," said Joy.

Deedee tried to **wipe** it up with her napkin, but that only made it worse. "Now I have to start all over!" she **complain**ed.

Deedee remained in the cafeteria long after her friends left to go play. She still had one question to answer, and one last toe to eat.

It didn't seem fair that her friends were outside playing, while she was stuck inside.

"Stupid Ron," she muttered. "Stupid Maurecia. Stupid Joy. They're the ones with **stinky** feet!"

When at last she finished, she put her dishes in the dish tray, and **dump**ed her **trash**. She hurried out of the **lunchroom**, and down the stairs.

Once outside, she saw them playing three-square,[4] and wasn't sure if she even wanted to join them.

Suddenly, her face filled with **horror**. "Oh, no!" she called out, and then pulled her hair with both hands.

She didn't have her homework, or her history book! She turned and ran back into the building.

---

4 **three-square** 세 사람이 하는 four-square 게임. four-square는 네 사람이 네 개의 정사각형으로 이루어진 코트의 각 모서리에 서서 서로 공을 주고받는 게임을 말한다.

Miss Mush and Mr. Pepperadder were busy wiping the **counter** with dish**rag**s when Deedee came **rush**ing up to them.

"Hi, Deedee, did you want seconds?" Miss Mush asked **hopeful**ly. "We put everything away, but I'd be happy to heat up another plate."

Out of breath, Deedee explained about her book and homework.

Neither Miss Mush nor Mr. Pepperadder remembered seeing it.

"And I've already dumped all the trash," said Mr. Pepperadder.

There were four large **dumpster**s in the back of Wayside School. A pair of feet was sticking up out of one of them.

Upside down, **buried** in the trash, Deedee tried to read every **wrinkle**d and **soggy** piece of paper as she **dug** through half-eaten feetballs, **strand**s of spaghetti, **drippy** milk **carton**s, apple **core**s, pickle **slice**s, and *who-knows-what-else?*[5]

"It's impossible! There's no way!" she cried.

Then, just when all hope seemed lost, a noise came from somewhere deep inside the dumpster next to hers.

"Found it!" called Ron.

Rustling sounds could be heard from inside the other two

5　who-knows-what-else 그 밖에 여러 가지 것. 기타 등등.

dumpsters, as well.

"Hooray!" cheered Maurecia.

"Wow, what a relief!" shouted Joy.

Yes, there were six other feet sticking up from the dumpsters.

They were the Unbreakables. Not even the Cloud of Doom could destroy their friendship.

But that was only the first test. The **ultimate** test was still to come.

16. A SHORT CHAPTER
ABOUT A LONG BOOK

Read a book. Write a book report. Draw a picture.

That was the **assign**ment Mrs. Jewls put up on the board.

(Don't worry. You haven't already read this chapter. Mrs. Jewls assigned lots of book reports. For some reason, she thought reading was important.)

Whenever Jason looked at the board, he got a heavy feeling in **the pit of his stomach**—almost as heavy as the 999-page book he **lug**ged around in his backpack. It was like his own

Cloud of Doom that he took wherever he went.

He didn't know how he'd ever read it. His book report was already three weeks late.

One time his bookmark fell out. It took him twenty minutes just to find his place.

He was very disappointed to discover he was only on page six.

"Jason, is your book report ready yet?" Mrs. Jewls asked him each day he walked into class.

"Sorry, Mrs. Jewls," he told her. "It's a really, really, really long book."

He always answered the same way, although the number of *really*s varied.

"How do you like your book?" Allison asked him.

"Have you finished it yet?" asked Rondi.

The two girls **giggle**d.

He wondered if anyone had ever read a book with 999 pages. Maybe the author never even finished writing it. Perhaps she quit after 300 pages, **figuring** nobody would ever get that far anyway.

That evening, however, something strange happened.

Jason was trying to get through page twenty-six, when suddenly he laughed. He read some more, and laughed again.

It was as if he and the character had become friends. He read for an entire hour without realizing it.

When he reached page seventy, something sad happened, and he hoped his sister didn't **notice** his tears.

He **stay**ed **up** all night. He read about exciting battles, and strange and **goofy** animals. No matter how tired he got, he kept needing to know what happened next.

The next day during **recess**, while everyone else played, Jason preferred to sit by himself with his book. He even liked the kissing parts, but had to keep **glancing** around, to make sure Allison and Rondi couldn't see what he was reading.

The two girls came toward him.

"He'll never finish it," said Allison.

"**No way**," Rondi agreed.

"Shh," said Jason. "I'm trying to read."

17. THE BEST PRINCIPAL EVER!!!

Mrs. Jewls went from desk to desk, handing back everyone's history homework. "Nice job, Eric," she said to one of the Erics. "Well done, Eric," she said to another. "You better study the history of **cabbage**," she told the third Eric. "The Ultimate Test is coming."

The third Eric, naturally, was Eric Ovens. He thought he knew all about the history of cabbage, and felt bad when he saw his homework grade. Then he realized that Mrs. Jewls had given him Eric Bacon's paper by mistake.

It **turn**ed **out** Eric Bacon had Eric Fry's homework, and Eric Fry had his.

They **switch**ed papers.

Mrs. Jewls **moved on**. "Nice job, Deedee, although your paper smelled **somewhat** strange."

She stopped at Jason's desk and shook her head. "I was very disappointed, Jason."

"Sorry," Jason muttered. He could **barely** hold his head up. "I was up all night reading."

"He'll never finish his book, Mrs. Jewls," said Allison.

Suddenly, the classroom door **swung** open and **bang**ed against the wall. Everyone turned to see Mr. Kidswatter.

"Good morning, children," he said.

They stared at him. He had never been inside their classroom before.

Mr. Kidswatter loudly **clear**ed **his throat**. "I said, 'Good morning, children . . .'"

Mrs. Jewls hurried to the front of the room. She **wave**d her hands like an orchestra[1] **conductor**.

"Good morning, Mr. Kidswatter," the children said in **unison**.

The principal smiled. "What's all this?" he asked, pointing to the twenty-seven plastic **containers stack**ed against the wall.

"Toenails," said Paul.

"Also fingernails," added Leslie so the principal wouldn't

---

1 orchestra 오케스트라. 관악기, 타악기, 현악기 등 여러 가지 악기로 이루어진 합주.

think the class was **weird**.

"Well, I'm glad to see you're doing important work here," said Mr. Kidswatter.

"Would you like to **donate** a toenail, or maybe a fingernail?" asked Mrs. Jewls.

Mr. Kidswatter **curl**ed his fingers as he **examine**d his nails. "No, I'm still using mine. Anyway, that's not why I'm here. I'm looking for a student to bang the gong on Friday. I **figure**d I'd start at the top, and work my way down, until I found someone **willing** to—"

Every arm **shot** up in the air. Calls of "Pick me" and "Ooh, ooh" could be heard from around the room.

"Oh," said Mr. Kidswatter. "I guess it won't take as long as I thought."

"Me, me," **beg**ged Bebe, **stretch**ing her arm high.

"No, me, me!" **urge**d Deedee.

It was impossible to know where Mr. Kidswatter was looking. He wore mirrored sunglasses,[2] even indoors.

Joy had both hands raised, **doubling** her chances of being picked. "You're the best principal ever!!!" she called out.

Mr. Kidswatter's head turned. "YOU!!!" he **boom**ed, pointing his finger.

Everybody **groan**ed, except for the one person he had chosen.

---

2 **mirrored sunglasses** 밖에서 봤을 때 거울처럼 보이는 필름을 렌즈에 부착해서, 다른 사람이 눈을 볼 수 없게 만든 선글라스.

"Me?" Stephen asked **meek**ly.

"You?" asked Mr. Kidswatter, sounding somewhat surprised. "Yes, you!" he declared. "I chose you, didn't I? And I don't make mistakes!"

He **strode** toward Stephen, then placed his big hands on both sides of Stephen's desk and **lean**ed over. "Be in my office on Friday, at two minutes before three o'clock!" he ordered. "You will get one, and only one, swing of the mallet, so you better not miss! You must hit the very center of the gong, at **exact**ly three o'clock. Not a second early! Not a second late!! There are no second chances!!!"

Stephen's right leg was shaking.

The principal **straighten**ed up and headed toward the door. "Good-bye, children," he said.

He stopped.

He waited.

He folded his arms across his **chest**.

Mrs. Jewls waved her arms like an orchestra conductor.

"Good-bye, Mr. Kidswatter," everyone said together.

As soon as the principal was gone, everyone **crowd**ed around Stephen's desk.

"You are so lucky!" said Jason.

"This is the best thing that has ever happened to anyone in our class!" said Jenny.

"You better not **blow** it!" said Joy. "Or else no kid will ever get to ring the gong again!"

"Can you even lift the mallet?" asked Terrence.

Stephen didn't say anything. He hadn't heard a word they said.

It was as if the moment Mr. Kidswatter had said, "YOU!!!" someone had banged a gong inside Stephen's head.

GONNN-nnnn-NNNNN-nnnnn-NNNNN-nnnnn-NNNNNGGGG!!!

18. THE MIRROR

Dr. Pickle kept two things on his desk. One was a **bust** of Sigmund Freud.[1]

A *bust* is a **statue** of someone's head, neck, and shoulders. Sigmund Freud was the most famous **psychologist** ever. He was Dr. Pickle's hero.

Dr. Freud also had a **beard**.

The second thing on Dr. Pickle's desk was a **handheld** mirror. Dr. Pickle checked his beard at least five times per day, to make sure it was **trim**med just right.

---

1 Sigmund Freud 지그문트 프로이트. 오스트리아 출신의 심리학자이자 신경과 의사로 정신분석학의 창시자이다. 잠재의식을 바탕으로 한 심층 심리학을 수립하였다.

Now, however, that was the least of his worries. He looked at his face in the mirror. His **cheek** was **puff**ed **out**. His **tongue** was **stick**ing **out**. One eye was closed. One **eyebrow** was raised.

He looked like a big **doofus**!

He gently swung his pickle stone between his face and the mirror.

"I am getting sleepy," he said to himself. "By the **count** of five, I will fall asleep. One . . . two . . . thruppledub.[2]" His head **plop**ped down on his desk.

This would normally be the time when Dr. Pickle would tell his **patient** what she was supposed to do when she woke up. But he was his own patient. And both patient and doctor were sleeping.

Sometime later, a car **horn blare**d. It sounded like there was an angry driver right behind him.

Dr. Pickle woke up. He had no idea how long he'd been sleeping. It took him a moment to remember who he was, where he was, and why he had tried to **hypnotize** himself.

He picked up the mirror and checked his face. No change.

"Now what am I going to do?" he asked.

That was strange.

He had felt his mouth move when he spoke, but the mouth in the mirror didn't move.

---

2   thruppledub 주인공이 '셋(three)'을 세다 도중에 잠이 들며 내는 소리.

He brought a hand to his face. He could see his hand touching the face in the mirror too.

The cheek in the mirror was still all puffed out, but his own cheek felt soft and flat. He moved his tongue around inside his mouth, even though the tongue in the mirror was sticking out at him.

He set the mirror on his desk.

"This is very interesting," he said aloud. Clearly, the face **shift**s to whoever **stare**s at it, he realized.

He turned the mirror over, facedown.

He hadn't read about this in any of his **psychiatry** books. He slowly raised the mirror, caught a **glimpse** of the **hideous** face that was still there, then quickly lowered it back down on his desk.

This discovery would make him famous! He picked up the bust of Sigmund Freud. "Even more famous than you," he said to it.

But would all that **fame** be **worth** it? What if someone else's face got **stuck** along the way?

"What would you do?" he asked Dr. Freud.

There is a reason it is called a bust. It was made of **bronze**, and felt heavy in his hand.

He **flip**ped the mirror over, and **slam**med Sigmund Freud down on top of it.

The face **shatter**ed.

Up in Mrs. Jewls's class, Kathy suddenly felt very **dizzy** and **confus**ed.

She looked at the sentence she had just written. "I can't read this!" she **exclaim**ed. "It's backward."

"Let me see," said D.J., taking it from her. "How did you do that? That is so cool!"

"Warm!" Kathy replied.

19. PUSH-DOWNS

Stephen lay on the **playground**, **surround**ed by his **classmates**. He **grunt**ed as he pushed down on the **blacktop** with all his **might**.

Nothing happened.

"You can do it!" urged Maurecia.

"Push harder, Stephen!" **encourage**d Joe.

Stephen pushed harder. He grunted louder.

Still, nothing.

Louis, the **yard** teacher, blew his **whistle**. "What's going on here?" he asked as he **made his way** to Stephen.

"Stephen is trying to do a push-down," said Dameon.

"You mean a push-up,[1]" **correct**ed Kathy.

"Why do you have to be so **opposite** all the time?" asked Dameon. "Stephen isn't pushing *up*. He's pushing *down*!"

"So he can go up," said Myron.

Kathy didn't mean to be opposite. She'd discovered she liked being nice and having friends. She just really thought they were called *push-ups*.

"How many has he done so far?" asked Louis.

"None," said Jason. "But he's trying really hard."

Louis **kneel**ed and then **pat**ted Stephen on the back. "Keep at it, Stephen," he encouraged. "Every day you'll get a little stronger. In a month, I **bet** you'll be able to do five push-downs."

"A month!" exclaimed Deedee. "Stephen doesn't have a month."

"He has to bang the gong on Friday!" explained Ron.

Louis raised one **eyebrow**. His **mustache twitch**ed. "I guess he really is the best principal ever!!!" he **mutter**ed.

"What?" asked Mac.

"**Never mind**," said Louis. "Push hard, Stephen. The mallet is made of **solid iron**."

Stephen grunted louder than ever. He didn't move. "I can't do it, Louis," he **gasp**ed. "Talk to Mr. Kidswatter. Tell him to

---

1   push-up 푸시업 또는 팔 굽혀 펴기. 엎드려뻗친 자세에서 짚은 팔을 굽혔다 폈다 하는 운동.

pick somebody else!"

"Ooh, me!" exclaimed Joy.

"Mr. Kidswatter is the smartest principal in the school," said Louis. "He must have had a very good reason for choosing you."

@. @. @.

"Would you like to **donate** a toe**nail**, or maybe a fingernail?" Mrs. Jewls asked.

Mr. Kidswatter **examine**d his nails. "No, I'm still using mine. I need a student to bang the gong on Friday."

The next thing he knew all the little **brat**s had their arms in the air, and they were making strange noises, like "Ooh, ooh!" and "Me, me!"

"You're the best principal ever!!!" someone shouted.

Those were magic words. He turned to see who had shouted them, when suddenly he saw HER—that **awful** girl who had given him that awful face.

"YOU!!!" he **boom**ed, pointing at Dana.

Dana had a **mosquito bite** on her **ankle**, however, and at that moment, she **bent** down to **scratch** it.

Stephen sat behind Dana.

@. @. @.

He lay on the blacktop, staring up at the awful Cloud. "I'm **doom**ed," he **moan**ed.

"Look, Stephen, I don't know what will happen on Friday,"

96

Louis admitted. "I don't know if you'll hit the gong, or drop the mallet on your toe. But I know this. You have to try. Or else you will regret it every day for the rest of your life. And whenever you hear a gong, your heart will fill with a **terrible** sadness."

"You really don't hear gongs all that often," Myron **point**ed **out**. "I mean, except here."

"Even if you make a **million** dollars someday," Louis continued. "You could buy your own gong, and hit it every day, all alone in your great big **mansion**. But it won't be the same."

"That is so sad," said Leslie.

Paul **sniff**ed back a tear.

"So, what do you say, Stephen?" asked Louis. "You want to give it one more try?"

Stephen wished Louis hadn't mentioned dropping the mallet on his toe. Now that was all he could think about.

He **sigh**ed, and then **roll**ed back over. He pushed as hard as he could.

"You can do it, Stephen!" urged Allison.

"Push!" said Jason.

"Up!" encouraged Kathy. "I mean down. I mean up. I mean . . ."

Now she was really **confus**ed.

Stephen rose an inch² off the ground, then **collaps**ed.

---

2 inch 길이의 단위 인치. 1인치는 약 2.54센티미터이다.

Everyone cheered.

"One more," urged Louis. "And then we'll go to the monkey bars[3] and do some pull-downs.[4]"

---

3 **monkey bars** 정글짐. 아이들이 오르내리며 놀도록 만든 운동 기구. 철봉을 가로세로로 얽어서 만든다.

4 **pull-down** 'push-up'을 'push-down'으로 잘못 말하고 있는 것에서 유추할 수 있듯이, 'pull-up'을 'pull-down'으로 잘못 말하고 있다. 'pull-up'은 봉을 잡고 매달린 상태에서 팔의 힘으로 몸을 들어 올려 봉 위까지 올라가게 하는 운동으로 '턱걸이'라고도 불린다.

20. INSIDE THE CLOSET

Jason did it! He finished reading all 999 pages.

He was so tired, he didn't know how he **made it** up the stairs to Mrs. Jewls's class. He fell asleep somewhere around the fourth floor and **awoke** on the twenty-eighth.

"Did you finish your book, yet?" Allison asked him when he entered the classroom.

She and Rondi **giggle**d.

"Yep," said Jason.

The girls' mouths dropped open.

His book report only had to be one page, but Jason had written ten pages. It was impossible to write only one page about a 999-page book.

He wondered if anybody had ever written a book with more pages. Probably not. There was probably a law against writing a book with a thousand pages or more.

He brought the ten pages, and his three pictures, to Mrs. Jewls's desk. "I guess if somebody writes a book with nine hundred and ninety-nine pages, it has to be really good," he said. "Or else nobody would ever read it."

"I don't know," Mrs. Jewls admitted. "I've never read a book that long."

Jason sleepily handed over all his papers.

"Where's your paper clip?" asked Mrs. Jewls.

"It got all **bent** in my backpack," he explained, too tired to think about what he was saying. "Unbent really. I guess the nine-hundred-and-ninety-nine-page book was too heavy for it."

He showed Mrs. Jewls his paper clip, now unbent into a **crook**ed line.

Mrs. Jewls put her hand to her mouth, **horrified**. "You bent your paper clip?" she **gasp**ed.

"Unbent," said Jason.

Mrs. Jewls stood up. "You better come with me!" she exclaimed. She **grab**bed Jason by his ear and **yank**ed him toward the door.

"Ow," he **whimper**ed.

Whispers could be heard from all around the room.

"He read a nine-hundred-and-ninety-nine-page book!"

"But he bent his paper clip."

"He wrote a ten-page book report."

"But he bent his paper clip."

"No, he unbent it."

"Everyone stop talking, now!" ordered Mrs. Jewls. "Do not leave your seats for any reason!" She pulled Jason out of the room and **slam**med the classroom door behind her.

She **drag**ged him straight to the closet that wasn't there.

Jason read the **sign**s. *"KEEP BACK!" "DO NOT OPEN DOORS!" "DANGER!" "CALL THE* **FIRE DEPARTMENT** *IF YOU SMELL SOMETHING UNUSUAL!"*

He sniffed.

He didn't smell anything.

Yet.

Mrs. Jewls turned the **dial** on the padlock as she quietly said the **combination** to herself. "Twenty-four . . . seventeen . . . six."

The **lock** opened.

"But you said it wasn't there," Jason pointed out.

"Of course it's there," said Mrs. Jewls. "Hold this." She gave Jason one end of the heavy chain.

He remained where he was as Mrs. Jewls took the other end and walked four times around the closet, un**wrap**ping it. Then she took Jason's end from him and **toss**ed the chain aside.

It **clang**ed against the floor.

A **steel** bar, held in place by two **clamp**s, still **block**ed the closet doors. The locks on the clamps had letters instead of numbers.

Jason watched as Mrs. Jewls set one lock to ACBD and the other lock to BDBC.

The clamps **snap**ped open.

"I'm really sorry about the paper clip, Mrs. Jewls," said Jason.

"It's a little late for that now, don't you think?" said his teacher. She lifted the steel bar and tossed it aside. A loud *CLANK* **echo**ed down and up the stairs.

Mrs. Jewls walked down several steps. Jason watched, **amaze**d, as she **slid** open a secret **compartment** hidden in the third step from the top.

She **remove**d two keys, one red and one green.

Each closet door had a keyhole; one was green, the other red. Mrs. Jewls put the green key in the red hole, and the red key in the green hole.

"I have to turn them toward each other, at **precise**ly the same time," she said, "or else it will **trigger** the **siren**s and smoke screen.[1]"

---

1 **smoke screen** 연막. 군사 작전 등에서 행동이나 물체를 은폐하기 위해 인공적으로 피우는 짙은 연기.

Jason **held his breath** as he watched her turn the keys.

The doors **click**ed open.

Ever since the closet first appeared, he and his friends had been trying to guess what was inside it. They imagined all kinds of **horrible** things, but what Jason saw now was worse than anything they ever imagined.

The closet was empty.

"Don't lock me in there, Mrs. Jewls!" he **plead**ed. "I didn't do it **on purpose**. The book was too heavy!"

He tried to remember all that he had seen and heard. *Third step from the top. Red key in green hole. 27-6-14. ABDC.*

It was too much! It was **slip**ping out of his brain faster than he could remember.

"CALL THE FIRE DEPARTMENT IF YOU SMELL SOMETHING UNUSUAL!"

"I don't want to become an unusual smell!" he cried.

"What are you **blabber**ing about?" asked Mrs. Jewls. "Why would I lock you in the closet?"

She bent over.

Jason looked again. The closet wasn't completely empty, after all. There, in the back corner, was a small cardboard[2] box.

Mrs. Jewls picked it up. A price **tag** stuck to its side read, "89¢.[3]"

---

2 cardboard 판지. 두껍고 단단하게 널빤지 모양으로 만든 종이.

3 ¢ 센트 기호. 센트는 미국, 캐나다 등의 화폐 단위로 1달러의 1/100이다.

Mrs. Jewls opened the top **flap** and removed a paper clip.

"Now, don't tell anyone where you got this," she said as she handed it to him.

"I won't," he promised.

She put the box back in the closet, then shut and locked the doors, turning the **color-code**d keys in opposite directions. She returned the keys to their secret hiding place.

She **grunt**ed as she lifted the steel bar, and then again when she set it in place. She snapped the clamps shut and **spun** the dials on the locks.

Jason picked up one end of the chain and walked four times around the closet. Mrs. Jewls **secure**d the padlock.

"I'm very proud of you, Jason, for finishing the whole book," she said.

"I was kind of sorry when it ended," said Jason.

Teacher and student returned to class.

21. BREATHE

Stephen stared at the clock on the wall.

What if he couldn't lift the mallet? What if he dropped it on his toe? What if he dropped it on Mr. Kidswatter's toe? He could be **expel**led!

"Breathe," said Jason from the desk next to him.

Stephen took a breath.

He stared at the clock.

What if someone left a skateboard on the stairs? Then he might **trip** over it on his way to the gong. If he broke his leg, Mr. Kidswatter would **yell** at him for being late!

"Breathe," said Rondi from the desk on his other side.

Stephen took a breath.

He stared at the clock. Sometimes, it seemed the hands didn't move at all. Other times, he'd **blink**, and it would be half an hour later.

Time didn't always **make sense** at Wayside School.

For lunch, Miss Mush made **pepper**-only pizza.[1] Stephen ate his **slice**, but did not remember eating it. His only **clue** was that he was very **thirsty** and his **tongue** and lips burned.

He returned to his seat in Mrs. Jewls's class. He stared at the clock.

Jenny was late coming back from lunch. "Sorry, Mrs. Jewls," she said. "I can't find my skateboard."

"Oh, no!" Stephen shouted.

"Are you all right, Stephen?" Mrs. Jewls asked him.

"Why did he have to pick me?" Stephen moaned.

"If you didn't want to do it, why'd you raise your hand?" asked Mac.

"Everyone else had their hands raised," Stephen explained. "I mean, I guess I was excited about it at the time, but now . . ."

"You **have cold feet**," said Mrs. Jewls.

---

1 pepper-only pizza 글자 그대로 피망(pepper)만을 올린 피자라는 뜻으로, '페퍼로니(pepperoni)' 피자와 유사한 발음으로 말장난을 하고 있다. 페퍼로니 피자는 이탈리아식 소시지를 올린 대중적인 피자의 한 종류이다.

"Yes!" exclaimed Stephen. He wondered how Mrs. Jewls knew that. His feet felt like two **block**s of ice. **No wonder** she was a teacher! But what did his **frozen** feet have to do with ringing the gong?

"Breathe," said Mrs. Jewls.

Stephen took a breath.

Mrs. Jewls's class always had music on Friday afternoons. "I'm sorry, we don't have musical **instrument**s today," she **announce**d. "They were sent out to be cleaned, and we haven't gotten them back yet."

What if the gong was being washed too? Would he have to **bang** it on a different day?

"Breathe," said Kathy.

Stephen took a breath.

"So just use what you were born with!" said Mrs. Jewls. "And a one, and a two . . ."

Dana loudly **blew her nose**. Ron **twiddle**d his lips. Mac **puff**ed **out** his cheek and **pop**ped it with a **flick** of a finger. Calvin and Bebe **whistle**d. Joe **stood on his head** and sang "**Jingle** Bells."

Paul pulled Leslie's **pigtail**s. She **shriek**ed, **squeal**ed, or **squawk**ed, **depend**ing **on** the pull.

"Stop the music!" Mrs. Jewls suddenly shouted, and the room became **instant**ly quiet.

"Stephen, you're late," she told him. "I'm sorry. I **was** so **carried away** by the music, I didn't **notice** the time."

"Time?" said Stephen.

"Now, Stephen!" said Mrs. Jewls.

He remained frozen in his chair.

Mrs. Jewls asked Jason and Rondi to help.

They moved to either side of Stephen and slowly lifted him to a standing **position**. "It's time, **buddy**," said Jason.

"Time," Stephen repeated.

He took one step, then stopped.

"Now the other leg," said Rondi.

He took another step.

"You can do it, Stephen!" cheered Kathy.

"Bang that gong like no one ever banged it before!" called Joy.

Stephen walked across the room. He stepped out the door. Behind him, he heard the entire class shout together.

"Breathe!"

Stephen took a breath.

22. THE MOMENT

Stephen was worrying his way down the stairs when suddenly he **spot**ted Jenny's skateboard, right in the middle of a step. He stepped over it.

Well, that was easy.

And just like that, his fears **vanish**ed. Not even the Cloud of Doom worried him.

He quickly hurried the rest of the way down. He didn't want to be late. When he reached the second floor, he could see Louis below, **wheel**ing the gong into place.

"Louis!" he shouted, and then jumped down the final eight steps. "Am I late?"

"You're right **on time**," said the yard teacher.

The gong was **gigantic**, almost twice as big as Stephen. He had never stood so close to it before. In the center was a small red **dot**.

The **iron** mallet hung from a **hook**. The mallet was longer than his arm, and thicker too.

"Have you been doing your push-downs?" Louis asked.

Stephen **nod**ded. "I'm almost up to two," he said **confident**ly.

Mr. Kidswatter stepped out of his office. He took one look at Stephen and asked, "Who are you?"

"This is Stephen," said Louis. "You chose him to **bang** the gong today?"

"Him? Why would I choose him?"

"Because you're the best **principal** ever!!!" said Louis.

"Well, yes, that's true," said Mr. Kidswatter.

"I'll do my best, sir," said Stephen.

"That's what worries me," said the principal.

Louis handed Stephen two **cotton** balls.

As Stephen was **stuff**ing them in his ears, Louis unhooked the mallet.

He held it out to Stephen.

Stephen **wobble**d as he took the mallet with both hands. Louis helped him raise it to his shoulder.

Mr. Kidswatter checked his watch, and then started the **countdown**.

"Ten! Nine! Eight!"

He had to shout the numbers, so Stephen could hear him through the cotton balls.

"Seven! Six!"

Stephen **tighten**ed his **grip** on the handle.

"Five! Four!"

Stephen **groan**ed loudly as he slowly raised the iron mallet up off his shoulder. It was a good thing he'd been doing all those push-downs.

"Three!"

Stephen **stagger**ed, but maintained his **balance**.

"Two!"

He **concentrate**d on the red dot.

"One!!!"

He **swung** with all his **might** . . . and missed!

He didn't just miss the red dot. He missed the gong.

Louis jumped out of the way as the **weight** of the mallet pulled Stephen around in a circle.

The second time around, the mallet banged into the gong, right on the dot.

GONNNNNN—nnnnnn—NNNNNN—nnnnnn—NNNNNN—nnnnnn . . .

Despite the cotton balls, the sound **echo**ed inside Stephen's

skull, and **rattled** his bones.

. . . *NNNNNN—nnnnnn—NNNNNN—nnnnnn—*
NNNNNNN—

It traveled up the stairs, **all the way** to the thirtieth floor.

. . . *nnnnnn-NNNNNNG!*

"He did it!" shouted Mac.

"Yay, Stephen!" **yell**ed Jenny.

Everyone in Mrs. Jewls's class **whoop**ed and **holler**ed.

Louis kept Stephen from falling over, and took the mallet from him. He hooked it to the **frame**, and then he and Stephen wheeled the gong into the principal's office.

Mr. Kidswatter was already there, standing by the door. The principal held out his big hand and said, "Well done, Stephen!"

In the history of Wayside School, Stephen was the only kid to ever shake Mr. Kidswatter's hand.

In the future, whenever Stephen feels worried, or **frustrated**, or just **plain** sad, his mind will take him back to the moment the mallet **struck** the gong. He will close his eyes and see the red dot. His hands will feel the weight of the iron mallet. He will hear the sound of the gong **bouncing back and forth** between his ears, and will feel the **vibration**s in his bones.

And he will smile.

23. BLAME IT ON THE CLOUD

Mrs. Jewls went from desk to desk as she handed back the **arithmetic** test. "I'm very disappointed in you, Joy," she said. "You need to learn your sixes and sevens."

Joy had gotten an F. That **awful** letter was written in red ink, and there was a circle around it.

"But it wasn't my fault, Mrs. Jewls," Joy **complain**ed. "It's the Cloud of **Doom**. It made me change my answers!"

"Hmmm," said Mrs. Jewls as she took another look at Joy's test. She made two little **stroke**s with her red pen, changing the F to a B.

Joy smiled.

The door **swung** open and Bebe walked in more than fifteen minutes late.

"Bebe, you need to put your name on the board under DISCIPLINE," Mrs. Jewls told her.

"Don't blame me," said Bebe. "I left my house **on time**. The Cloud of Doom slowed me down."

"Oh. Okay, then," said Mrs. Jewls.

Leslie screamed.

Mrs. Jewls turned.

"Paul pulled my **pigtails**!" she **accused**. "Both at the same time!"

"Paul, what do you have to say for yourself?" **demand**ed Mrs. Jewls.

Paul **shrugged**. "Cloud-a-Doom?" he tried.

Leslie turned around and shook her **fist** at Paul. "I'll doom you, you ugly **bug sniff**er!"

"Leslie, that's no way to talk!" said Mrs. Jewls.

"It wasn't me, Mrs. Jewls," Leslie said sweetly. "The Cloud of Doom made me say it."

"Well, apologize to Paul for calling him ugly."

"But I didn't call him ugly," said Leslie. "He sniffs ugly bugs."

Jenny and D.J. laughed. Mrs. Jewls **glared** at them.

"Cloud-a-Doom," they said at the same time.

Mrs. Jewls continued to hand back the tests. "You can do

better, Terrence," she said, when she came to him.

Terrence **crumple**d his test into a ball and brought it to the front of the room, where he dropped it in the **trash**. He stood there a moment, **staring** at the trash basket.

"Terrence, return to your seat!" ordered Mrs. Jewls.

He stayed where he was.

"Terrence, do you have a problem?" asked Mrs. Jewls.

"No," said Terrence. "No problem." He kicked the basket. It **sail**ed end over end across the classroom, **spill**ing trash along the way.

Mac raised both arms like a football ref.[1] "Three points!" he **declare**d.

"Terrence!" **exclaim**ed Mrs. Jewls.

"Sorry, the Cloud of Doom made me do it," said Terrence.

"Mac," said Mrs. Jewls. "You **know better**."

"Cloud of—"

"Enough!" shouted Mrs. Jewls. "I **get it**. It's hard with that cloud hanging over us all the time. But you can't blame it for everything that goes wrong. You have to take **responsibility**. And that means working extra hard so things don't go wrong! So, I'm **doubling** all your homework."

"That's not fair!" complained Benjamin.

Mrs. Jewls told Benjamin to write his name on the

---

1 ref 운동 경기의 심판을 가리키는 'referee'의 구어적인 줄임말.

blackboard under the word DISCIPLINE.

"The **Ultimate** Test will start Monday," Mrs. Jewls declared. "It will take three days to **complete**, and you better be prepared, cloud or no cloud!"

There were lots of **groan**s.

Mrs. Jewls returned to Joy's desk. She crossed out the B, and this time gave her an F minus.

"Terrence, there's a **broom** in the back closet. I want you to pick up the trash basket and **sweep** the floor. Mac will help you.

"Everyone else, get in line behind Benjamin, and write your names on the blackboard under DISCIPLINE."

There were more **moan**s and groans as everyone rose from their seats.

"Except you, Todd," ordered Mrs. Jewls. "You're the only one who's been good."

Todd sat back down. He **scratch**ed his head.

"You used to be a nice teacher," said Rondi as she **made her way** to the blackboard.

"Why are you so mean?" asked Allison.

Mrs. Jewls just shrugged, and said, "Cloud-a-Doom."

Above them, the dark cloud continued to **churn**, as it turned itself inside out again and again. No one **hardly** noticed it anymore, but it continued to grow larger and more powerful every day.

Lightning flashed inside the cloud, where no one could see it. **Thunder boom**ed where no one could hear it. What happened in the cloud, stayed in the cloud.

For now.

24. THE ULTIMATE TEST,
DAY ONE

The four Unbreakables met by the **flagpole** before school. "Don't worry, Maurecia," said Joy. "When you get sent back to **kindergarten**, I will still be your friend."

"Thanks," said Maurecia. "I know you'll do great. Nobody can jump rope[1] like you can."

"True," Joy agreed.

"And Ron's **memorized** every page in the **dictionary**," said Deedee.

---

1 **jump rope** 줄넘기. 여기서는 '줄넘기를 하다' 라는 뜻의 동사로 쓰였다.

Ron smiled. "Joy's a good **spell**er too," he **point**ed **out**. "You always get a hundred percent on your spelling tests."

"True," Joy agreed.

"And one of Deedee's legs is shorter than the other," said Maurecia.

Deedee smiled. "Just lucky I guess," she admitted.

They **lock**ed **thumb**s and **pinkies** and shouted, "Unbreakable!"

Maurecia **glance**d up at the Cloud of Doom, then followed her friends into the school building.

"I hope everyone's ready," Mrs. Jewls **greet**ed her class. "You just need to remember everything you've learned in your whole life."

The children looked nervously around.

The test would **last** three days. Each day would have several minor tests, and one **Major** Event. On day one, the Major Event was a spelling bee.[2]

"You mean we have to spell the words *out loud*?" asked Joy.

"That's how a spelling bee works," said Mrs. Jewls.

Joy did a lot better when she could write the words. She was a master of **fudge-squiggle**s. If she didn't know the letter, she made a fudge-squiggle that could have been any number of letters. Mrs. Jewls always gave her the benefit of the **doubt**.[3]

---

2 spelling bee 단어를 듣고 철자를 맞추는 대회.

3 give someone the benefit of the doubt '~의 말을 믿어 주다'라는 뜻으로 남에 대해 미심쩍은 점이 있지만 그렇지 않음을 증명할 수 없는 경우에 사용하는 숙어.

All the children stood along the wall as they waited for their turns. If they missed a word, they would have to sit down.

Mac couldn't spell *curious*. Leslie missed *squawked*. Jason went out on *confidential*.

"**Dilly-dally**," said Mrs. Jewls.

"Dilly-dally," Todd repeated. He got every letter right, but **left out** the hyphen.[4]

"It's not even a letter," he **protest**ed, when Mrs. Jewls told him to sit down.

Jenny missed *skateboard*.

Joy was next.

"Helicopter," said Mrs. Jewls.

"Helicopter," Joy repeated. "H-e-l—" She was **stuck**. She didn't know if there was one or two l's, and she didn't know if the letter after that was an e or an i. If she could have written it, she could have made the perfect fudge-squiggles to cover all the possibilities.

She returned to her seat.

Deedee was **eliminate**d on *eliminated*. A short leg didn't help with spelling.

After a while, only three students remained: John, Ron, and Maurecia.

"**Spectacle**," said Mrs. Jewls.

---

4 **hyphen** 하이픈(-). 붙임표라고도 불리는 문장 부호로, 낱말을 합치거나 음절을 나눌 때 사용한다.

"Spectacle," John repeated. "S-k-e-p-t-i-c-a-l."

Only Ron and Maurecia remained.

"Orchestra," said Mrs. Jewls.

Murmurs could be heard around the room. Nobody thought Ron could do it.

"Orchestra," Ron repeated, and then spelled it perfectly.

"**Vacuum**," said Mrs. Jewls.

Maurecia wasn't sure if there were two c's and one u, or two u's and one c, but she guessed right.

Mrs. Jewls closed her dictionary. "Well, that's all the dictionary words," she announced. "I guess I'll have to use words that aren't in the dictionary."

It was Ron's turn.

"Thruppledub," said Mrs. Jewls.

Ron had memorized the entire dictionary. How was he supposed to spell un-dictionary words? "May I have the **definition**?" he asked.

"It's when you **count** to three, and fall asleep in the middle," said Mrs. Jewls.

"Oh, that's easy," Ron said, then **correct**ly spelled the nonword.

"Fudge-squiggle," said Mrs. Jewls.

Maurecia spelled it perfectly. She even **include**d the hyphen, having learned from Todd's earlier mistake.

"Whummph," said Mrs. Jewls.

Again Ron asked for the definition.

"It's the sound made by a jump rope as it brushes against the ground," explained Mrs. Jewls.

Ron **gave** it **his best shot**. "W-h-u-m-p-h."

"I'm sorry, Ron," said Mrs. Jewls. "There are two m's in whummph."

"I win!" Maurecia exclaimed.

The class cheered.

Ron felt **cheat**ed. If it's a **made-up** word, who gets to decide the number of m's?

Maurecia's smile was big and bright.

Ron was not smiling.

25. JUMP ROPE ARITHMETIC

On day two, the **Major** Event was Jump Rope Arithmetic. It is just what you'd expect from the name. The children had to answer arithmetic problems while jumping rope.

They earned one point for each jump of a rope. They could choose either to use one rope, or two at a time. Two ropes were harder, but the points added up more quickly.

If they answered a problem wrong, or **trip**ped over a rope, they were done.

Joy, of course, chose two ropes. This was her special **talent**, like Joe's **upside-down** "**Jingle** Bells," or Dana's funny faces.

"Four plus seven?" asked Mrs. Jewls.

Whummph. "Eleven," replied Joy. *Whummph.*

Two points, and she'd only had to answer one question.

Whummph. "Three **times** nine?" *Whummph.*

"Twenty"—*whummph*—"seven." *Whummph.*

She continued with ease, **skip**ping lightly over the ropes while **rattling off** answers. Louis and Miss Nogard turned the ropes for her.

Miss Nogard was everyone's favorite **substitute** teacher, especially Louis's.

By the time Joy reached sixty-five points, nearly everybody else in her class had finished jumping.

Ron had earned twenty-three points.

Deedee only got to six. Jumping rope wasn't easy for her, since one leg was shorter than the other.

D.J. had the highest score so far, with eighty-four points.

In the history of the Ultimate Test, nobody had ever broken a hundred.

Whummph-whummph.

"Twelve **divide**d by four?" asked Mrs. Jewls.

Whummph-whummph. "Three," said Joy. *Whummph-whummph.*

A circle of children had formed around her. They cheered each correct answer.

"Go, Joy, go!" shouted Mac.

When she reached eighty points, even Mrs. Jewls started to get excited.

"Thirty-eight"—*whummph*—"plus fourteen?" *Whummph.*

"Fifty-two!" *Whummph-whummph.*

She was now **tied** with D.J.!

"One hundred and"—*whummph*—"forty-three"—*whummph*—"divided by" —*whummph*— "eleven?"

"Thirteen!"

Everyone took up Mac's call. "Go, Joy, go! Go, Joy, go!" they **chant**ed.

Louis's and Miss Nogard's arms were getting tired, but they continued to **twirl** the ropes. They knew they were a part of history.

Joy was now up to ninety-nine!

"Go, Joy, go! Go, Joy, go!"

Whummph-whummph. "Twenty-nine times four?" shouted Mrs. Jewls.

Whummph-whummph. "One hundred and sixteen," Joy easily answered.

Everyone **whoop**ed and **holler**ed. "That's a new world record!" exclaimed Deedee.

Whummph-whummph. "Six times seven?"

Whummphraaaapp!

Joy lay **sprawl**ed across the **blacktop**. Sixes and sevens always tripped her up.

Still, she had broken one hundred, and set a new world record!

Her **classmates rush**ed up to her.

"You're the best ever!" said Kathy.

"True," Joy agreed.

There was one jumper left.

Whummph.

"Sixteen minus eleven?"

Whummph.

"Five," said Maurecia.

Maurecia used only one rope. Miss Mush and Mr. Pepperadder turned it for her.

She jumped with both feet at the same time, and **held her breath** every time she jumped.

Whummph.

"Nine times eight?"

Whummph.

"Seventy-two."

Whummph.

Joy continued to lie on the blacktop as she listened to the slow whummphing. She imagined the **solid** gold **trophy** with her name on it. Her picture would be in newspapers all around the world. She'd go on TV, where famous people would ask her questions about jumping rope and arithmetic. Maybe they'd put her in a movie.

When she came out of her **daydream**, she was surprised to hear the jump rope still whummphing.

"Zero times a thousand."

Whummph.

"Zero."

Joy sat up to see that a circle of kids had **surround**ed Maurecia. They cheered every one of her answers.

Whummph.

She headed over and **poke**d Todd in the back of his neck. "What's her score so far?"

"Sixty-six," he told her.

Joy wasn't too worried. She was sure her best friend would whummphraaaappp at any moment.

She didn't start to worry until Maurecia reached eighty.

Whummph.

"Sixteen times seventeen."

Whummph.

"Two hundred and seventy-two."

Whummph.

Well, sure, Joy thought **bitter**ly. Sixteens and seventeens were a lot easier than sixes and sevens.

🍎 🍎 🍎

In the end, Maurecia whummphraaaapped on an easy one, two

plus three.

She was probably just tired. She had been jumping for almost an hour and had earned 211 points.

Joy didn't see her fall. She had quit watching long before.

26. THE ULTIMATE, ULTIMATE TEST

Yes, that's two *ultimates*.

The word *ultimate* has two meanings. It could mean *final*, or it could mean *most important*.

The **Stairway** Quiz was both. It was the final event of the third day, and it counted double.

The students were **worn out** before they started. They'd already had the science **crawl**, right and left **handwriting**, animal **imitation**s, **upside-down** singing, and **blindfold**ed smelling.

The Stairway Quiz would require knowledge, **stamina**, and most important, speed.

This was Deedee's special talent.

Deedee was a pretty fast runner on flat ground, but she was even faster going up and down stairs. That was because her left leg was a little bit shorter than her right leg. Or maybe it was the other way around. Either way, it gave her an **obvious advantage**.

Louis, the **yard** teacher, stood next to the bottom step. "On your mark!" he called out. "Get set![1]"

Louis **blew** his **whistle**.

The children rushed past him, knees **pump**ing and **elbows flail**ing.

Deedee started way back in the **pack**, but **besides** her un**even** legs, she had another advantage. She was **skinny** and short. She could **squeeze** past the slower kids ahead of her.

And they were all slower than Deedee.

As she neared the third floor, only Dameon remained ahead of her.

A man with a black **mustache** was waiting on the **landing**.

"How many quarts[2] in a gallon?[3]" he asked Dameon.

"Eight," said Dameon.

---

1 **on your mark, get set** '제자리에! 준비!'라는 뜻으로, 육상 경기 등에서 참가자들에게 자신의 출발 위치에 선 다음 달릴 준비를 하라고 알리는 말.

2 **quart** 액체나 곡물의 부피 단위인 쿼트. 1쿼트는 1/4갤런으로 약 0.95리터이다.

3 **gallon** 액체나 곡물의 부피 단위인 갤런. 1갤런은 4쿼트로 약 3.78리터이다.

Dameon was sent back down to the first floor.

"Name a city in England," he said to Deedee.

"London!" Deedee shouted, then continued on up.

Dr. Pickle was waiting on the fourth floor. "Are dreams real?" he asked.

Deedee was **stump**ed. She could hear other kids **charging** up the stairs behind her. She hated to have to go back down.

"They're real dreams," she said.

Dr. Pickle **rub**bed his **beard**. "Very interesting answer," he said, and let her pass.

By the time she reached the ninth floor, she could only hear **distant footstep**s behind her.

"What do you call someone who writes books?" asked Mrs. Surlaw.

"You don't *call* them," said Deedee. "You must never **interrupt** a great author during her moment of **inspiration**."

"I think you said the **correct** answer in there somewhere," the **librarian** decided.

On the twelfth floor, the man with the mustache was waiting again. Deedee wondered how he had gotten ahead of her.

"Name the largest river in the United States."

Deedee couldn't remember its name, but she knew how to spell it. "M-i-s-s-i-s-s-i-p-p-i![4]"

Miss Mush asked the question on the fifteenth floor. "How many **points** on a fork?"

Deedee formed a picture of a fork in her mind, but when she tried to count the points, they **blur**red.

"Three?" she tried.

"I'm so sorry, Deedee," said Miss Mush.

She didn't have to go **all the way** back down to the bottom, just to the tenth.

Ron was coming up the other way. "Hi, Deedee," he **greet**ed her.

"Hi, Ron," said Deedee. "Hope you studied your forks and spoons?"

She reached the tenth, answered another question there, then again on the eleventh and twelfth.

Ron was coming down.

"Hi, Ron."

"Hi, Deedee."

She reached Miss Mush a second time.

---

4 Mississippi 미시시피 강. 미국 중앙부를 북쪽에서 남쪽으로 관통하며 흐르는 강으로, 미국에서 가장 긴 강이자 세계에서 세 번째로 가장 긴 강이다.

"What was Christopher Columbus's[5] favorite vegetable?" asked the lunch lady.

Deedee knew that one. "**Cabbage!**"

She had spent two whole nights studying the history of cabbage.

When she reached the eighteenth floor, the man with the mustache was there again.

"Are zebras black with white **stripe**s, or white with black stripes?"

Deedee thought it was the same thing, but knew that had to be wrong. "The first one," she guessed.

"Was that white with black stripes, or black with white stripes?"

"I don't remember," said Deedee.

"Me neither," the man admitted, and let her pass.

A tall, thin woman asked the next question. She looked like a teacher, but Deedee had never seen her before. Strangely, the woman had one very long finger**nail** on her pinky.

"Please **recite** the **alphabet** backward."

Deedee had to close her eyes to **concentrate**. "Z, Y, X . . ."

---

5 **Christopher Columbus** 크리스토퍼 콜럼버스. 이탈리아의 탐험가로 지구가 둥글다는 것을 믿고 대서양을 서쪽으로 항해하여 신대륙을 발견했다.

It took her a long time. In her mind, Deedee had to keep saying the alphabet forward, in order to **figure out** the next backward letter.

She could hear footsteps coming closer, and then Maurecia came up **alongside** her.

"What are you stopping for?" Maurecia asked.

Deedee looked around. The woman with the long fingernail was gone. "C, B, A!" she finished, **just in case**.

Deedee and Maurecia continued up together, reaching the twentieth floor at the same time. The mustache man was back again.

"How many toes does a three-toed sloth[6] have?" he asked.

That had to be the easiest question yet, thought Deedee. "Three," she said.

"Twelve," said Maurecia.

Deedee was sent back down to the fifteenth floor.

Now she really had to **turn on the jets**. She **leap**ed around and over the other kids on her way down, and then, using her uneven legs, she **practically** flew back up the stairs, as she answered all the questions correctly.

She **shot** past Maurecia between the twenty-eighth and

6　three-toed sloth 세발가락나무늘보. 나무늘보의 한 종으로 털이 길고 거칠며 발가락에 세 개의 갈고리발톱이 있다. 동작이 매우 느리고 나무에 매달려 나뭇잎과 열매 등을 따 먹는다.

twenty-ninth floors, answered a question about the different kinds of **dirt**, and then finally reached the top of the stairs where Mrs. Jewls was waiting.

"How many points on a fork?" Mrs. Jewls asked.

"I already had that question," Deedee said as she took several long deep breaths. Her heart was **pound**ing.

"Good, then you know the answer."

Once again, Deedee tried to picture a fork in her mind. It was either three or four.

"Twelve!" she declared, still **confuse**d about the sloth, with its three toes and four feet.

She **trudge**d back down.

"Hi, Deedee," said Maurecia on her way up.

Deedee didn't say hi back.

After school, only three of the Unbreakables could be seen by the flagpole.

Maurecia was still inside the school. Photographers were **snap**ping her picture, and she was being questioned by newspaper reporters from all around the world.

When she finally came outside, she was carrying a **giant trophy**.

"Sorry I took so long," she said.

"You must think you're really great," said Joy.

Maurecia shrugged.

"Well, you should!" said Ron.

"Because you are!" said Deedee.

Maurecia set down her trophy and said, "You guys are the greatest friends ever!"

They held out their hands, **lock**ed pinkies and **thumb**s, and shouted, "Unbreakable!"

Friends stick by each other when one is down. That is a true test of friendship.

But sometimes, it is harder to stick by a friend who is up.

That is the ultimate test of friendship.

27. KACHOOGA BOOP

The **Ultimate** Test was over, and nobody was sent back to **kindergarten**. Mrs. Jewls had made up the test so that every one of her students had a chance to shine, using his or her special **talent**.

"Anyone with nail **clipping**s?" she asked.

Myron came to the front of the room and dropped thirty-seven clippings into the nail **bucket**. Nineteen came from toes, and eighteen from fingers. He started to do the math on the board.

$$
\begin{array}{r}
999{,}962 \\
+\ 37 \\
\hline
9
\end{array}
$$

He was suddenly **startled** by a very loud *kachooga boop!* He dropped the **chalk**.

This was the bell nobody in the class had ever heard before, not even Mrs. Jewls.

Then came another *kachooga*, followed by two boops.

"What's it mean, Mrs. Jewls?" shouted Leslie.

"Everybody keep calm," said Mrs. Jewls.

Kachooga boop! Boop! Boop!

Mrs. Jewls hurried to the back **closet**.

It started up again.

Kachooga boop!

Kachooga boop! Boop!

Mrs. Jewls threw open the closet door and started **toss**ing books and **supplies** out of the way.

Kachooga boop! Boop! Boop!

She finally **removed** a very large book, covered with **dust**.

"*The Complete Guide to Bells*," said Terrence, reading the book's title over Mrs. Jewls's shoulder.

Mrs. Jewls sat on the floor, turning the pages until she got to the index.[1] The kachooga booping continued, making it difficult for her to **concentrate**.

She found it. "*Kachooga boop—page 297.*" She quickly turned to that page.

Suddenly, a loud *BOOM* shook the classroom. The lights went out.

This time nobody screamed. They were too **scare**d.

Mrs. Jewls **lit** a candle. In the **flicker**ing light, she read aloud from page 297.

"If you hear a *kachooga*, followed by one, two, and then three boops, you should . . ." She stopped and **blew** a cloud of dust off the page, then tried to find where she had **left off**. ". . . one, two, and then three boops, you should **run for your lives**. A Cloud of **Doom** is about to destroy everything." She dropped the book. "Everybody outside!" she ordered.

Another *BOOM* shook the classroom so hard that the clock fell off the wall.

The children ran to the door, but it wouldn't open.

"The paper clip closet must have fallen over!" said Dameon. "It's **block**ing the door!"

"Paper clip closet?" asked Mrs. Jewls. She **glare**d at Jason.

"Sorry," he said.

Jason couldn't keep a secret.

Todd, Maurecia, Dameon, and Allison all pushed together, but the door wouldn't **budge**.

---

1 **index** 인덱스 또는 색인. 책 속의 내용 중에서 중요한 단어나 항목, 인명 등을 쉽게 찾아 볼 수 있도록 일정한 순서에 따라 별도로 배열하여 놓은 목록.

"Let Stephen in there," **urge**d Kathy. "He's been doing all those push-downs."

With Stephen's help, they pushed the door open.

Sirens **wail**ed from the closet, which lay on the ground. A smoke screen filled the area.

In the light of Mrs. Jewls's candle, they could see that the chains and **steel** bar had been **shatter**ed. Paper clips were **strew**n all over the floor.

Benjamin and Rondi started picking them up.

"Leave them!" shouted Mrs. Jewls.

Now they knew it was serious.

Mrs. Jewls told everyone to hold hands as she led the way down the **staircase**.

Paul **grab**bed Leslie's **pigtail**.

"What are you doing?" she **demand**ed.

"It's either that or your hand," he said.

"Okay, then," Leslie agreed.

The kachooga booping continued as more loud booms shook the school.

A **gust** of wind blew out Mrs. Jewls's candle, and the class continued down in darkness.

Joe stepped on a skateboard, which somebody had left in the middle of the stairs. He fell, pulling John down with him. Who pulled down Dana. Who pulled down Jenny. Who pulled down Rondi. Who pulled down Terrence. The chain reaction[2] ended with Dameon pulling down Mrs. Jewls.

The class lay sprawled across the stairs as the school shook around them.

"We're doomed!" Mac wailed.

"Look!" **exclaim**ed Bebe.

A door had opened, and there was a light coming from inside a classroom.

A teacher stood in the **doorway**. "Quick. Come inside," she **beckon**ed. "You'll be safe here."

She had a long fingernail on her **pinky**.

---

2 **chain reaction** 연쇄 반응. 어떤 하나의 사건을 계기로 하여 잇달아 관련된 사건이 일어나는 일.

28. THE TEACHER WITH
THE LONG FINGERNAIL

Like **moths**, the children went to the light.

"Welcome, welcome, glad you're here, come in," the woman said as they **file**d past and joined the other kids in her class.

"I'm sorry I don't have enough desks, but we'll **make do.** Please find a place on the floor for now."

The children did as they were told. They felt safe, even if a bit uncomfortable. They could no longer feel the school shake, or hear the kachooga boops.

"Miss Zarves," said Mrs. Jewls. "It's so good to see you! How long has it been?"

"Feels like forever," said Miss Zarves.

"I never **bump** into you in the teachers' **lounge**," said Mrs. Jewls. "We must just keep missing each other."

"I try not to bump into people," said Miss Zarves.

Miss Zarves was tall and thin. Her skirt and blouse were **neat** and **trim**. Her short hair looked shiny and **silky**, and smelled like strawberry shampoo. Everything about her was neat and **orderly**, except for that one fingernail.

"And how's Mavis?" asked Miss Zarves.

Mavis was Mrs. Jewls's daughter.

"**Adorable**," said Mrs. Jewls. "But they grow up so fast, don't they?"

"I wouldn't know," said Miss Zarves.

"You don't look like you've aged a day," said Mrs. Jewls.

"Very nice of you to say," said Miss Zarves.

Mrs. Jewls wasn't just being nice. Miss Zarves hadn't changed one bit—except for her fingernail, of course, which had grown **considerably** longer.

Calvin walked between the two teachers. "Excuse me, Miss Zarves," he said. "I think I'm supposed to give you this."

He handed Miss Zarves a folded piece of paper that was so old, it **tore** as Miss Zarves unfolded it. She **strain**ed to read the **fade**d writing.

"Oh, okay," she said to Mrs. Jewls, then dropped the note in the **trash**.

"Is that the note I gave you to give Miss Zarves?" Mrs. Jewls asked Calvin.

Calvin **shrugged**. "I just found it in my pocket," he said, sounding even more surprised than Mrs. Jewls.

Mrs. Jewls **stared** at him. "You told me you gave it to her," she **accused**.

"I don't think I ever said that," said Calvin.

Mrs. Jewls continued to stare as he returned to his seat on the floor.

"We were just about to have our history review," said Miss Zarves. "Who's your best history student?"

"Myron," Mrs. Jewls answered, without **hesitation**.

Myron had gotten the highest score on the history **portion** of the **Ultimate** Test.

"Myron, stand up, please," said Miss Zarves.

He stood.

"What kind of shoes did Mary Bopkins[1] like to wear?" Miss Zarves asked him.

"Who?" asked Myron.

The kids from Miss Zarves's class **giggled**.

"No laughing," said Miss Zarves. "We don't laugh at stupid people. Don't feel bad, Myron. You may be stupid now, but

---

1 Mary Bopkins 뮤지컬 영화 '메리 포핀스(Mary Poppins)'의 동명의 주인공과 비슷한 발음을 사용하여 언어유희적으로 만들어 낸 가상의 인물. 메리 포핀스는 개구쟁이 남매를 돌보는 마법사 보모로, 우산을 타고 하늘에서 내려오는 모습으로 유명하다.

once you've been in my class for a few years, you'll know the history of everybody. Mark, would you please tell Myron the answer?"

"*A few years?*" Myron asked, but Miss Zarves **ignore**d the question.

Mark Miller stood up. "Which Mary Bopkins do you mean?" he asked. "The one born in 1801 in Boston,[2] or the one born in 1954 in San Francisco?[3]"

"Boston," said Miss Zarves.

"Red boots," said Mark.

"Excellent," said Miss Zarves.

"Who's Mary Bopkins?" asked Mrs. Jewls. "Was she famous?"

"Why?" asked Miss Zarves. "Does your class only study famous people? Do you think famous people are more important than people who aren't famous?"

"But there isn't enough time to study *everyone*," said Mrs. Jewls.

"We don't play favorites in my class," said Miss Zarves.

She went to the back **closet** and took out several giant **stack**s of papers. "This is everyone born in 1837." She went around the room, handing each student a stack of a hundred

---

2 **Boston** 보스턴. 미국 동부를 대표하는 항구 도시로, 전통적인 문화와 교육의 중심지이다.

3 **San Francisco** 샌프란시스코. 미국 서부를 대표하는 항구 도시로, 국제적인 상업과 공업이 발달했다.

pages or more. "When you finish studying a page, please pass it on to someone else."

Myron stared **helpless**ly at his stack. "I can't even read this," he **complain**ed. "I think it's Chinese."

"Well, yes, a lot of people were born in China," said Miss Zarves.

She handed Myron a Chinese **dictionary** and said, "You'll need this."

It is impossible to say how long Myron sat there, **fumbling** through the dictionary as the kids around him were passing around their **sheet**s of paper.

He might have been there an hour. Or a day. Or a week.

Time passes slowly when you're trying to read a Chinese dictionary.

Even if you're Chinese.

He **glance**d up and **spot**ted a pair of **scissors** on Mark Miller's desk. He got an idea.

"Hey, Mark, can I borrow those for a sec?[4]" Myron asked.

"Sure," said Mark.

Myron took the scissors, then walked bravely to the front of the room.

He didn't know if his plan would work. In fact, it really

---

4 for a sec (= for a second) '잠시만', '잠깐'이라는 뜻.

didn't **make** any **sense**, but it was his only h-o-p-e.

"Excuse me, Miss Zarves. I can trim your fingernail for you, if you like," he offered.

"My fingernail?" asked Miss Zarves, **astonish**ed by such a **suggestion**. "Which one?"

"The long one on the end," said Myron.

Miss Zarves looked at her hand. "Hmm, now that you mention it, it has gotten long. I guess I hadn't **notice**d, because it grew so slowly."

She held out her hand.

Myron **press**ed hard on the scissors and **snip**ped it off.

"That does feel better," said Miss Zarves. "Thank you, Myron."

Myron held the fingernail up in the air.

Except, he was no longer standing in the front of the classroom. He was standing on the stairs, and everyone else from Mrs. Jewls's class lay **sprawl**ed across the **staircase**.

"A **million**!" he shouted **triumphant**ly.

29. AFTER THE STORM

The boops and **booms** had stopped, and the lights were back on.

Myron and the others had to step over all sorts of objects as they **made their way** back up toward their classroom. The stairs were **strew**n with books, papers, **cafeteria tray**s, musical **instrument**s, an air pump, a giant **stuff**ed walrus, and even a **bust** of Sigmund Freud.

Between the twenty-sixth and twenty-seventh floors, the stairs were completely **block**ed off by Mr. Kidswatter's **enormous** desk. They all had fun climbing over it, **including** Mrs. Jewls.

Once back in class, Myron dropped Miss Zarves's finger**nail** into the **bucket**, which, **unfortunate**ly, was empty. Sadly, the other nine hundred thousand, nine hundred, and ninety-nine **clipping**s were gone.

Myron would have written 1,000,000 on the **blackboard** anyway, but there was no blackboard.

The **chalk** was there, however.

It was as if everything inside Wayside School had been **shuffle**d like a **deck** of cards and **dealt out** randomly to every floor.

(Mrs. Jewls's blackboard was **eventually** discovered in the library. Fingernails and toenails would continue to be found for years to come, sometimes in very strange places.)

The sun shined. The sky was as blue as Allison's eyes. Birds **chirp**ed as they flew about.

There had been no birds during the dark days of doom.

Louis, the **yard** teacher, **shovel**ed snow off the **roof**. Among other things, the cloud had **dump**ed huge amounts of snow. The **playground sparkle**d white.

Louis had to be careful. The snow was **pack**ed high above the **guardrail**s and was very **slippery**. "**Look out**, below!" he shouted as he tossed a shovelful of snow over the edge.

Down below the kids were playing a kind of **reverse** dodgeball. It was the boys against the girls. Every time Louis shouted, "Look out below!" they did the **opposite**.

Eric Ovens **charged** past Jenny and dived face-first, **sliding** across the snow-covered ground. Louis's **clump smack**ed him right on the head.

"One point!" he exclaimed.

Recess was three hours today. The kids had been sent out to play, while the teachers were **stuck** with cleaning up the **mess** made by the storm.

Just as Mrs. Jewls had **predict**ed, now that the Cloud of Doom was gone, the world had become a happier place. The only thing missing was a rainbow.

"Look out below!" Louis called from the other side of the school.

They **race**d around the building. Leslie dived toward the falling clump. "One point," she **declare**d.

"**No way**, Miss **Piggy-tail**s," said Terrence. "It missed you!"

"Did not!" Leslie **insist**ed. "See, look at all the snow in my hair."

"That's ground snow," argued Terrence.

Dana came to Leslie's **defense**. "Some of it came from the ground," she agreed. "But four **flake**s came from the air. I saw them."

"How can you see four **snowflake**s?" asked Paul.

"Super glasses!" said Dana, pointing to her **spectacle**s. She picked four snowflakes out of Leslie's hair. "One, two, three, and four. Just like I told you."

"That **proves** it!" declared Bebe. "One point!"

Paul **scowl**ed. He remained **skeptical** of her spectacles.

Up on the roof, Louis **spot**ted something **stick**ing **out** of the snow. It was purple and green, with some yellow **dot**s.

He tried to pull it free, but it was stuck. He pulled hard.

It still wouldn't **budge**.

He gave it one hard **yank**!

The umbrella **jerk**ed free, but Louis's feet **slip**ped out from under him. He fell on his bottom and slid backward across the roof.

"Look out below!" he shouted as he went over the edge.

The children ran to the call. They were quite surprised when they looked up and saw the yard teacher coming toward them.

Louis looked down. He didn't want to hurt the children.

He considered trying a Mary Poppins, but he was holding the wrong end of the umbrella, and there wasn't time to change his **grip** and try to open it.

His best chance was to grab the top of the **flagpole**.

Wayside School had an extra-tall flagpole so it wouldn't look **puny** next to the building.

Louis **reach**ed **out** for it but missed.

The next thing he knew, he was **spin**ning wildly in circles.

The **curved** handle of the umbrella had **hook**ed the pole.

Louis **whirl**ed **dizzily** around it as he slowly moved down the pole. By the time he reached the ground, he must have circled the flagpole more than a thousand times.

Sharie ran to him.

To Louis, it looked like there were six Sharies, all spinning like **top**s.

"Thanks, Louis—you're the best!" said Sharie, taking her umbrella. "But really, there was no big **rush**. You could have just used the stairs."

30. RAINBOW

There was no **stove** in the **cafeteria** kitchen. An **enormous pot** hung from a thick chain above a **blazing** fire.

"Lower the pot," ordered Miss Mush.

Mr. Pepperadder turned the **squeaky** crank,[1] and the pot came down.

"What will it be today?" he asked.

"Shh!" said Miss Mush.

Mr. Pepperadder **knew better**. You must never **interrupt** a great artist during her moment of **inspiration**.

---

1   crank 크랭크. 왕복 운동과 회전 운동을 서로 변환할 수 있는 기계 장치로, 물체를 들어올리릴 때나 자전거 페달 등에 사용된다.

Miss Mush's eyes were closed. She **rub**bed her **chin**. She wanted to make something truly special after the **Storm** of **Doom**. "Rainbow stew!²" she **declare**d as she raised her wooden spoon high above her head.

"**Brilliant!**" agreed Mr. Pepperadder.

"What do we have that's red?" asked Miss Mush.

Mr. Pepperadder looked over his **inventory** list. "Red **cabbage**," he said. "Beets,³ strawberries, red **peppers**."

Miss Mush **wave**d the wooden spoon and said, "**Toss** them in the pot!"

Flames **shot** up as Mr. Pepperadder threw in the **ingredient**s. He had to **shield** his eyes from the smoke.

"What about yellow?" asked Miss Mush.

"Yellow squash,⁴ bananas, yellow peppers, yellow onions . . ."

"Start with the bananas," said Miss Mush, "and then we'll **see about** the onions."

Mr. Pepperadder started to **peel** a banana, but Miss Mush stopped him.

"The peel is the part that's yellow," she **remind**ed him. "If I wanted white, I would have asked for peeled bananas."

---

2 stew 스튜. 고기를 큼직하게 썰어서 버터로 볶다가, 양파, 감자, 당근 등을 차례로 넣고 물을 부어 푹 끓인 음식.

3 beet 비트. 빨간 뿌리를 지닌 우리나라의 강화 순무와 비슷한 채소. 아삭한 식감과 풍부한 영양소로 샐러드를 비롯한 여러 요리에 사용된다.

4 squash 스쿼시. 레몬, 오렌지 등의 과일즙에 탄산수를 넣어 희석한 다음 설탕을 넣은 음료수.

"Sorry," said Mr. Pepperadder. He tossed fifty-seven bushels[5] of bananas, peels and all, into the pot.

There was a loud **hiss**ing noise, as **steam** filled the room.

Some cooks considered things like taste, or perhaps **nutrition**, when preparing a meal. For rainbow stew, color was all that mattered.

Miss Mush **stir**red the pot with a large stick. "Perhaps a little black now, for **definition**," she said.

Mr. Pepperadder read from his list. "Poppy **seed**s,[6] burnt toast, my shoes . . ."

High above them, in Mrs. Jewls's class, several children **held their noses**.

"What's that smell?" asked Calvin.

"Miss Mush must be cooking something," said Bebe.

"It smells like shoes," said Myron.

D.J. **sniff**ed. "Black shoes," he said. "With hard **sole**s, and no **lace**s."

"You can smell the laces?" asked Kathy.

"No," said D.J. "I just told you there weren't any laces."

Mr. Kidswatter's voice came over the speaker. "GOOD MORNING, STUDENTS. IT'S ANOTHER GREAT DAY

---

5 bushel 곡물이나 과일의 중량 단위인 부셸. 1부셸은 8갤런으로 약 30리터이다.

6 poppy seed 양귀비씨. 양귀비꽃의 씨앗으로 아삭한 식감과 고소하고 달콤한 향미를 지녀 빵, 샐러드, 파스타 등의 토핑으로 활용된다.

HERE AT—"

There was the sound of paper **rustling**.

"—WAYSIDE SCHOOL. FOR LUNCH TODAY, MISS MUSH WILL BE **SERVING** RAINBOW STEW. IT WILL BE THE GREATEST LUNCH EVER!"

Fifteen floors beneath them, Miss Mush felt her **stomach tighten**. She too heard Mr. Kidswatter's morning **announce**ment. Now the **pressure** was on.

She climbed a **ladder** and **stare**d down into the **bubbling** pot. Her face was covered with **soot** and **sweat**. "Something orange," she decided.

"How about oranges?" suggested Mr. Pepperadder.

"Too **obvious**," said Miss Mush.

"Carrots?"

"I suppose . . ." said Miss Mush, although carrots didn't *feel* right to her.

Inspiration **struck**! "Eighteen **pumpkins**!" she **exclaim**ed.

Each pumpkin made a **giant splash**, as Miss Mush and Mr. Pepperadder **took turns** tossing them into the pot.

After all the pumpkins were added to the stew, a tiny smile **crept** across Miss Mush's face.

It was a smile that all great artists know well. After years of self-**doubt**, she started to believe that she was on the **verge** of creating something truly wonderful.

But it was just a quick smile, and then back to work!

The doubts always return.

The lunch bell kaboinked, and the children **descend**ed upon the cafeteria.

"Rainbow Stew," said Benjamin. "It sounds like it could be good."

"Don't let the name **fool** you," **warn**ed Todd. "The better the name, the worse it tastes."

"Remember when she made 'Midnight Madness'?" asked Paul.

"Don't even say it!" **snap**ped Leslie. "I was up all night, running around in circles."

Miss Mush and Mr. Pepperadder stood **shoulder to shoulder** as the children **lined up**. They had finished the stew only moments before.

"I hope they like it," Miss Mush **whisper**ed.

"They will," Mr. Pepperadder **assure**d her. He wore short pants, black socks, and no shoes.

Miss Mush hoped he was right, but all her doubts had returned. Her **apron** was **splotch**ed with lots of bright colors, but the rainbow stew looked like **lumpy grayish**-brown mud.

She didn't understand it. What had happened to all the colors?

Maurecia reached the front of the line. Miss Mush **scoop**ed some rainbow stew into a **bowl** and handed it to her.

"Thank you, Miss Mush," said Maurecia, always **polite**.

"Sorry, it was supposed to be a bit more colorful," explained Miss Mush. "I don't know what went wrong."

Joy was next.

"Sorry," Miss Mush said again as she handed a bowl to Joy.

"Sorry, Ron," she said. "Sorry, Deedee. Sorry, Joe. Sorry, John. Sorry, sorry, sorry . . . ."

Allison and Rondi sat at one end of a long table. "Are you going to eat it?" Rondi asked Allison.

"I have a tangerine[7] in my pocket," said Allison. "Maybe I'll just eat that."

Rondi watched as Allison slowly **removed** the entire peel in just one piece.

Deedee **count**ed the **point**s on her fork.

D.J. **swirl**ed his plastic fork through the gray **muck**. "Well, here goes," he announced.

He **poke**d his fork into something **solid**. It could have been a vegetable, or maybe a piece of meat, or perhaps part of a shoe.

He lowered his fork. "Maybe later," he said.

"Looks delicious!" Kathy said **enthusiastic**ally. She took a big spoonful, brought it to her mouth, and **swallow**ed.

---

7   **tangerine** 감귤. 오렌지와 비슷하나 더 말랑말랑하고 달콤한 즙이 풍부한 귤의 한 종류.

"Yummy!" she declared.

The other kids couldn't be sure. They could never tell anymore when Kathy was speaking in **opposite**s.

Calvin **stab**bed something **gooey** with his fork. He brought it to his mouth, **chew**ed a while, and then chewed some more.

"Well?" asked Bebe.

Calvin wasn't sure how to **describe** it. "Red," he said at last.

"Red?" questioned Allison. "That's a color, not a taste."

"And blue," said Calvin.

Rondi took a **bite**. She chewed awhile. "Purple!" she declared.

"I taste yellow!" said Todd.

Dana swallowed. "Pink!" she exclaimed.

John finished chewing, then swallowed. "Kind of a blue green," he said.

"It's delicious," said Sharie. "Purple and green with yellow **polka dot**s."

The more they chewed, the more colors they tasted.

"That's **silly**," said Allison. She took a bite.

Her eyes shone. She tasted orange, with green and purple **stripe**s, and a black **outline**.

"Do you like it?" asked Rondi.

"Only the best lunch ever!" said Allison.

Mr. Pepperadder **grab**bed and shook Miss Mush's arm. "They like it!" he said excitedly. "Look at them! They really like it."

Miss Mush didn't say a word. A tear **roll**ed down her **sweaty** and **sooty cheek**.

"Did you write down the **recipe**?" he asked.

Miss Mush shook her head. "There is no recipe," she whispered. "No two rainbows are the same."

She **gaze**d out across the **lunchroom**. This was all she ever wanted.

Everybody chewed.

WAYSIDE SCHOOL
BENEATH THE CLOUD OF DOOM

LOUIS SACHAR

ILLUSTRATED BY TIM HEITZ

Contents

'아동 도서계의 노벨상!' 미국 최고 권위의 아동 문학상

뉴베리 상(Newbery Award)은 미국 도서관 협회에서 해마다 미국 아동 문학 발전에 가장 크게 이바지한 작가에게 수여하는 아동 문학상입니다. 1922년에 시작된 이 상은 미국에서 가장 오랜 역사를 지닌 아동 문학상이자, '아동 도서계의 노벨상'이 라 불릴 만큼 높은 권위를 자랑하는 상입니다.

뉴베리 상은 그 역사와 권위만큼이나 심사 기준이 까다롭기로 유명한데, 심사단은 책의 주제 의식은 물론 정보의 깊이와 스토리의 정교함, 캐릭터와 문체의 적정성 등을 꼼꼼히 평가하여 수상작을 결정합니다.

그해 최고의 작품으로 선정된 도서에게는 '뉴베리 메달(Newbery Medal)'이라고 부르 는 금색 메달을 수여하며, 최종 후보에 올랐던 주목할 만한 작품들에게는 '뉴베리 아너(Newbery Honor)'라는 이름의 은색 마크를 수여합니다.

뉴베리 상을 받은 도서는 미국의 모든 도서관에 비치되어 더 많은 독자들을 만나 게 되며, 대부분 수십에서 수백만 부가 판매되는 베스트셀러가 됩니다. 뉴베리 상 을 수상한 작가는 그만큼 필력과 작품성을 인정받게 되어, 수상 작가의 다른 작품 들 또한 수상작 못지않게 커다란 주목과 사랑을 받습니다.

왜 뉴베리 수상작인가?
쉬운 어휘로 쓰인 '검증된' 영어원서!

뉴베리 수상작들은 '검증된 원서'로 국내 영어 학습자들에게 큰 사랑을 받고 있습 니다. 뉴베리 수상작이 원서 읽기에 좋은 교재인 이유는 무엇일까요?

1. 아동 문학인 만큼 어휘가 어렵지 않습니다.
2. 어렵지 않은 어휘를 사용하면서도 '문학상'을 수상한 만큼 문장의 깊이가 상당 합니다.
3. 적당한 난이도의 어휘와 깊이 있는 문장으로 구성되어 있기 때문에 초등 고학 년부터 성인까지, 영어 초보자부터 실력자까지 모든 영어 학습자들이 읽기에 좋습니다.

실제로 뉴베리 수상작은 국제중·특목고에서는 입시 필독서로, 대학교에서는 영어 강독 교재로 다양하고 폭넓게 활용되고 있습니다. 이런 이유로 뉴베리 수상작은 한국어 번역서보다 오히려 원서가 훨씬 많이 판매되는 기현상을 보이고 있습니다.

'베스트 오브 베스트'만을 엄선한 「뉴베리 컬렉션」

「뉴베리 컬렉션」은 뉴베리 메달 및 아너 수상작, 그리고 뉴베리 수상 작가의 유명 작품들을 엄선하여 한국 영어 학습자들을 위한 최적의 교재로 재탄생시킨 영어원서 시리즈입니다.

1. 어휘 수준과 문장의 난이도, 분량 등 국내 영어 학습자들에게 적합한 정도를 종합적으로 검토하여 선정하였습니다.
2. 기존 원서 독자층 사이의 인기도까지 감안하여 최적의 작품들을 선별하였습니다.
3. 판형이 좁고 글씨가 작아 읽기 힘들었던 원서 디자인을 대폭 수정하여, 판형을 시원하게 키우고 읽기에 최적화된 영문 서체를 사용하여 가독성을 극대화하였습니다.
4. 함께 제공되는 워크북은 어려운 어휘를 완벽하게 정리하고 이해력을 점검하는 퀴즈를 덧붙여 독자들이 원서를 보다 쉽고 재미있게 읽을 수 있도록 구성하였습니다.
5. 기존에 높은 가격에 판매되어 구입이 부담스러웠던 오디오북을 부록으로 제공하여 리스닝과 소리 내어 읽기에까지 원서를 두루 활용할 수 있도록 했습니다.

루이스 새커(Louis Sachar)는 현재 미국에서 가장 인기 있는 아동 문학 작가 중 한 사람입니다. 그는 1954년 미국 뉴욕에서 태어났으며 초등학교 보조 교사로 일한 경험을 바탕으로 쓴 「웨이사이드 스쿨(Wayside School)」 시리즈로 잘 알려져 있습니다. 그 외에도 그는 「마빈 레드포스트(Marvin Redpost)」 시리즈, 『There's a Boy in the Girls' Bathroom(여자화장실에 남자가 있다고?)』, 『The Boy Who Lost His Face(얼굴을 잃어버린 소년)』 등 20여 권의 어린이책을 썼습니다. 그가 1998년에 발표한 『Holes』는 독자들의 큰 사랑을 받으며 National Book Award 등 많은 상을 수상하였고, 마침내 1999년에는 뉴베리 메달을 수상하였습니다. 2006년에는 『Holes』의 후속편 『Small Steps』를 출간하였습니다.

「Wayside School」 시리즈는 저자 루이스 새커가 학점 이수를 위해 힐사이드 초등학교(Hillside Elementary School)에서 보조 교사로 일한 경험을 바탕으로 쓴 책입니다. 그곳의 학생들은 루이스를 운동장 선생님(Louis the Yard Teacher)라고 불렀다고 합니다. 이 시리즈의 주인공들은 힐사이드 초등학교에서 루이스가 만난 아이들의 이름에서 따왔고, 저자 자신을 반영한 인물인 운동장 선생님 루이스도 등장합니다.

웨이사이드 스쿨은 원래는 1층 건물에 30개의 교실을 지을 예정이었지만, 1층에 1개의 교실이 있는 30층 건물로 지어졌습니다. (학교를 지은 건설업자는 매우 미안하다고 했습니다.) 책의 주인공들은 30층에 있는 학급의 아이들 30명이고, 이들은 모두 별나고 이상합니다.

각 장마다 별나고 이상하며 때로는 초현실적인 일이 일어나는 웨이사이드 스쿨 시리즈는 미국 어린이들의 마음을 사로잡았습니다. 어린이들이 직접 선정하는 IRA-CBC Children's Choice에 선정되었고, 900만 부 이상의 판매를 올렸습니다. 또한 TV 애니메이션 시리즈로도 제작되어 큰 사랑을 받고 있습니다.

원서 본문

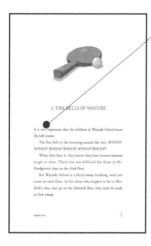

내용이 담긴 원서 본문입니다.
원어민이 읽는 일반 원서와 같은 텍스트지만,
암기해야 할 중요 어휘들은 볼드체로 표시되
어 있습니다. 이 어휘들은 지금 들고 계신 워
크북에 챕터별로 정리되어 있습니다.

학습 심리학 연구 결과에 따르면, 한 단어씩
따로 외우는 단어 암기는 거의 효과가 없다고
합니다. 단어를 제대로 외우기 위해서는 문맥
(context) 속에서 단어를 암기해야 하며, 한 단
어당 문맥 속에서 15번 이상 마주칠 때 완벽하
게 암기할 수 있다고 합니다.

이 책의 본문에서는 중요 어휘를 볼드체로 강조하여, 문맥 속의 단어들을 더 확
실히 인지(word cognition in context)하도록 돕고 있습니다. 또한 대부분의 중요 단
어들은 다른 챕터에서도 반복해서 등장하기 때문에 이 책을 읽는 것만으로도 자
연스럽게 어휘력을 향상시킬 수 있습니다.

또한 본문 하단에는 내용 이해를 돕기 위한
'각주'가 첨가되어 있습니다. 각주는 군이 암기
할 필요는 없지만, 알아 두면 도움이 될 만한
정보를 설명하고 있습니다. 각주를 참고하면
스토리를 더 깊이 있게 이해할 수 있어 원서를
읽는 재미가 배가됩니다.

워크북(Workbook)

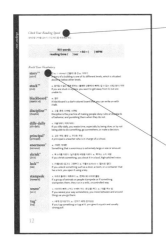

Check Your Reading Speed

해당 챕터의 단어 수가 기록되어 있어, 리딩 속도를 측정할 수 있습니다. 특히 리딩 속도를 중시하는 독자들이 유용하게 사용할 수 있습니다.

Build Your Vocabulary

본문에 볼드 표시되어 있는 단어들이 정리되어 있습니다. 리딩 전·후에 반복해서 보면 원서를 더욱 쉽게 읽을 수 있고, 어휘력도 빠르게 향상될 것입니다.

단어는 〈스펠링 – 빈도 – 발음기호 – 품사 – 한글 뜻 – 영문 뜻〉 순서로 표기되어 있으며 빈도 표시(★)가 많을수록 필수 어휘입니다. 반복해서 등장하는 단어는 빈도 대신 '복습'으로 표기되어 있습니다. 품사는 아래와 같이 표기했습니다.

n. 명사 ｜ a. 형용사 ｜ ad. 부사 ｜ v. 동사

conj. 접속사 ｜ prep. 전치사 ｜ int. 감탄사 ｜ idiom 숙어 및 관용구

Comprehension Quiz

간단한 퀴즈를 통해 읽은 내용에 대한 이해력을 점검해 볼 수 있습니다.

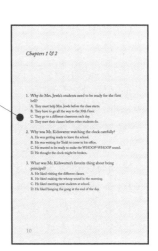

「뉴베리 컬렉션」 이렇게 읽어 보세요!

아래와 같이 프리뷰(Preview) → 리딩(Reading) → 리뷰(Review) 세 단계를 거치면서 읽으면, 더욱 효과적으로 영어 실력을 향상할 수 있습니다.

1. 프리뷰(Preview) : 오늘 읽을 내용을 먼저 점검하자!

• 워크북을 통해 오늘 읽을 챕터에 나와 있는 단어들을 쭉 훑어봅니다. 어떤 단어들이 나오는지, 내가 아는 단어와 모르는 단어는 어떤 것들이 있는지 가벼운 마음으로 살펴봅니다.

• 평소처럼 하나하나 쓰면서 암기하려고 하지는 마세요! 익숙하지 않은 단어들을 주의 깊게 보되, 어차피 리딩을 하면서 점차 익숙해질 단어라는 것을 기억하며 빠르게 훑어봅니다.

• 뒤 챕터로 갈수록 '복습'이라고 표시된 단어들이 늘어나는 것을 알 수 있습니다. '복습' 단어인데도 여전히 익숙하지 않다면 더욱 신경을 써서 봐야겠죠? 매일매일 꾸준히 읽는다면, 익숙한 단어들이 점점 많아진다는 것을 몸으로 느낄 수 있습니다.

2. 리딩(Reading) : 내용에 집중하며 빠르게 읽어 나가자!

• 프리뷰를 마친 후 바로 리딩을 시작합니다. 방금 살펴봤던 어휘들을 문장 속에서 다시 만나게 되는데, 이 과정에서 단어의 쓰임새와 어감을 자연스럽게 익히게 됩니다.

• 모르는 단어나 이해되지 않는 문장이 나오더라도 멈추지 말고 전체적인 맥락을 파악하면서 속도감 있게 읽어 나가세요. 이해되지 않는 문장들은 따로 표시를 하되, 일단 넘어가고 계속 읽는 것이 좋습니다. 뒷부분을 읽다 보면 자연히 이해가 되는 경우도 있고, 정 이해가 되지 않는 부분은 리딩을 마친 이후에 따로 리뷰하는 시간을 가지면 됩니다. 문제집을 풀듯이 모든 문장을 분석하면서 원서를 읽는 것이 아니라, 리딩을 할 때는 리딩에만, 리뷰를 할 때는 리뷰에만 집중하는 것이 필요합니다.

• 볼드 처리된 단어의 의미가 궁금하더라도 워크북을 바로 펼치지 마세요. 정 궁금하다면 한 번씩 참고하는 것도 나쁘진 않지만, 워크북과 원서를 번갈아 보면서 읽는 것은 리딩의 흐름을 끊고 단어 하나하나에 집착하는 좋지 않은 리딩 습관을 심어 줄 수 있습니다.

• 같은 맥락에서 번역서를 구해 원서와 동시에 번갈아 보는 것도 좋은 방법이 아닙니다. 한글 번역을 가지고 있다고 해도 일단 영어로 읽을 때는 영어에만 집중하고 어느 정도 분량을 읽은 후에 번역서와 비교하도록 하세요.

모든 문장을 일일이 번역해서 완벽하게 이해하려는 것은 오히려 좋지 않은 리딩 습관을 심어 주어 장기적으로는 바람직하지 않은 결과를 얻을 수 있습니다. 처음부터 완벽하게 이해하려고 하는 것보다는 빠른 속도로 2~3회 반복해서 읽는 방식이 실력 향상에 더 도움이 됩니다. 만일 반복해서 읽어도 내용이 전혀 이해되지 않아 곤란하다면 책 선정에 문제가 있다고 할 수 있습니다. 그럴 때는 좀 더 쉬운 책을 골라 실력을 다진 뒤 다시 도전하는 것이 좋습니다.

• 초보자라면 분당 150단어의 리딩 속도를 목표로 잡고 리딩을 합니다. 분당 150단어는 원어민이 말하는 속도로, 영어 학습자들이 리스닝과 스피킹으로 넘어가기 위해 가장 기초적으로 달성해야 하는 단계입니다. 분당 50~80단어 정도의 낮은 리딩 속도를 가지고 있는 경우는 대부분 영어 실력이 부족해서라기보다 '잘못된 리딩 습관'을 가지고 있어서 그렇습니다. 이해력이 조금 떨어진다고 하더라도 분당 150단어까지는 속도에 대한 긴장감을 놓치지 말고 속도감 있게 읽어 나가도록 하세요.

3. 리뷰(Review) : 이해력을 점검하고 꼼꼼하게 다시 살펴보자!

• 해당 챕터의 Comprehension Quiz를 통해 이해력을 점검해 봅니다.

• 오늘 만난 어휘들을 다시 한번 복습합니다. 이때는 읽으면서 중요하다고 생각했던 단어를 연습장에 써 보면서 꼼꼼하게 외우는 것도 좋습니다.

• 이해가 되지 않는다고 표시해 두었던 부분도 주의 깊게 분석해 봅니다. 다시 한번 문장을 꼼꼼히 읽고, 어떤 이유에서 이해가 되지 않았는지 생각해 봅니다. 따로 메모를 남기거나 노트를 작성하는 것도 좋은 방법입니다.

• 사실 꼼꼼히 리뷰하는 것은 매우 고된 과정입니다. 원서를 읽고 리뷰하는 시간을 가지는 것이 영어 실력 향상에 많은 도움이 되기는 하지만, 이 과정을 철저히 지키려다가 원서 읽기의 재미를 반감시키는 것은 바람직하지 않습니다. 그럴 때는 차라리 리뷰를 가볍게 하는 것이 좋을 수 있습니다. '내용에 빠져서 재미있게', 문제집에서는 상상도 못할 '많은 양'을 읽으면서, 매일매일 조금씩 꾸준히 실력을 키워 가는 것이 원서를 활용하는 기본적인 방법이며, 영어 공부의 왕도입니다. 문제집 풀듯이 원서 읽기를 시도하고 접근해서는 실패할 수밖에 없습니다.

• 이런 방식으로 원서를 끝까지 다 읽었다면, 다시 반복해서 읽거나 오디오북을 활용하는 등 다양한 방식으로 원서 읽기를 확장해 나갈 수 있습니다. 이에 대한 자세한 안내가 워크북 말미에 실려 있습니다.

Chapters 1 & 2

1. Why do Mrs. Jewls's students need to be ready for the first bell?
   - A. They must help Mrs. Jewls before the class starts.
   - B. They have to go all the way to the 30th floor.
   - C. They go to a different classroom each day.
   - D. They start their classes before other students do.

2. Why was Mr. Kidswatter watching the clock carefully?
   - A. He was getting ready to leave the school.
   - B. He was waiting for Todd to come to his office.
   - C. He wanted to be ready to make the WHOOP-WHOOP sound.
   - D. He thought the clock might be broken.

3. What was Mr. Kidswatter's favorite thing about being principal?
   - A. He liked visiting the different classes.
   - B. He liked making the whoop sound in the morning.
   - C. He liked meeting new students at school.
   - D. He liked banging the gong at the end of the day.

4. Why did Todd have a sick feeling in his stomach?
   A. The Ultimate Test would start the next day.
   B. Mrs. Jewls asked him a difficult question.
   C. He ate too much mac and cheese.
   D. He could not find his homework assignment.

5. What did Terrence do before he got to school?
   A. He kicked ninety-nine different things.
   B. He cleaned his bedroom.
   C. He organized his stuffed animals.
   D. He bought some cereal.

6. How did Mrs. Jewls think the students could understand how big a million is?
   A. She thought they should practice multiplying numbers.
   B. She thought they should win one million dollars.
   C. She thought they should collect one million things.
   D. She thought they should count to one million.

7. What did the students think when Terrence cut his toenail in class?
   A. Everyone thought it was bad behavior.
   B. Everyone thought it was funny.
   C. Some thought it was funny and some thought it was rude.
   D. Some thought it was gross and some thought it was funny.

chapter one

Check Your Reading Speed

1분에 몇 단어를 읽는지 리딩 속도를 측정해 보세요.

$$\frac{901 \text{ words}}{\text{reading time ( ) sec}} \times 60 = (\quad) \text{ WPM}$$

Build Your Vocabulary

story**
[stɔ́:ri]

① n. (건물의) 층 ② n. 이야기
A story of a building is one of its different levels, which is situated above or below other levels.

stuck**
[stʌk]

a. 움직일 수 없는, 꼼짝 못하는; (불쾌한 상황에서) 빠져나갈 수 없는; (대답 등이) 막힌
If you are stuck in a place, you want to get away from it, but are unable to.

blackboard*
[blǽkbɔ̀:rd]

n. 칠판
A blackboard is a dark-colored board that you can write on with chalk.

discipline**
[dísəplin]

n. 규율, 훈육; 단련법, 수련법
Discipline is the practice of making people obey rules or standards of behavior, and punishing them when they do not.

dilly-dally
[díli-dæ̀li]

v. 꾸물거리다, 미적거리다
If you dilly-dally, you waste time, especially by being slow, or by not being able to do something, go somewhere, or make a decision.

principal*
[prínsəpəl]

n. 교장; 학장, 총장; a. 주요한, 주된
A principal is a teacher who is in charge of a school.

enormous*
[inɔ́:rməs]

a. 거대한, 막대한
Something that is enormous is extremely large in size or amount.

shriek*
[ʃri:k]

v. 꽥 소리를 지르다; (날카롭게) 비명을 지르다; n. 꽥 하는 소리; 비명
If you shriek something, you shout it in a loud, high-pitched voice.

lock**
[lak]

v. (자물쇠로) 잠그다; 고정하다; n. 자물쇠 (unlock v. (열쇠로) 열다)
If you unlock something such as a door, a room, or a container that has a lock, you open it using a key.

stampede
[stæmpíːd]

v. 우르르 몰리다; 재촉하다; n. (한쪽으로) 우르르 몰림
If a group of animals or people stampede or if something stampedes them, they run in a wild, uncontrolled way.

weave*
[wiːv]

v. 이리저리 빠져 나가다, 누비며 가다; (옷감을) 짜다; n. (직물) 짜는 법
If you weave your way somewhere, you move between and around things as you go there.

tug*
[tʌg]

v. (세게) 잡아당기다; n. (갑자기 세게) 잡아당김
If you tug something or tug at it, you give it a quick and usually strong pull.

ceiling^{**}
[síːliŋ]

n. 천장
A ceiling is the horizontal surface that forms the top part or roof inside a room.

clang
[klæŋ]

n. 쨍그랑 하는 소리; v. 쨍그랑 하고 울리다
Clang is a loud ringing sound like metal being hit.

count^{***}
[kaunt]

v. (수를) 세다; 계산에 넣다; n. (하나부터 순서대로 세는) 셈; 계산
When you count, you say all the numbers one after another up to a particular number.

land^{***}
[lænd]

v. 내려앉다, 착륙하다; 도착하다; n. 육지, 땅; 지역
When someone or something lands, they come down to the ground after moving through the air or falling.

roof^{**}
[ruːf]

n. 지붕
The roof of a building is the covering on top of it that protects the people and things inside from the weather.

make it

idiom 가다; 성공하다, 해내다
If you make it to somewhere, you succeed in reaching there.

lounge^{*}
[laundʒ]

n. (호텔·클럽 등의) 휴게실; (공항 등의) 대합실; v. 느긋하게 있다
In a hotel, club, or other public place, a lounge is a room where people can sit and relax.

scary
[skέəri]

a. 무서운, 겁나는
Something that is scary is rather frightening.

slam^{*}
[slæm]

v. 세게 치다, 놓다; 쾅 닫다; n. 쾅 하고 닫기; 쾅 하는 소리
If you slam something on, you put, move, or hit it against or onto a surface with great force.

horn^{*}
[hɔːrn]

n. (차량의) 경적; (양·소 등의) 뿔
On a vehicle such as a car, the horn is the device that makes a loud noise as a signal or warning.

dash^{*}
[dæʃ]

v. 서둘러 가다; n. 황급히 달려감, 질주
If you dash somewhere, you run or go there quickly and suddenly.

sore^{**}
[sɔːr]

a. 아픈, 따가운; n. 상처
If part of your body is sore, it causes you pain and discomfort.

blare
[blɛər]

v. (소리를) 요란하게 울리다; n. 요란한 소리
If something such as a siren or radio blares or if you blare it, it makes a loud, unpleasant noise.

recess^{*}
[risés]

n. (학교의) 쉬는 시간; (의회·위원회 등의) 휴회 기간
A recess is a break between classes at a school.

ding
[diŋ]

n. 딩동, 땡 하는 소리; v. 딩동, 땡 하는 소리를 내다
Ding is a ringing sound, like the sound of a bell.

bang^{*}
[bæŋ]

v. 쾅 하고 치다; 쾅 하고 닫다; n. 쾅 하는 소리
If you bang on something or if you bang it, you hit it hard, making a loud noise.

giant[*] [dʒáiənt]	v. 거대한; 위대한; n. (이야기 속의) 거인 Something that is described as giant is much larger or more important than most others of its kind.
iron[**] [áiərn]	n. 철, 쇠; 철분; 다리미 Iron is an element which usually takes the form of a hard, dark grey metal. It is used to make steel, and also forms part of many tools, buildings, and vehicles.
glum [glʌm]	a. 침울한 (glumly ad. 침울하게) Someone who is glum is sad and quiet because they are disappointed or unhappy about something.
mark[***] [ma:rk]	n. 표시, 부호; 자국, 흔적; v. (표·기호 등으로) 표시하다 A mark is a written or printed symbol, for example a letter of the alphabet.
assign[*] [əsáin]	v. (일·책임 등을) 맡기다; 선임하다, 파견하다 (assignment n. 과제, 임무) An assignment is a task or piece of work that you are given to do, especially as part of your job or studies.
worksheet [wə́:rkʃiːt]	n. (학습용) 연습 문제지 A worksheet is a specially prepared page of exercises designed to improve your knowledge or understanding of a particular subject.
even[***] [íːvən]	a. 짝수의; 평평한; 균등한; ad. ~조차; 훨씬 An even number can be divided exactly by two. For example, 2, 4, and 6 are even numbers.
odd[**] [ad]	a. 홀수의; 이상한, 특이한 An odd number is a whole number that cannot be divided exactly by two. For example, 1, 3, and 5 are odd numbers.
experiment[***] [ikspérəmənt]	n. (과학적인) 실험; v. (과학적인) 실험을 하다 An experiment is a scientific test which is done in order to discover what happens to something in particular conditions.
stomach[**] [stʌ́mək]	n. 위(胃), 속; 복부, 배 Your stomach is the organ inside your body where food goes after it has been eaten and where it starts to be digested.
ultimate[*] [ʌ́ltəmət]	a. 궁극적인, 최종적인; 최고의, 최상의; n. 극치 You use ultimate to describe the final result or aim of a long series of events.
warn[***] [wɔːrn]	v. 주의를 주다, 경고하다, 조심하라고 하다 If you warn someone about something such as a possible danger or problem, you tell them about it so that they are aware of it.
last[**] [læst]	v. (특정한 시간 동안) 계속되다; ad. 맨 끝에, 마지막에 If an event, situation, or problem lasts for a particular length of time, it continues to exist or happen for that length of time.
kindergarten [kíndərgàːrtn]	n. 유치원 A kindergarten is an informal kind of school for very young children, where they learn things by playing.

14

clap[*]
[klæp]

v. 박수를 치다, 손뼉을 치다; n. 박수 (소리)
When you clap, you hit your hands together to show appreciation or attract attention.

stun[*]
[stʌn]

v. (놀람·기쁨으로) 어리벙벙하게 하다; 기절시키다 (stunned a. 어안이 벙벙한)
If you are stunned by something, you are extremely shocked or surprised by it and are therefore unable to speak or do anything.

disbelief
[dìsbilí:f]

n. 믿기지 않음, 불신감
Disbelief is not believing that something is true or real.

erase[*]
[iréis]

v. (지우개 등으로) 지우다; (완전히) 없애다
If you erase something such as writing or a mark, you remove it, usually by rubbing it with a cloth.

wipe[*]
[waip]

v. 지우다; (먼지·물기 등을) 닦다; n. 닦기
If you wipe away or wipe off dirt or liquid from something, you remove it, for example by using a cloth or your hand.

remove[**]
[rimú:v]

v. 없애다; 치우다; 옮기다; 떼다; (옷 등을) 벗다
If you remove something, you get rid of it and make it disappear.

basement[**]
[béismənt]

n. (건물의) 지하층
The basement of a building is a floor built partly or completely below ground level.

mustache[*]
[mʌ́stæʃ]

n. 콧수염
A man's mustache is the hair that grows on his upper lip.

snap[*]
[snæp]

v. 탁 하고 움직이다; 딱딱거리다; 톡 쏘다; 사진을 찍다; n. 찰칵 하는 소리
If you snap something into a particular position, or if it snaps into that position, it moves quickly into that position, with a sharp sound.

attaché case
[ətǽʃei kèis]

n. (작은) 서류 가방
An attaché case is a flat case for holding documents.

bald[*]
[bɔ:ld]

a. 대머리의, 머리가 벗겨진
Someone who is bald has little or no hair on the top of their head.

solid[**]
[sálid]

a. (다른 물질이 섞이지 않고) 순수한; 단단한; 고체의; n. 고체, 고형물
If an object is made of solid gold or solid wood, for example, it is made of gold or wood all the way through, rather than just on the outside.

chapter two

Check Your Reading Speed

1분에 몇 단어를 읽는지 리딩 속도를 측정해 보세요.

$$\frac{687\text{words}}{\text{reading time (\quad) sec}} \times 60 = (\quad) \text{ WPM}$$

Build Your Vocabulary

million***
[míljən]

n. 100만; a. 수많은
A million or one million is the number 1,000,000.

stuff*
[stʌf]

v. (빽빽이) 채워 넣다; (재빨리) 쑤셔 넣다; n. 일, 것; 물건
(stuffed animal n. (솜으로 채워 넣은) 봉제 인형)
Stuffed animals are toys that are made of cloth filled with a soft material and which look like animals.

counter*
[káuntər]

n. (주방의) 조리대; (식당 등의) 카운터, 기다란 대; (은행·상점 등의) 계산대
A counter is a long table, board, or cabinet top in a kitchen that is used to serve or prepare food.

flagpole
[flǽgpoul]

n. 깃대
A flagpole is a tall pole on which a flag can be displayed.

stretch**
[streʧ]

v. (팔·다리를) 뻗다; 기지개를 켜다; 펼쳐지다; n. (길게) 뻗은 구간; 기간
If you stretch your arm or leg, you move it away from your body in order to reach something.

call on

idiom (이름을 불러서) 학생에게 시키다; (사람을) 방문하다
If a teacher calls on students in a class, he or she asks them to answer a question or give their opinion.

correct***
[kərékt]

a. 맞는, 정확한; 적절한, 옳은; v. 바로잡다, 정정하다
If something is correct, it is in accordance with the facts and has no mistakes.

pause**
[pɔːz]

v. (말·일을 하다가) 잠시 멈추다; 일시 정지시키다; n. (말·행동 등의) 멈춤
If you pause while you are doing something, you stop for a short period and then continue.

impress*
[imprés]

v. 깊은 인상을 주다, 감명을 주다; 강하게 남다 (impressed a. 감명을 받은)
If something impresses you, you feel great admiration for it.

pay attention

idiom 주의를 기울이다; 관심을 갖다
If you pay attention to someone, you watch them, listen to them, or take notice of them.

nail**
[neil]

n. 손톱, 발톱; 못; v. 못으로 박다
Your nails are the thin hard parts that grow at the ends of your fingers and toes.

awake***
[əwéik]

v. (awoke-awoken) 깨다, 깨우다; (감정을) 불러일으키다; a. 잠들지 않은, 깨어 있는
When you awake or when something awakes you, you wake up.

times
[taimz]

prep. ~으로 곱한
You use times in arithmetic to link numbers or amounts that are multiplied together to reach a total.

rest***
[rest]

v. 받치다, 기대다; 쉬다, 휴식을 취하다; n. 휴식; 나머지
If you rest something somewhere, you put it there so that its weight is supported.

overcoat*
[óuvərkòut]

n. 외투, 오버코트
An overcoat is a thick warm coat that you wear in winter.

multiply**
[mʌltəplài]

v. 곱하다; 크게 증가하다; 증식하다
If you multiply one number by another, you add the first number to itself as many times as is indicated by the second number. For example, 2 multiplied by 3 is equal to 6.

arithmetic*
[ərίθmətik]

n. 산수, 연산; 산술, 계산
Arithmetic is the part of mathematics that is concerned with the addition, subtraction, multiplication, and division of numbers.

numb*
[nʌm]

a. 멍한; (신체 부위가) 감각이 없는; v. (신체 부위에) 감각이 없게 만들다
When you are numb, you are unable to think, feel, or react normally because of something that shocks or upsets you.

throb*
[θrab]

v. (몸이) 욱신거리다; 고동치다, 울리다; n. 욱신거림; 진동
If part of your body throbs, you feel a series of strong and usually painful beats there.

exclaim*
[ikskléim]

v. 소리치다, 외치다
If you exclaim, you cry out suddenly in surprise, strong emotion, or pain.

pumpkin*
[pʌ́mpkin]

n. 호박
A pumpkin is a large, round, orange vegetable with a thick skin.

fit***
[fit]

v. (모양·크기가) 맞다; (제자리에) 끼우다; a. 적합한, 알맞은
If something fits somewhere, it can be put there or is designed to be put there.

reject**
[ridʒékt]

v. 거부하다, 거절하다; n. 불량품, 불합격품
If you reject something such as a proposal, a request, or an offer, you do not accept it or you do not agree to it.

count^{복습}
[kaunt]

v. (수를) 세다; 계산에 넣다; n. (하나부터 순서대로 세는) 셈; 계산
When you count, you say all the numbers one after another up to a particular number.

take it

idiom (비난·고통 등을) 견디다, 참다; 이해하다
If you say that you can take it, you mean that you are able to bear or tolerate something difficult or unpleasant such as stress, criticism or pain.

stare*
[stɛər]

v. 빤히 쳐다보다, 응시하다; n. 빤히 쳐다보기, 응시
If you stare at someone or something, you look at them for a long time.

horrify
[hɔ́ːrəfài]

v. 소름 끼치게 만들다 (horrified a. 충격받은, 겁에 질린)
If someone is horrified, they feel shocked or disgusted, usually because of something that they have seen or heard.

bend**
[bend]

v. (bent-bent) (무엇을) 구부리다; (몸이나 머리를) 굽히다, 숙이다; n. 굽이, 굽은 곳
If you bend something that is flat or straight, you use force to make it curved or to put an angle in it.

out of shape

idiom 제 모양이 아닌, 형태가 찌그러진; 건강이 안 좋은, 몸매가 엉망인
If something is out of shape, it is no longer in its proper or original shape, for example because it has been damaged or wrongly handled.

scissors*
[sízərz]

n. 가위
Scissors are a small cutting tool with two sharp blades that are screwed together.

snip
[snip]

v. (가위로 싹둑) 자르다; n. 싹둑 자르기
If you snip something, you cut it quickly using sharp scissors.

gross*
[grous]

a. 역겨운; 아주 무례한
If you describe something as gross, you think it is very unpleasant.

instant*
[ínstənt]

a. 즉각적인; n. 순간, 아주 짧은 동안 (instantly ad. 즉각, 즉시)
You use instant to describe something that happens immediately.

demand***
[dimǽnd]

v. 요구하다; 강력히 묻다, 따지다; n. 요구 (사항)
If you demand something such as information or action, you ask for it in a very forceful way.

clipping
[klípiŋ]

n. 잘라 낸 조각, 오려 낸 것
Clippings are small pieces of something that have been cut from something larger.

hobble
[habl]

v. 다리를 절다, 절뚝거리다; 방해하다
If you hobble, you walk in an awkward way with small steps, for example because your foot is injured.

outstretch
[àutstrétʃ]

v. 펴다, 뻗다; 확장하다 (outstretched a. 한껏 뻗은)
If a part of the body of a person or animal is outstretched, it is stretched out as far as possible.

genius*
[dʒíːnjəs]

n. 천재; 천재성; 특별한 재능
A genius is a highly talented, creative, or intelligent person.

announce**
[ənáuns]

v. 발표하다, 알리다; (공공장소에서) 방송으로 알리다
If you announce something, you tell people about it publicly or officially.

Chapters 3 & 4

1. Why did Kathy keep saying "down"?
    A. She wanted to go downstairs.
    B. She wanted to argue with DJ.
    C. She wanted the class to quiet down.
    D. She wanted help getting down.

2. Why was Dana crying?
    A. She lost her giraffe book.
    B. A page of her book was torn.
    C. She didn't get the book she wanted.
    D. The giraffe in the book got lost.

3. Which of the following was NOT a suggestion the students gave DJ to cure his hiccups?
    A. Eating a lemon
    B. Standing on his head and drinking water
    C. Sucking in a big breath of air
    D. Holding his tongue while saying the Pledge of Allegiance

4. How did Dr. Pickle cure DJ's hiccups?
   A. He scared DJ by shouting.
   B. He made DJ fall asleep.
   C. He asked DJ to count to five.
   D. He patted DJ on the back.

5. Why did Dana write an extra-long book report?
   A. She could write faster than other students.
   B. She really liked the book *The Lost Giraffe*.
   C. She wanted to get a good grade.
   D. She did not know which parts were important.

6. What did Mrs. Jewls do at the beginning of the year?
   A. She gave each student a paper clip.
   B. She taught the students about paper clips.
   C. She bought a new box for her paper clips.
   D. She sorted the paper clips by color.

7. Why was Mrs. Jewls proud of Calvin?
   A. He said he wanted to be a paper clip bender.
   B. He was kind to other students in the class.
   C. He did not lose his paper clip.
   D. He helped Mrs. Jewls find some lost items.

chapter three

Check Your Reading Speed

1분에 몇 단어를 읽는지 리딩 속도를 측정해 보세요.

$$\frac{697 \text{ words}}{\text{reading time ( ) sec}} \times 60 = (\quad) \text{ WPM}$$

Build Your Vocabulary

insist**
[insíst]

v. 고집하다, 주장하다, 우기다
If you insist that something is the case, you say so very firmly and refuse to say otherwise, even though other people do not believe you.

opposite**
[ápəzit]

n. 반대(되는 것); a. (정)반대의; 건너편의; 맞은편의
The opposite of someone or something is the person or thing that is most different from them.

instant^{복습}
[ínstənt]

a. 즉각적인; n. 순간, 아주 짧은 동안 (instantly ad. 즉각, 즉시)
You use instant to describe something that happens immediately.

streak*
[striːk]

v. (줄 같이) 기다란 자국을 내다; 전속력으로 가다; n. 줄무늬
If something streaks a surface, it makes long stripes or marks on the surface.

sob*
[sab]

v. (흑흑) 흐느끼다, 흐느껴 울다; n. 흐느껴 울기, 흐느낌
When someone sobs, they cry in a noisy way, breathing in short breaths.

snap^{복습}
[snæp]

v. 딱딱거리다, 톡 쏘다; 탁 하고 움직이다; 사진을 찍다; n. 찰칵 하는 소리
If someone snaps at you, they speak to you in a sharp, unfriendly way.

hiccup
[híkʌp]

n. 딸꾹질; 딸꾹 하는 소리; v. 딸꾹질을 하다, 딸꾹 하는 소리를 내다
When you have hiccups, you make repeated sharp sounds in your throat, often because you have been eating or drinking too quickly.

stand on one's head

idiom 물구나무를 서다
If you stand on your head, you balance upside down with the top of your head and your hands on the ground.

tongue**
[tʌŋ]

n. 혀; 언어
Your tongue is the soft movable part inside your mouth which you use for tasting, eating, and speaking.

pledge*
[pledʒ]

n. 맹세, 서약; v. 맹세하다, 약속하다
When someone makes a pledge, they make a serious promise that they will do something.

allegiance*
[əlíːdʒəns]

n. (국가·정당·종교 등에 대한) 충성
Your allegiance is your support for and loyalty to a particular group, person, or belief.

22

suggestion**
[səgdʒésʧən]

n. 제안, 의견; 암시
If you make a suggestion, you put forward an idea or plan for someone to think about.

pucker
[pʌ́kər]

v. (입술 등을) 오므리다; 주름잡다, 구겨지다; n. 주름
If you pucker your lips or if your lips pucker, you squeeze them together and out.

patriotic*
[pèitriátik]

a. 애국적인, 애국심이 강한
Someone who is patriotic loves their country and feels very loyal toward it.

hop*
[hap]

v. 급히 가다; 깡충깡충 뛰다; n. 깡충 뛰기
If you hop somewhere, you move there quickly or suddenly.

dummy
[dʌ́mi]

n. 멍청이, 바보; 인체 모형; a. 모조의, 가짜의
If you call a person a dummy, you mean that they are stupid or foolish.

knock**
[nak]

v. (문 등을) 두드리다; n. 문 두드리는 소리
If you knock on something such as a door or window, you hit it, usually several times, to attract someone's attention.

pointy
[pɔ́inti]

a. 끝이 뾰족한; 가시가 돋은
Something that is pointy has a thin, sharp point at one end.

beard*
[biərd]

n. (턱)수염
A man's beard is the hair that grows on his chin and cheeks.

rub**
[rʌb]

v. (손·손수건 등을 대고) 문지르다; (두 손 등을) 맞비비다; n. 문지르기, 비비기
If you rub a part of your body, you move your hand or fingers backward and forward over it while pressing firmly.

chin**
[ʧin]

n. 턱
Your chin is the part of your face that is below your mouth and above your neck.

mutter*
[mʌ́tər]

v. 중얼거리다; 투덜거리다; n. 중얼거림
If you mutter, you speak very quietly so that you cannot easily be heard, often because you are complaining about something.

couch*
[kauʧ]

n. 소파, 긴 의자
A couch is a long, comfortable seat for two or three people.

swing**
[swiŋ]

v. (swung-swung) (전후·좌우로) 흔들(리)다; 휙 움직이다; n. 흔들기; 휘두르기
If something swings or if you swing it, it moves repeatedly backward and forward or from side to side from a fixed point.

back and forth
[bǽk ən fɔ́ːrθ]

ad. 앞뒤(좌우)로; 여기저기에, 왔다 갔다
If someone or something moves back and forth, they repeatedly move in one direction and then in the opposite direction.

soothe*
[suːð]

v. (마음을) 달래다; (통증 등을) 누그러뜨리다 (soothing a. 달래는)
If you soothe someone who is angry or upset, you make them feel calmer.

psychiatrist*
[saikáiətrist]

n. 정신과 의사
A psychiatrist is a doctor who treats people suffering from mental illness.

pat*
[pæt]

v. 쓰다듬다, 토닥거리다; n. 쓰다듬기, 토닥거리기
If you pat something or someone, you tap them lightly, usually with your hand held flat.

shrug*
[ʃrʌg]

v. (두 손바닥을 위로 하고) 어깨를 으쓱하다; n. 어깨를 으쓱하기
If you shrug, you raise your shoulders to show that you are not interested in something or that you do not know or care about something.

counselor*
[káunsələr]

n. (학교의) 학생 상담 교사; 의논 상대자
A counselor is a person whose job is to give advice to people who need it, especially advice on their personal problems.

hallway
[hɔ́:lwèi]

n. 복도; 통로; 현관
A hallway in a building is a long passage with doors into rooms on both sides of it.

annoy***
[ənɔ́i]

v. 짜증나게 하다; 귀찮게 하다 (annoying a. 성가신)
Someone or something that is annoying makes you feel fairly angry and impatient.

proper***
[prápər]

a. 제대로 된, 적절한; 올바른, 정당한
The proper thing is the one that is correct or most suitable.

wise****
[waiz]

a. 지혜로운, 현명한, 슬기로운
A wise person is able to use their experience and knowledge in order to make sensible decisions and judgments.

greet***
[gri:t]

v. 인사하다; 환영하다; 반응을 보이다
When you greet someone, you say 'hello' or shake hands with them.

definite***
[défənit]

a. 분명한, 뚜렷한; 확실한, 확고한 (definitely ad. 분명히, 틀림없이)
You use definitely to emphasize that something is the case, or to emphasize the strength of your intention or opinion.

chapter four

Check Your Reading Speed

1분에 몇 단어를 읽는지 리딩 속도를 측정해 보세요.

$$\frac{641 \text{ words}}{\text{reading time ( ) sec}} \times 60 = (\quad) \text{ WPM}$$

Build Your Vocabulary

assign^{복습}
[əsáin]

v. (일·책임 등을) 맡기다; 선임하다, 파견하다 (assignment n. 과제, 임무)
An assignment is a task or piece of work that you are given to do, especially as part of your job or studies.

mark^{복습}
[maːrk]

n. 표시, 부호; 자국, 흔적; v. (표·기호 등으로) 표시하다 (question mark n. 물음표)
A question mark is the punctuation mark '?' which is used in writing at the end of a question.

erase^{복습}
[iréis]

v. (지우개 등으로) 지우다; (완전히) 없애다 (eraser n. 지우개)
An eraser is an object, usually a piece of rubber or plastic, which is used for removing something that has been written using a pencil or a pen.

crayon
[kréian]

n. 크레용
A crayon is a pencil containing colored wax or clay, or a rod of colored wax used for drawing.

nub
[nʌb]

n. 덩어리, 조각; 요지, 핵심
A nub is a small rounded piece of something, especially a piece that is left after the rest has been eaten or used.

crumb
[krʌm]

n. (빵·케이크의) 부스러기; 약간, 소량
Crumbs are tiny pieces that fall from bread, biscuits, or cake when you cut it or eat it.

moan[*]
[moun]

v. 투덜거리다, 불평하다; 신음하다; n. 투덜거림, 불평; 신음
To moan means to complain or speak in a way which shows that you are very unhappy.

sigh[*]
[sai]

v. 한숨을 쉬다, 한숨짓다; n. 한숨
When you sigh, you let out a deep breath, as a way of expressing feelings such as disappointment, tiredness, or pleasure.

glare[*]
[glɛər]

v. 노려보다; 환하다, 눈부시다; n. 노려봄; 환한 빛, 눈부심
If you glare at someone, you look at them with an angry expression on your face.

demand^{복습}
[dimǽnd]

v. 강력히 묻다, 따지다; 요구하다; n. 요구 (사항)
If you demand something such as information or action, you ask for it in a very forceful way.

remind[*]
[rimáind]

v. 상기시키다, 다시 한번 알려 주다
If someone reminds you of a fact or event that you already know about, they say something which makes you think about it.

slam ^{복습}
[slæm]

v. 세게 치다, 놓다; 쾅 닫다; n. 쾅 하고 닫기; 쾅 하는 소리
If you slam something on, you put, move, or hit it against or onto a surface with great force.

responsibility**
[rispÀnsəbíləti]

n. 책임, 책무
If you have responsibility for something or someone, or if they are your responsibility, it is your job or duty to deal with them and to take decisions relating to them.

drawer**
[drɔːr]

n. 서랍
A drawer is part of a desk, chest, or other piece of furniture that is shaped like a box and is designed for putting things in.

dismay*
[disméi]

n. 실망, 경악; v. 크게 실망시키다, 경악하게 하다
Dismay is a strong feeling of worry, disappointment, or unhappiness you feel when something unpleasant happens.

spoil**
[spɔil]

v. (아이를) 버릇없게 키우다; 망치다, 버려 놓다; 상하다 (spoiled a. 버릇없는)
A spoiled person, especially a child, is rude and behaves badly because they have always been given what they want and allowed to do what they want.

loop*
[luːp]

n. 고리; v. 고리 모양을 만들다; 고리 모양으로 이동하다
A loop is a curved or circular shape in something long, for example, in a piece of string.

gleam*
[gliːm]

v. 어슴푸레 빛나다; (눈빛이 어떤 감정을 보이며) 반짝거리다; n. 어슴푸레한 빛
If an object or a surface gleams, it reflects light because it is shiny and clean.

melt**
[melt]

v. (감정 등이) 누그러지다; 녹다; n. 용해
If something such as your feelings melt, they suddenly disappear and you no longer feel them.

marvel*
[máːrvəl]

v. 경이로워하다, 경탄하다; n. 놀라운 일, 경이
If you marvel at something, you express your great surprise, wonder, or admiration.

magnificent*
[mægnífəsnt]

a. 훌륭한, 참으로 아름다운, 감명 깊은
If you say that something or someone is magnificent, you mean that you think they are extremely good, beautiful, or impressive.

masterpiece*
[mǽstərpiːs]

n. 걸작, 명작
A masterpiece is an extremely good painting, novel, film, or other work of art.

talent*
[tǽlənt]

n. (타고난) 재능, 재주; 재능 있는 사람 (talented a. 재능 있는)
Someone who is talented has a natural ability to do something well.

wire**
[waiər]

n. 철사; 전선, (전화기 등의) 선; v. 전선을 연결하다
A wire is a long thin piece of metal that is used to fasten things or to carry electric current.

stiff**
[stif]

a. 뻣뻣한; 딱딱한, 경직된; 심한; ad. 몹시, 극심하게
Something that is stiff is firm or does not bend easily.

wiggly
[wígli]

a. 꾸불꾸불한, 물결 모양의
Something wiggly is wavy and has many curves in it.

polish*
[páliʃ]

v. (윤이 나도록) 닦다; 다듬다; n. (광택 나도록) 닦기; 윤
If you polish something, you put polish on it or rub it with a cloth to make it shine.

precise*
[prisáis]

a. 정확한, 정밀한; 엄밀한, 꼼꼼한
Something that is precise is exact and accurate in all its details.

bend^{복습}
[bend]

v. (무엇을) 구부리다; (몸이나 머리를) 굽히다, 숙이다; n. 굽이, 굽은 곳
If you bend something that is flat or straight, you use force to make it curved or to put an angle in it.

rush**
[rʌʃ]

n. 분주함; 혼잡; v. 급히 움직이다, 서두르다
A rush is a situation in which you need to go somewhere or do something very quickly.

handful*
[hǽndfùl]

n. 몇 안 되는 수; 줌, 움큼
A handful of people or things is a small number of them.

switch*
[switʃ]

v. 전환하다, 바꾸다; n. 스위치
If you switch to something different, for example to a different system, task, or subject of conversation, you change to it from what you were doing or saying before.

admire**
[ædmáiər]

v. 감탄하며 바라보다; 존경하다, 칭찬하다
If you admire someone or something, you look at them with pleasure.

notice***
[nóutis]

v. 알아채다, 인지하다; 주목하다, 관심을 기울이다; n. 신경 씀, 알아챔
If you notice something or someone, you become aware of them.

Chapters 5 & 6

1. Why did Eric Ovens think he would have a day of glory?
   A. He got the highest score on the test.
   B. He found some paper clips for Mrs. Jewls.
   C. He brought a lot of nail clippings to class.
   D. He helped the class to win a prize.

2. What was the real reason that Eric Fry had kept his hand in a fist?
   A. He was angry at the other students.
   B. He was holding some nail clippings.
   C. He was making his hand feel warmer.
   D. He was trying to show people that he was tough.

3. How did Eric Bacon get so many nail clippings?
   A. He asked his family members for them.
   B. He got them from his neighbors.
   C. He had really long toenails.
   D. He took them from another student.

4. What was Kathy's odd behavior?
   A. She was being nice to everyone.
   B. She was always late for class.
   C. She finished her work quickly.
   D. She wore strange clothes.

5. How did Dr. Pickle feel about Kathy's attitude when she first entered his office?
   A. He got very angry about it.
   B. He thought that it was very interesting.
   C. He was sad about what she said to him.
   D. He wanted Kathy to leave the office.

6. What was Dr. Pickle's theory for helping Kathy?
   A. He tried to introduce her to a new friend.
   B. He tried to teach her some nice things to say.
   C. He tried to turn her opposites into double opposites.
   D. He tried to warn her about her attitude.

7. What was wrong with Kathy's homework?
   A. It was missing some pages.
   B. It had some spelling errors.
   C. It was written backward.
   D. It had very small letters.

Check Your Reading Speed

1분에 몇 단어를 읽는지 리딩 속도를 측정해 보세요.

$$\frac{752 \text{ words}}{\text{reading time ( ) sec}} \times 60 = (\quad) \text{ WPM}$$

Build Your Vocabulary

sneaky
[sníːki]

a. 교활한, 엉큼한
If you describe someone as sneaky, you disapprove of them because they do things secretly rather than openly.

trustworthy*
[trʌ́stwərði]

a. 신뢰할 수 있는, 믿을 수 있는
A trustworthy person is reliable, responsible, and can be trusted completely.

overlook*
[ouvərlúk]

v. 간과하다; 눈감아 주다; 내려다보다; n. (높이 있어) 전망이 좋은 곳
If you overlook a fact or problem, you do not notice it, or do not realize how important it is.

patient**
[péiʃənt]

a. 인내심 있는; n. 환자 (patiently ad. 끈기 있게, 참을성 있게)
If you are patient, you stay calm and do not get annoyed, for example when something takes a long time, or when someone is not doing what you want them to do.

attendance*
[əténdəns]

n. 출석, 참석; 참석자 수, 참석률 (take attendance idiom 출석을 확인하다)
If someone take attendance, they check who is present and who is not present at a place and mark this information on a list of names.

glory*
[glɔ́ːri]

n. 영광, 영예; 자랑스러운 것
Glory is the fame and admiration that you gain by doing something impressive.

nail복습
[neil]

n. 손톱, 발톱; 못; v. 못으로 박다
Your nails are the thin hard parts that grow at the ends of your fingers and toes.

clipping복습
[klípiŋ]

n. 잘라 낸 조각, 오려 낸 것
Clippings are small pieces of something that have been cut from something larger.

blackboard복습
[blǽkbɔ̀ːrd]

n. 칠판
A blackboard is a dark-colored board that you can write on with chalk.

whisper*
[hwíspər]

v. 속삭이다, 소곤거리다, 귓속말을 하다; n. 속삭임, 소곤거리는 소리
When you whisper, you say something very quietly.

jinx
[dʒiŋks]

v. 불운을 가져오다; n. 불길한 것, 징크스
To jinx means to cause a person or group to experience bad luck.

besides**
[bisáidz]

ad. 게다가, 뿐만 아니라; prep. ~외에
Besides is used to emphasize an additional point that you are making, especially one that you consider to be important.

mock*
[mak]

v. 놀리다, 조롱하다; a. 거짓된, 가짜의
If someone mocks you, they show or pretend that they think you are foolish or inferior, for example by saying something funny about you, or by imitating your behavior.

make one's way

idiom 나아가다, 가다
When you make your way somewhere, you walk or travel there.

declare***
[diklέər]

v. 선언하다, 공표하다; 분명히 말하다
If you declare something, you state officially and formally that it exists or is the case.

fist*
[fist]

n. 주먹
Your hand is referred to as your fist when you have bent your fingers in toward the palm.

bucket*
[bʌ́kit]

n. 양동이, 들통
A bucket is a round metal or plastic container with a handle attached to its sides.

clap^{복습}
[klæp]

v. 박수를 치다, 손뼉을 치다; n. 박수 (소리)
When you clap, you hit your hands together to show appreciation or attract attention.

halfway*
[hǽfwèi]

ad. (거리·시간상으로) 중간에, 가운데쯤에
Halfway means in the middle of a place or between two points, at an equal distance from each of them.

million^{복습}
[míljən]

n. 100만; a. 수많은
A million or one million is the number 1,000,000.

hop^{복습}
[hap]

v. 급히 가다; 깡충깡충 뛰다; n. 깡충 뛰기
If you hop somewhere, you move there quickly or suddenly.

triumphant
[traiʌ́mfənt]

a. 의기양양한; 크게 성공한, 큰 승리를 거둔 (triumphantly ad. 의기양양하게)
Someone who is triumphant has gained a victory or succeeded in something and feels very happy about it.

go wild

idiom 열광하다
If someone or something goes wild, they behave in a very excited uncontrolled way.

gasp*
[gæsp]

v. (숨이 막히는 듯) 헉 소리를 내다; 숨이 턱 막히다; n. (숨이 막히는 듯) 헉 하는 소리
When you gasp, you take a short quick breath through your mouth, especially when you are surprised, shocked, or in pain.

skeptical
[sképtikəl]

a. 의심 많은, 회의적인
If you are skeptical about something, you have doubts about it.

spectacle^{복습}
[spéktəkl]

n. (기이한·놀라운) 모습, 상황; 장관, 광경; 구경거리; (pl.) 안경
A spectacle is a strange or interesting sight.

warn^{복습}
[wɔːrn]

v. 주의를 주다, 경고하다, 조심하라고 하다
If you warn someone about something such as a possible danger or problem, you tell them about it so that they are aware of it.

challenge[**]
[ʧǽlindʒ]
v. 도전장을 내밀다; 도전하다; 도전 의식을 북돋우다; n. 도전; 저항
If you challenge someone, you invite them to compete or fight with you in some way.

stare[복습]
[stɛər]
v. 빤히 쳐다보다, 응시하다; n. 빤히 쳐다보기, 응시
If you stare at someone or something, you look at them for a long time.

dump[*]
[dʌmp]
v. (아무렇게나) 내려놓다; 버리다; n. (쓰레기) 폐기장
If you dump something somewhere, you put it or unload it there quickly and carelessly.

divide[***]
[diváid]
v. (여러 부분들로) 나누다, 가르다; (몫을) 나누다; (수를) 나누다
If you divide people or something into smaller groups or parts, they become separated into smaller parts.

pile[**]
[pail]
n. 무더기, 더미; (차곡차곡) 쌓아 놓은 것; v. (물건을 차곡차곡) 쌓다
A pile of things is a mass of them that is high in the middle and has sloping sides.

announce[복습]
[ənáuns]
v. 발표하다, 알리다; (공공장소에서) 방송으로 알리다
If you announce something, you tell people about it publicly or officially.

wrap[**]
[ræp]
v. (포장지 등으로) 싸다, 포장하다; (무엇의 둘레를) 두르다; n. 포장지
(wrapping paper n. 포장지)
When you wrap something, you fold paper or cloth tightly round it to cover it completely, for example in order to protect it or so that you can give it to someone as a present.

donate[*]
[dóuneit]
v. 기부하다, 기증하다; 헌혈하다
If you donate something to a charity or other organization, you give it to them.

erase[복습]
[iréis]
v. (지우개 등으로) 지우다; (완전히) 없애다
If you erase something such as writing or a mark, you remove it, usually by rubbing it with a cloth.

mutter[복습]
[mʌ́tər]
v. 중얼거리다; 투덜거리다; n. 중얼거림
If you mutter, you speak very quietly so that you cannot easily be heard, often because you are complaining about something.

glum[복습]
[glʌm]
a. 침울한 (glumly ad. 침울하게)
Someone who is glum is sad and quiet because they are disappointed or unhappy about something.

urge[*]
[əːrdʒ]
v. 재촉하다; 충고하다, 설득하려 하다; n. (강한) 욕구, 충동
If you urge someone to do something, you try hard to persuade them to do it.

bother[*]
[báðər]
v. 신경 쓰다, 애를 쓰다; 신경 쓰이게 하다, 괴롭히다; 귀찮게 하다; n. 성가심
If you bother to do something, you take the time or trouble to do it.

grab[*]
[græb]
v. (와락·단단히) 붙잡다; ~을 잡으려고 하다; n. 와락 잡아채려고 함
If you grab something, you take it or pick it up suddenly and roughly.

amaze[*]
[əméiz]

v. (대단히) 놀라게 하다 (amazingly ad. 놀랍게도)

You say that something is amazing when it is very surprising and makes you feel pleasure, approval, or wonder.

exclaim ^{복습}
[ikskléim]

v. 소리치다, 외치다

If you exclaim, you cry out suddenly in surprise, strong emotion, or pain.

Check Your Reading Speed

1분에 몇 단어를 읽는지 리딩 속도를 측정해 보세요.

$$\frac{847 \text{ words}}{\text{reading time ( ) sec}} \times 60 = (\quad) \text{ WPM}$$

Build Your Vocabulary

opposite^{복습}
[ápəzit]

n. 반대(되는 것); a. (정)반대의; 건너편의; 맞은편의
The opposite of someone or something is the person or thing that is most different from them.

notice^{복습}
[nóutis]

v. 알아채다, 인지하다; 주목하다, 관심을 기울이다; n. 신경 씀, 알아챔
If you notice something or someone, you become aware of them.

odd^{복습}
[ad]

a. 이상한, 특이한; 홀수의
If you describe someone or something as odd, you think that they are strange or unusual.

talent^{복습}
[tǽlənt]

n. (타고난) 재능, 재주; 재능 있는 사람 (talented a. 재능 있는)
Someone who is talented has a natural ability to do something well.

insult[*]
[insʌ́lt]

v. 모욕하다; n. 모욕
If someone insults you, they say or do something that is rude or offensive.

improve^{**}
[imprú:v]

v. 개선하다, 향상시키다 (improvement n. 개선, 향상)
If there is an improvement in something, it becomes better.

attitude^{**}
[ǽtitjùːd]

n. 태도, 자세; 반항적인 태도
Your attitude to something is the way that you think and feel about it, especially when this shows in the way you behave.

psychiatrist^{복습}
[saikáiətrist]

n. 정신과 의사
A psychiatrist is a doctor who treats people suffering from mental illness.

pat^{복습}
[pæt]

v. 쓰다듬다, 토닥거리다; n. 쓰다듬기, 토닥거리기
If you pat something or someone, you tap them lightly, usually with your hand held flat.

hiccup^{복습}
[híkʌp]

n. 딸꾹질; 딸꾹 하는 소리; v. 딸꾹질을 하다, 딸꾹 하는 소리를 내다
When you have hiccups, you make repeated sharp sounds in your throat, often because you have been eating or drinking too quickly.

counselor^{복습}
[káunsələr]

n. (학교의) 학생 상담 교사; 의논 상대자
A counselor is a person whose job is to give advice to people who need it, especially advice on their personal problems.

beard^{복습}
[biərd]

n. (턱)수염
A man's beard is the hair that grows on his chin and cheeks.

stroke[*]
[strouk]

v. 쓰다듬다, 어루만지다; 달래다; n. (손으로) 쓰다듬기; (글씨나 그림의) 획
If you stroke someone or something, you move your hand slowly and gently over them.

sniff[*]
[snif]

v. 냄새를 맡다; 코를 훌쩍이다; n. 냄새 맡기; 콧방귀 뀌기
If you sniff something or sniff at it, you smell it by taking air in through your nose.

comment[**]
[káment]

v. 견해를 밝히다, 논평하다; n. 언급, 논평
If you comment on something, you give your opinion about it or you give an explanation for it.

couch[복습]
[kautʃ]

n. 소파, 긴 의자
A couch is a long, comfortable seat for two or three people.

lumpy
[lámpi]

a. 울퉁불퉁한, 덩어리진
Something that is lumpy contains or is covered with small solid pieces.

complain[**]
[kəmpléin]

v. 불평하다, 항의하다
If you complain about a situation, you say that you are not satisfied with it.

experiment[복습]
[ikspérəmənt]

n. (과학적인) 실험; v. (과학적인) 실험을 하다
An experiment is a scientific test which is done in order to discover what happens to something in particular conditions.

pop[*]
[pap]

v. 불쑥 나타나다; 불쑥 움직이다; 펑 하고 터뜨리다; 펑 하는 소리를 내다; n. 펑 하고 터지는 소리
If something pops, it suddenly appears, especially when not expected.

sloppy
[slápi]

a. 엉성한, 대충 하는; 헐렁한
If you describe someone's work or activities as sloppy, you mean they have been done in a careless and lazy way.

skinny
[skíni]

a. 깡마른, 비쩍 여윈; (물건의) 폭이 좁은
A skinny person is extremely thin, often in a way that you find unattractive.

bore[*]
[bɔːr]

v. 지루하게 하다 (boring a. 재미없는, 지루한)
Someone or something boring is so dull and uninteresting that they make people tired and impatient.

unfortunate[*]
[ʌnfɔ́ːrtʃənət]

a. 운이 없는, 불운한, 불행한 (unfortunately ad. 불행하게도, 유감스럽게도)
You can use unfortunately to introduce or refer to a statement when you consider that it is sad or disappointing, or when you want to express regret.

cure[**]
[kjuər]

n. 치유법; 해결책; v. (사람·동물을) 낫게 하다; (문제를) 고치다
A cure for an illness is a medicine or other treatment that makes a sick person healthy.

patient[복습]
[péiʃənt]

n. 환자; a. 인내심 있는
A patient is a person who is receiving medical treatment from a doctor or hospital.

positive**
[pázətiv]

a. 긍정적인; 확신하는; 분명한 (positively ad. 긍정적으로)
If you are positive about things, you are hopeful and confident, and think of the good aspects of a situation rather than the bad ones.

theory**
[θíːəri]

n. (개인적인) 의견; 이론; 학설
If you have a theory about something, you have your own opinion about it which you cannot prove but which you think is true.

drawer^{복습}
[drɔːr]

n. 서랍
A drawer is part of a desk, chest, or other piece of furniture that is shaped like a box and is designed for putting things in.

swing^{복습}
[swiŋ]

v. (swung-swung) (전후·좌우로) 흔들(리)다; 획 움직이다; n. 흔들기; 휘두르기
If something swings or if you swing it, it moves repeatedly backward and forward or from side to side from a fixed point.

back and forth^{복습}
[bæk ən fɔ́ːrθ]

ad. 앞뒤(좌우)로; 여기저기에, 왔다 갔다
If someone or something moves back and forth, they repeatedly move in one direction and then in the opposite direction.

count^{복습}
[kaunt]

n. (하나부터 순서대로 세는) 셈; 계산; v. (수를) 세다; 계산에 넣다
A count is an act of saying numbers in order, up to a particular number.

pointy^{복습}
[pɔ́inti]

a. 끝이 뾰족한; 가시가 돋은
Something that is pointy has a thin, sharp point at one end.

reach out

idiom (손·팔을) 뻗다; 접근하다, 연락하다; 추구하다, 노력하다
If you reach out, you move your arm and hand to take or touch something.

solid^{복습}
[sálid]

a. 단단한; 고체의; (다른 물질이 섞이지 않고) 순수한; n. 고체, 고형물
A substance that is solid is very hard or firm.

stick out

idiom ~을 내밀다, 튀어나오게 하다
If you stick out part of your body, you extend it away from your body.

weird*
[wiərd]

a. 기이한, 기묘한; 기괴한, 섬뜩한
If you describe something or someone as weird, you mean that they are strange.

hesitate***
[hézətèit]

v. 망설이다, 주저하다; 거리끼다
If you hesitate to do something, you delay doing it or are unwilling to do it, usually because you are not certain it would be right.

amaze^{복습}
[əméiz]

v. (대단히) 놀라게 하다 (amazing a. 놀라운)
You say that something is amazing when it is very surprising and makes you feel pleasure, approval, or wonder.

note***
[nout]

v. 언급하다; 주목하다; n. 메모; 음, 음표; 편지, 쪽지
When you note something, you make particular mention of it or remark upon it.

wise ^{복습}
[waiz]

a. 지혜로운, 현명한, 슬기로운
A wise person is able to use their experience and knowledge in order to make sensible decisions and judgments.

sigh ^{복습}
[sai]

v. 한숨을 쉬다, 한숨짓다; n. 한숨
When you sigh, you let out a deep breath, as a way of expressing feelings such as disappointment, tiredness, or pleasure.

figure out

idiom (생각한 끝에) ~을 이해하다; (양·비용을) 계산하다
If you figure out someone or something, you come to understand them by thinking carefully.

Chapters 7 & 8

1. What did Mac think was the most curious thing about the closet?

   A. It was wrapped in chains and had a padlock on it.

   B. It had a lot of warning signs all over it.

   C. It was not something he noticed near the classroom before.

   D. It had a very strange smell coming from it.

2. Why did Mac put on his catcher's mask outside the closet?

   A. He thought it would help him to see through the keyhole.

   B. He was getting ready to play some sports.

   C. He did not want to lose the mask again.

   D. He wanted to be safe before trying to open the closet.

3. What did the students do when they saw the signs on the closet?

   A. They went to find Mrs. Jewls.

   B. They sniffed around the closet.

   C. They called the fire department.

   D. They tried to open the closet.

4. What did Joy do to try to get picked by Mrs. Jewls?

    A. She stood up on her chair so she could be seen.

    B. She ran to the front of the classroom.

    C. She shouted loudly to Mrs. Jewls.

    D. She put up two arms and waved them around.

5. Why was Mrs. Jewls worried about the safety railing?

    A. It was built too close to the edge.

    B. It was easy for students to slip under it.

    C. It was covered in wet paint.

    D. It was broken in some places.

6. What did Bebe do while Mrs. Jewls pointed out clouds?

    A. She drew pictures of clouds and other things.

    B. She asked Mrs. Jewls a lot of questions.

    C. She took notes about the names of the clouds.

    D. She started to take a nap on a pillow.

7. Why did Mrs. Jewls let out a gasp?

    A. One of the students said a bad word.

    B. One of the students nearly fell off the edge.

    C. She saw a dark cloud in the distance.

    D. She heard the sound of a storm.

Check Your Reading Speed

1분에 몇 단어를 읽는지 리딩 속도를 측정해 보세요.

$$\frac{683 \text{ words}}{\text{reading time ( ) sec}} \times 60 = (\quad) \text{ WPM}$$

Build Your Vocabulary

closet*
[klázit]

n. 벽장
A closet is a piece of furniture with doors at the front and shelves inside, which is used for storing things.

curious**
[kjúəriəs]

a. 호기심이 많은; 궁금한; 별난
Someone who is curious wants to find out about something.

serve***
[sə:rv]

v. (식당 등에서 음식을) 제공하다; 도움이 되다, 기여하다; n. (테니스 등에서) 서브
When you serve food and drink, you give people food and drink.

besides복습
[bisáidz]

prep. ~외에; ad. 게다가, 뿐만 아니라
Besides means other than someone or something.

appoint**
[əpɔ́int]

v. 임명하다, 지명하다; (시간·장소를) 정하다 (self-appointed a. 자칭의)
A self-appointed leader or ruler has taken the position of leader or ruler without anyone else asking them or choosing them to have it.

describe**
[diskráib]

v. (~이 어떠한지를) 말하다, 묘사하다
If you describe a person, object, event, or situation, you say what they are like or what happened.

cafeteria*
[kæfətíəriə]

n. (학교·회사 등의) 구내식당; 카페테리아
A cafeteria is a lunchroom or dining hall, as in a factory, office, or school, where food is often served from counters.

include**
[inklú:d]

v. 포함하다; ~을 (~에) 포함시키다
If one thing includes another thing, it has the other thing as one of its parts.

hardly***
[há:rdli]

ad. 거의 ~ 아니다; 거의 ~할 수가 없다; 막 ~하자마자
You use hardly to modify a statement when you want to emphasize that it is only a small amount or detail which makes it true, and that therefore it is best to consider the opposite statement as being true.

worth**
[wə:rθ]

a. ~해 볼 만한, ~할 가치가 있는; (금전 등의 면에서) ~의 가치가 있는; n. 가치, 값어치
If something is worth a particular action, or if an action is worth doing, it is considered to be important enough for that action.

all the way

idiom 내내, 시종; 완전히
You use all the way to emphasize how long a distance is.

playground*
[pléigràund]

n. (학교의) 운동장; 놀이터
A playground is a piece of land, at school or in a public area, where children can play.

story^{복습}
[stɔ́:ri]

① n. (건물의) 층 ② n. 이야기
A story of a building is one of its different levels, which is situated above or below other levels.

giant^{복습}
[dʒáiənt]

a. 거대한; 위대한; n. (이야기 속의) 거인
Something that is described as giant is much larger or more important than most others of its kind.

wrap^{복습}
[ræp]

v. (무엇의 둘레를) 두르다; (포장지 등으로) 싸다, 포장하다; n. 포장지
When you wrap something such as a piece of paper or cloth round another thing, you put it around it.

lock^{복습}
[lak]

v. (자물쇠로) 잠그다; 고정하다; n. 자물쇠
When you lock something such as a door, drawer, or case, you fasten it, usually with a key, so that other people cannot open it.

steel**
[sti:l]

n. 강철; v. (~에 대비해서) 마음을 단단히 먹다
Steel is a very strong metal which is made mainly from iron.

clamp*
[klæmp]

v. (죄는 기구로) 고정시키다; 꽉 물다; n. 죄는 기구, 죔쇠
When you clamp one thing to another, you fasten the two things together with a clamp.

sign***
[sain]

n. 표지판, 간판; 징후, 조짐; v. 서명하다; (손으로) 신호를 보내다
A sign is a piece of wood, metal, or plastic with words or pictures on it.

fire department
[fáiər dipà:rtmənt]

n. 소방서, 소방대
The fire department is an organization which has the job of putting out fires.

sniff^{복습}
[snif]

v. 냄새를 맡다; 코를 훌쩍이다; n. 냄새 맡기; 콧방귀 뀌기
If you sniff something or sniff at it, you smell it by taking air in through your nose.

budge
[bʌdʒ]

v. 약간 움직이다, 꼼짝하다; 의견을 바꾸다
If someone or something will not budge, they will not move.

peer*
[piər]

v. 유심히 보다, 눈여겨보다; n. 또래
If you peer at something, you look at it very hard, usually because it is difficult to see clearly.

knock^{복습}
[nak]

v. (문 등을) 두드리다; n. 문 두드리는 소리
If you knock on something such as a door or window, you hit it, usually several times, to attract someone's attention.

press**
[pres]

v. (무엇에) 바짝 대다; 누르다; 꾹 밀어 넣다 n. 언론
If you press something somewhere, you push it firmly against something else.

shrug^{복습}
[ʃrʌg]

v. (두 손바닥을 위로 하고) 어깨를 으쓱하다; n. 어깨를 으쓱하기
If you shrug, you raise your shoulders to show that you are not interested in something or that you do not know or care about something.

make it^{복습}

idiom 가다; 성공하다, 해내다
If you make it to somewhere, you succeed in reaching there.

rattle*
[rǽtl]

v. 덜거덕거리게 하다; 덜거덕거리다; 당황하게 하다; n. 덜거덕거리는 소리
When something rattles or when you rattle it, it makes short sharp knocking sounds because it is being shaken or it keeps hitting against something hard.

determine*
[ditə́:rmin]

v. 알아내다, 밝히다; 결정하다
To determine a fact means to discover it as a result of investigation.

shudder*
[ʃʌ́dər]

v. (공포·추위 등으로) 몸을 떨다, 몸서리치다; n. 몸이 떨림, 전율
If you shudder, you shake with fear, horror, or disgust, or because you are cold.

boost*
[bu:st]

n. 밀어 올리기; 격려; 증가; v. 신장시키다, 북돋우다
If you give someone a boost, you lift them up, so that they can reach something that is high up.

cup*
[kʌp]

v. 두 손을 동그랗게 모아 쥐다; n. 컵, 잔
If you cup your hands, you make them into a curved shape like a cup.

grip**
[grip]

v. 꽉 잡다, 움켜잡다; n. 꽉 붙잡음; 통제, 지배
If you grip something, you take hold of it with your hand and continue to hold it firmly.

shimmy
[ʃími]

v. (손과 다리를 이용하여) 재빨리 ~을 타고 오르내리다; 몸을 흔들며 움직이다
When you shimmy up or down something, you climb smoothly up or down it by holding it tightly with your arms and legs.

get away

idiom (~에서) 탈출하다, 벗어나다
If you get away from someone or some place, you escape from them or that place.

lounge^{복습}
[laundʒ]

n. (호텔·클럽 등의) 휴게실; (공항 등의) 대합실; v. 느긋하게 있다
In a hotel, club, or other public place, a lounge is a room where people can sit and relax.

hop^{복습}
[hap]

v. 급히 가다; 깡충깡충 뛰다; n. 깡충 뛰기
If you hop somewhere, you move there quickly or suddenly.

tangle*
[tǽŋgl]

v. 얽히다, 헝클어지다; n. (실·머리카락 등이) 엉킨 것; (혼란스럽게) 꼬인 상태
If something is tangled or tangles, it becomes twisted together in an untidy way.

complain^{복습}
[kəmpléin]

v. 불평하다, 항의하다
If you complain about a situation, you say that you are not satisfied with it.

never you mind

idiom ~은 묻지 마라 (말해 주지 않을 테니까)
You can say 'never you mind' to tell someone not to ask about something because it is not their concern or they should not know about it.

insist^{복습}
[insíst]

v. 고집하다, 주장하다, 우기다
If you insist that something is the case, you say so very firmly and refuse to say otherwise, even though other people do not believe you.

shuffle
[ʃʌfl]

v. 발을 끌며 걷다; (게임을 하기 위해 카드를) 섞다; 이리저리 움직이다;
n. 느릿느릿 걷기
If you shuffle somewhere, you walk there without lifting your feet properly off the ground.

adjust**
[ədʒʌ́st]

v. (매무새 등을) 바로잡다; 조정하다; 적응하다
If you adjust something such as your clothing or a machine, you correct or alter its position or setting.

cockeyed
[kákàid]

a. 비뚤어진, 삐딱한; 비현실적인
If something is cockeyed, it looks wrong because it is not straight, but sloping to one side.

Check Your Reading Speed

1분에 몇 단어를 읽는지 리딩 속도를 측정해 보세요.

$$\frac{730 \text{ words}}{\text{reading time ( ) sec}} \times 60 = (\quad) \text{ WPM}$$

Build Your Vocabulary

stretch 복습
[stretʃ]
v. (팔·다리를) 뻗다; 기지개를 켜다; 펼쳐지다; n. (길게) 뻗은 구간; 기간
If you stretch your arm or leg, you move it away from your body in order to reach something.

figure***
[fígjər]
v. 생각하다; 중요하다; n. (멀리서 흐릿하게 보이는) 사람; 수치; (중요한) 인물
If you figure that something is the case, you think or guess that it is the case.

double**
[dʌbl]
v. 두 배로 만들다; a. 두 배의, 갑절의; 이중의; n. 두 배, 갑절
When something doubles or when you double it, it becomes twice as great in number, amount, or size.

wave**
[weiv]
v. (손·팔을) 흔들다; 손짓하다; n. 파도, 물결; (손·팔·몸을) 흔들기
If you wave or wave your hand, you move your hand from side to side in the air, usually in order to say hello or goodbye to someone.

beg*
[beg]
v. 간청하다, 애원하다; 구걸하다
If you beg someone to do something, you ask them very anxiously or eagerly to do it.

urge 복습
[əːrdʒ]
v. 재촉하다; 충고하다, 설득하려 하다; n. (강한) 욕구, 충동
If you urge someone to do something, you try hard to persuade them to do it.

groan*
[groun]
v. 신음 소리를 내다; 끙끙거리다; n. 신음; 끙 하는 소리
If you groan, you make a long, low sound because you are in pain, or because you are upset or unhappy about something.

dirt**
[dəːrt]
n. 흙; 먼지, 때
You can refer to the earth on the ground as dirt, especially when it is dusty.

trudge
[trʌdʒ]
v. 터덜터덜 걷다; 느릿느릿 걷다; n. 터덜터덜 걷기
If you trudge somewhere, you walk there slowly and with heavy steps, especially because you are tired or unhappy.

gather**
[gǽðər]
v. (사람들이) 모이다; 모으다, 챙기다
If people gather somewhere or if someone gathers people somewhere, they come together in a group.

closet 복습
[klázit]
n. 벽장
A closet is a piece of furniture with doors at the front and shelves inside, which is used for storing things.

44

waist**
[weist]

n. 허리
Your waist is the middle part of your body where it narrows slightly above your hips.

giggle*
[gigl]

v. 킥킥거리다, 피식 웃다; n. 킥킥거림, 피식 웃음.
If someone giggles, they laugh in a childlike way, because they are amused, nervous, or embarrassed.

trapdoor
[trǽpdɔ:r]

n. (바닥·천장에 나 있는) 작은 문
A trapdoor is a small horizontal door in a floor, a ceiling, or on a stage.

roof ^{복습}
[ru:f]

n. 지붕
The roof of a building is the covering on top of it that protects the people and things inside from the weather.

tiptoe
[típtòu]

n. 발끝; v. 발끝으로 살금살금 걷다
If you do something on tiptoe or on tiptoes, you do it standing or walking on the front part of your foot, without putting your heels on the ground.

ladder*
[lǽdər]

n. 사다리
A ladder is a piece of equipment used for climbing up something or down from something.

tumble*
[tʌmbl]

v. 굴러 떨어지다; 폭삭 무너지다; n. (갑자기) 굴러 떨어짐; 폭락
If someone or something tumbles somewhere, they fall there with a rolling or bouncing movement.

railing
[réiliŋ]

n. 난간; 울타리
A fence made from metal bars is called a railing or railings.

slip*
[slip]

v. 미끄러지다; 슬며시 가다; (재빨리·슬며시) 놓다; n. (작은) 실수; 미끄러짐
If something slips, it slides out of place or out of your hand.

demand ^{복습}
[dimǽnd]

v. 강력히 묻다, 따지다; 요구하다; n. 요구 (사항)
If you demand something such as information or action, you ask for it in a very forceful way.

blank*
[blæŋk]

a. 멍한, 무표정한; (글자가 없는) 빈; n. 빈칸, 여백 (blankly ad. 멍하니)
If you look blank, your face shows no feeling, understanding, or interest.

pay attention ^{복습}

idiom 주의를 기울이다; 관심을 갖다
If you pay attention to someone, you watch them, listen to them, or take notice of them.

giant ^{복습}
[dʒáiənt]

n. (이야기 속의) 거인; a. 거대한; 위대한
A giant is an imaginary person who is very big and strong, especially one mentioned in old stories.

pillow*
[pílou]

n. 베개
A pillow is a rectangular cushion which you rest your head on when you are in bed.

swirl
[swə:rl]

v. 빙빙 돌다, 소용돌이치다; 빙빙 돌게 하다; n. 소용돌이
When something swirls, it moves around quickly in a circle.

dull**
[dʌl]

a. 흐릿한, 칙칙한; 따분한, 재미없는; v. 둔해지다, 약해지다
A dull color or light is not bright.

distance**
[dístəns]

n. (특정한 거리를 사이에 둔) 먼 곳; (공간상·시간상으로 떨어진) 거리
If you can see something in the distance, you can see it, far away from you.

gasp^{복습}
[gæsp]

v. (숨이 막히는 듯) 헉 소리를 내다; 숨이 턱 막히다; n. (숨이 막히는 듯) 헉 하는 소리
When you gasp, you take a short quick breath through your mouth, especially when you are surprised, shocked, or in pain.

exact***
[igzǽkt]

a. 정확한, 정밀한; 꼼꼼한, 빈틈없는 (exactly ad. 정확히, 꼭)
You use exactly before an amount, number, or position to emphasize that it is no more, no less, or no different from what you are stating.

vacuum*
[vǽkjuəm]

n. 진공청소기; 진공; v. 진공청소기로 청소하다
A vacuum or a vacuum cleaner is an electric machine that sucks up dust and dirt from carpets.

scramble*
[skrǽmbl]

v. 재빨리 움직이다; 서로 밀치다; n. 쟁탈전을 벌이기; (힘들게) 기어가기
If you scramble to a different place or position, you move there in a hurried, awkward way.

hatch*
[hætʃ]

n. (바닥·천장에 나 있는) 출입구; v. 부화하다; (계획 등을) 만들어 내다
A hatch is a door cut into the floor or ceiling of a ship, airplane, or building that people or things can move through.

atop
[ətáp]

prep. 꼭대기에, 맨 위에
If something is atop something else, it is on top of it.

toss*
[tɔ:s]

v. (가볍게·아무렇게나) 던지다; n. (고개를) 홱 젖히기
If you toss something somewhere, you throw it there lightly, often in a rather careless way.

steel^{복습}
[sti:l]

n. 강철; v. (~에 대비해서) 마음을 단단히 먹다
Steel is a very strong metal which is made mainly from iron.

slight**
[slait]

a. 약간의, 조금의; 작고 여윈
Something that is slight is very small in degree or quantity.

tremble*
[trembl]

n. 떨림, 전율; v. 떨다, 떨리다; (가슴이) 떨리다
A tremble is an act of shaking slightly in a way that you cannot control, for example because you are frightened, angry, or excited.

doom
[du:m]

n. 불운, 저주; 죽음, 파멸; v. 불행한 운명을 맞게 하다
Doom is a terrible future state or event which you cannot prevent.

darken*
[dá:rkən]

v. 어두워지다, 어둡게 만들다; 우울해지다
If something darkens or if a person or thing darkens it, it becomes darker.

Chapters 9 & 10

1. Why did Louis hear a loud bang?
   A. The Cloud of Doom made a noise like thunder.
   B. He accidentally dropped the air pump on the ground.
   C. The gong fell over while he was pushing it.
   D. He put too much air in a ball, and it exploded.

2. What did Louis plan to do with the ball?
   A. He planned to sew the broken pieces back together.
   B. He planned to throw it in the garbage.
   C. He planned to give it to one of the students.
   D. He planned to leave it in Mr. Kidswatter's office.

3. Why couldn't Louis hear Mr. Kidswatter when he got to the principal's office?
   A. Mr. Kidswatter was whispering to Louis.
   B. Mr. Kidswatter was too far away.
   C. Louis was talking on the phone.
   D. Louis had put cotton balls in his ears.

4. How did Louis get some money?
   A. He found it at the school.
   B. He wrote some books.
   C. He got a job at a bank.
   D. He won a prize in a contest.

5. What is Dana's special talent?
   A. Making funny faces
   B. Standing on her head
   C. Drawing beautiful pictures
   D. Singing "Jingle Bells"

6. Why did Jenny, Leslie, and Dana like the Patches ball?
   A. They did not know which way it would bounce.
   B. They thought it had beautiful colors.
   C. It was not as heavy as the other balls.
   D. It could bounce very high.

7. What made Dana's face pop back to normal?
   A. Louis blew a whistle loudly.
   B. Mr. Kidswatter patted her on the head.
   C. Todd told Dana a joke.
   D. Dana splashed some water on her face.

Check Your Reading Speed

1분에 몇 단어를 읽는지 리딩 속도를 측정해 보세요.

$$\frac{\textbf{727 words}}{\textbf{reading time (\quad) sec}} \times 60 = (\quad) \textbf{ WPM}$$

Build Your Vocabulary

yard**
[ja:rd]

n. (학교의) 운동장; 마당, 뜰; 정원
A yard is a flat area of concrete or stone that is next to a building and often has a wall around it.

doom^{복습}
[du:m]

n. 불운, 저주; 죽음, 파멸; v. 불행한 운명을 맞게 하다
Doom is a terrible future state or event which you cannot prevent.

cast***
[kæst]

v. (그림자를) 드리우다; (시선·미소 등을) 던지다; n. 깁스 (붕대)
If something casts a light or shadow somewhere, it causes it to appear there.

gloomy*
[glú:mi]

a. 어둑어둑한; 음울한; 우울한, 침울한
If a place is gloomy, it is almost dark so that you cannot see very well.

eerie
[íəri]

a. 괴상한, 으스스한
If you describe something as eerie, you mean that it seems strange and frightening, and makes you feel nervous.

chill*
[tʃil]

n. 오싹한 느낌; 냉기, 한기; v. 아주 춥게 만들다
If something sends a chill through you, it gives you a sudden feeling of fear or anxiety.

bang^{복습}
[bæŋ]

n. 쾅 하는 소리; v. 쾅 하고 치다; 쾅 하고 닫다
A bang is a sudden loud noise such as the noise of an explosion.

blacktop
[blǽktàp]

n. 아스팔트 도로; (포장에 쓰이는) 아스팔트; v. 아스팔트로 포장하다
Blacktop is a hard black substance which is used as a surface for roads, as well as a road covered with this substance.

wiggle
[wigl]

v. (좌우·상하로 짧게) 꿈틀꿈틀 움직이다
If you wiggle something or if it wiggles, it moves up and down or from side to side in small quick movements.

stick out^{복습}

idiom ~을 내밀다, 튀어나오게 하다
If you stick out part of your body, you extend it away from your body.

tongue^{복습}
[tʌŋ]

n. 혀; 언어
Your tongue is the soft movable part inside your mouth which you use for tasting, eating, and speaking.

wobbly
[wábli]

a. (불안정하게) 흔들리는, 기우뚱한; 불안정한, 떨리는
If you feel wobbly or if your legs feel wobbly, you feel weak and have difficulty standing up, especially because you are afraid, ill, or exhausted.

rubber**
[rʌ́bər]

n. 고무
Rubber is a strong, waterproof, elastic substance made from the juice of a tropical tree or produced chemically.

scatter**
[skǽtər]

v. 흩뿌리다; 황급히 흩어지게 만들다; n. 소수, 소량
If you scatter things over an area, you throw or drop them so that they spread all over the area.

playground^{복습}
[pléigràund]

n. (학교의) 운동장; 놀이터
A playground is a piece of land, at school or in a public area, where children can play.

explode*
[iksplóud]

v. 터지다, 폭발하다; (갑자기 강한 감정을) 터뜨리다
If an object such as a bomb explodes or if someone or something explodes it, it bursts loudly and with great force, often causing damage or injury.

bouncy
[báunsi]

a. 잘 튀는, 탱탱한; 활기 넘치는
A bouncy thing can bounce very well or makes other things bounce well.

afford**
[əfɔ́:rd]

v. (~을 살·할) 여유가 되다; 제공하다
If you say that you cannot afford to do something, you mean that you are not able to do it because you don't have enough money or time.

sew*
[sou]

v. 바느질하다, 깁다
When you sew something such as clothes, you make them or repair them by joining pieces of cloth together by passing thread through them with a needle.

principal^{복습}
[prínsəpəl]

n. 교장; 학장, 총장; a. 주요한, 주된
A principal is a teacher who is in charge of a school.

stuff^{복습}
[stʌf]

v. (재빨리) 쑤셔 넣다; (빽빽이) 채워 넣다; n. 일, 것; 물건
If you stuff something somewhere, you push it there quickly and roughly.

cotton**
[katn]

n. 솜; 면직물; 목화; a. 면으로 된
Cotton is a soft, white, downy substance consisting of the hairs or fibers attached to the seeds of particular plants.

wheel**
[hwi:l]

v. (바퀴 달린 것을) 밀다, 끌다; n. 바퀴; (자동차 등의) 핸들
If you wheel an object that has wheels somewhere, you push it along.

dull^{복습}
[dʌl]

a. 흐릿한, 칙칙한; 따분한, 재미없는; v. 둔해지다, 약해지다
A dull color or light is not bright.

dent
[dent]

v. 찌그러뜨리다; (자신감·명성을) 훼손하다; n. 움푹 들어간 곳 (dented a. 찌그러진)
If you dent the surface of something, you make a hollow area in it by hitting or pressing it.

iron^{복습}
[áiərn]

n. 철, 쇠; 철분; 다리미
Iron is an element which usually takes the form of a hard, dark grey metal. It is used to make steel, and also forms part of many tools, buildings, and vehicles.

hook**
[huk]

n. (갈)고리, 걸이; v. ~에 걸다; 갈고리로 잠그다
A hook is a bent piece of metal or plastic that is used for catching or holding things, or for hanging things up.

frame**
[freim]

n. (가구 · 건물 · 차량 등의) 뼈대; 틀, 액자; v. 틀에 넣다, 테를 두르다
The frame of an object such as a piece of furniture, vehicle, or other object is the structure or main supporting parts of it.

steady**
[stédi]

v. 균형을 잡다; 진정시키다, 가라앉히다; a. 꾸준한; 안정된
If you steady yourself, you get your balance again so that you do not fall.

countdown
[káuntdaun]

n. 카운트다운; (중요한 행사의) 초읽기
A countdown is the counting aloud of numbers in reverse order before something happens, for example before a spacecraft is launched.

dot*
[dat]

n. 점; v. 점을 찍다; 여기저기 흩어져 있다
A dot is a very small round mark or spot.

dead***
[ded]

a. 완전한, 정확한; 죽은; ad. 정확히 (dead center n. 정중앙)
Dead is used to mean 'complete' or 'absolute,' especially before the words 'center,' 'silence,' and 'stop.'

rattle^{복습}
[rǽtl]

v. 덜거덕거리다; 덜거덕거리게 하다; 당황하게 하다; n. 덜거덕거리는 소리
When something rattles or when you rattle it, it makes short sharp knocking sounds because it is being shaken or it keeps hitting against something hard.

echo*
[ékou]

v. (소리가) 울리다, 메아리치다; 그대로 따라 하다; n. (소리의) 울림, 메아리
If a sound echoes, it is reflected off a surface and can be heard again after the original sound has stopped.

flood
[flʌd]

v. 쇄도하다, 물밀듯이 밀려들다; 물에 잠기다; 범람하다; n. 쇄도, 폭주; 홍수
If you say that people or things flood into a place, you are emphasizing that they arrive there in large numbers.

wave^{복습}
[weiv]

v. (손 · 팔을) 흔들다; 손짓하다; n. 파도, 물결; (손 · 팔 · 몸을) 흔들기
If you wave or wave your hand, you move your hand from side to side in the air, usually in order to say hello or goodbye to someone.

no way

idiom (강한 거절의 의미로) 절대로 안 돼, 싫어; 말도 안 돼
You can say 'no way' for expressing surprise, or for telling someone that you do not believe them.

snap^{복습}
[snæp]

v. 딱딱거리다, 톡 쏘다; 탁 하고 움직이다; 사진을 찍다; n. 찰칵 하는 소리
If someone snaps at you, they speak to you in a sharp, unfriendly way.

recess^{복습}
[risés]

n. (학교의) 쉬는 시간; (의회 · 위원회 등의) 휴회 기간
A recess is a break between classes at a school.

rob**
[rab]

v. 털다, 도둑질하다
To rob is to to take something from someone illegally, as by force or threat of violence.

frown*
[fraun]

v. 얼굴을 찌푸리다; n. 찡그림, 찌푸림
When someone frowns, their eyebrows become drawn together, because they are annoyed or puzzled.

52

declare ^{복습}
[dikléər]

v. 분명히 말하다; 선언하다, 공표하다
If you declare something, you state something clearly and definitely.

exclaim ^{복습}
[ikskléim]

v. 소리치다, 외치다 (exclamation point n. 느낌표, 감탄 부호)
An exclamation point is the sign '!' which is used in writing to show that a word, phrase, or sentence is an exclamation.

suggestion ^{복습}
[səgdʒésʧən]

n. 제안, 의견; 암시
If you make a suggestion, you put forward an idea or plan for someone to think about.

Check Your Reading Speed

1분에 몇 단어를 읽는지 리딩 속도를 측정해 보세요.

$$\frac{844 \text{ words}}{\text{reading time ( ) sec}} \times 60 = (\quad) \text{ WPM}$$

Build Your Vocabulary

stuck^{복습}
[stʌk]

a. 움직일 수 없는, 꼼짝 못하는; (불쾌한 상황에서) 빠져나갈 수 없는; (대답 등이) 막힌
If something is stuck in a particular position, it is fixed tightly in this position and is unable to move.

talent^{복습}
[tǽlənt]

n. (타고난) 재능, 재주; 재능 있는 사람
Talent is the natural ability to do something well.

**stand on
one's head**^{복습}

idiom 물구나무를 서다
If you stand on your head, you balance upside down with the top of your head and your hands on the ground.

jingle
[dʒingl]

v. 짤랑짤랑 소리를 내다; n. 딸랑딸랑 울리는 소리
When something jingles or when you jingle it, it makes a gentle ringing noise, like small bells.

puff out

idiom (공기를 채워) 불룩하게 부풀리다
If you puff out your cheeks, you make them larger and rounder by filling them with air.

cheek**
[ʧiːk]

n. 뺨, 볼
Your cheeks are the sides of your face below your eyes.

opposite^{복습}
[ápəzit]

a. (정)반대의; 건너편의; 맞은편의; n. 반대(되는 것)
Opposite is used to describe the other of a pair that are corresponding or complementary in position, function, or nature.

eyebrow*
[áibràu]

n. 눈썹
Your eyebrows are the lines of hair which grow above your eyes.

crack up

idiom 마구 웃기 시작하다
If you crack up, you start laughing a lot.

goofball
[gúːfbɔ̀ːl]

n. 멍청이, 얼간이
If you describe someone or something as goofball, you think they are rather silly or ridiculous.

upside down
[Àpsaid dáun]

ad. (아래위가) 거꾸로
If something has been turned upside down, it has been turned around so that the part that is usually lowest is above the part that is usually highest.

pinky
[píŋki]

n. 새끼손가락
Your pinky is the smallest finger on your hand.

tug ^{복습}
[tʌg]

v. (세게) 잡아당기다; n. (갑자기 세게) 잡아당김
If you tug something or tug at it, you give it a quick and usually strong pull.

earlobe
[íərlòub]

n. 귓불
Your earlobes are the soft parts at the bottom of your ears.

bump[*]
[bʌmp]

v. 부딪치다; 마주치다; 덜컹거리며 가다; n. 쿵, 탁 (부딪치는 소리)
If you bump into something or someone, you accidentally hit them while you are moving.

warn ^{복습}
[wɔ:rn]

v. 주의를 주다, 경고하다, 조심하라고 하다
If you warn someone about something such as a possible danger or problem, you tell them about it so that they are aware of it.

weird ^{복습}
[wiərd]

a. 기이한, 기묘한; 기괴한, 섬뜩한 (weirdly ad. 기묘하게)
If you describe something or someone as weird, you mean that they are strange.

bounce back

idiom (병·곤경에서) 다시 회복되다
If you bounce back after a bad experience, you return very quickly to your previous level of success, enthusiasm, or activity.

settle^{***}
[setl]

v. 자리를 잡다; 해결하다; 진정되다
If something settles or if you settle it, it sinks slowly down and becomes still.

drift[*]
[drift]

v. (물·공기에) 떠가다; (서서히) 이동하다; n. 표류
When something drifts somewhere, it is carried there by the movement of wind or water.

patch[*]
[pæʧ]

n. 부분; (덧대는 용도의) 조각; 안대; n. 덧대다, 때우다
A patch is a small piece, scrap, or area of anything.

blow up

idiom 폭파하다, 터뜨리다
If someone blows something up or if it blows up, it is destroyed by an explosion.

raincoat[*]
[réinkòut]

n. 비옷
A raincoat is a waterproof coat.

gap^{**}
[gæp]

n. 간격, 틈, 구멍; 공백; 격차
A gap is a space between two things or a hole in the middle of something solid.

predict[*]
[pridíkt]

v. 예측하다, 예견하다
If you predict an event, you say that it will happen.

bounce[*]
[bauns]

v. 튀다; 튀기다; n. 튐, 튀어 오름
When an object such as a ball bounces or when you bounce it, it moves upward from a surface or away from it immediately after hitting it.

worm^{**}
[wə:rm]

n. 벌레; v. 꿈틀거리며 나아가다
A worm is a small animal with a long thin body, no bones and no legs.

sneaker
[sníːkər]

n. (pl.) 고무창을 댄 운동화
Sneakers are casual shoes with rubber soles.

doofus
[dúːfəs]

n. 멍청이, 얼간이
If you call someone a doofus, you think they are foolish and stupid.

fall for

idiom ~에게 속다, 사기당하다; 반하다
If you fall for a lie or trick, you believe it or are deceived by it.

trick**
[trik]

n. (골탕을 먹이기 위한) 장난; 속임수; v. 속이다, 속임수를 쓰다
A trick is an action that is intended to deceive someone.

mutter^{복습}
[mʌtər]

v. 중얼거리다; 투덜거리다; n. 중얼거림
If you mutter, you speak very quietly so that you cannot easily be heard, often because you are complaining about something.

dumb*
[dʌm]

a. 멍청한, 바보 같은; 말을 못 하는
If you say that something is dumb, you think that it is silly and annoying.

hang one's head

idiom 부끄러워 고개를 숙이다; 풀이 죽다, 낙담하다
If you hang your head, you are ashamed and discouraged.

tease*
[tiːz]

v. 놀리다, 장난하다; 괴롭히다; n. 남을 놀리기 좋아하는 사람
To tease someone means to laugh at them or make jokes about them in order to embarrass, annoy, or upset them.

get back at

idiom ~에게 복수하다, 앙갚음하다
If you get back at someone or get them back, you do something unpleasant to them in order to have revenge for something unpleasant that they did to you.

budge^{복습}
[bʌdʒ]

v. 약간 움직이다, 꼼짝하다; 의견을 바꾸다
If someone or something will not budge, they will not move.

nod**
[nad]

v. (고개를) 끄덕이다; n. (고개를) 끄덕임
If you nod, you move your head downward and upward to show that you are answering 'yes' to a question, or to show agreement, understanding, or approval.

on purpose

idiom 고의로, 일부러
If you do something on purpose, you do it intentionally.

swirl^{복습}
[swəːrl]

v. 빙빙 돌다, 소용돌이치다; 빙빙 돌게 하다; n. 소용돌이
When something swirls, it moves around quickly in a circle.

yard^{복습}
[jaːrd]

n. (학교의) 운동장; 마당, 뜰; 정원
A yard is a flat area of concrete or stone that is next to a building and often has a wall around it.

blow**
[blou]

v. (blew-blown) (호각 · 악기 등을) 불다; (입으로) 불다; (기회를) 날리다; n. 세게 때림
When a whistle or horn blows or someone blows it, they make a sound by blowing into it.

whistle**
[hwisl]

n. 호각, 호루라기; 휘파람 (소리); v. 호루라기를 불다; 휘파람을 불다
A whistle is a small metal tube which you blow in order to produce a loud sound and attract someone's attention.

poke*
[pouk]

v. (손가락 등으로) 쿡 찌르다; 쑥 내밀다; n. 찌르기, 쑤시기
If you poke someone or something, you quickly push them with your finger or with a sharp object.

make one's way^{복습}

idiom 나아가다, 가다
When you make your way somewhere, you walk or travel there.

lock^{복습}
[lak]

v. 고정하다; (자물쇠로) 잠그다; n. 자물쇠
If you lock something in a particular position or if it locks there, it is held or fitted firmly in that position.

stare^{복습}
[stɛər]

v. 빤히 쳐다보다, 응시하다; n. 빤히 쳐다보기, 응시
If you stare at someone or something, you look at them for a long time.

blink*
[bliŋk]

v. 눈을 깜박이다; (불빛이) 깜박거리다; n. 눈을 깜박거림
When you blink or when you blink your eyes, you shut your eyes and very quickly open them again.

pat^{복습}
[pæt]

v. 쓰다듬다, 토닥거리다; n. 쓰다듬기, 토닥거리기
If you pat something or someone, you tap them lightly, usually with your hand held flat.

instant^{복습}
[ínstənt]

a. 즉각적인; n. 순간, 아주 짧은 동안 (instantly ad. 즉각, 즉시)
You use instant to describe something that happens immediately.

pop^{복습}
[pap]

v. 불쑥 움직이다; 불쑥 나타나다; 펑 하고 터뜨리다; 펑 하는 소리를 내다;
n. 펑 하고 터지는 소리
If something pops, it moves suddenly and quickly, and usually unexpectedly.

plain**
[plein]

ad. 분명히, 완전히; a. 평범한; 솔직한; n. (pl.) 평원, 평지
You can use plain before an adjective in order to emphasize it.

pleasant**
[plézənt]

a. 쾌적한, 즐거운; 상냥한 (unpleasant a. 불쾌한)
If something is unpleasant, it gives you bad feelings, for example by making you feel upset or uncomfortable.

expression**
[ikspréʃən]

n. 표정; 표현, 표출
Your expression is the way that your face looks at a particular moment. It shows what you are thinking or feeling.

Chapters 11 & 12

1. How were the spelling words in Mrs. Jewls's class different from those in other classes?
   A. The students got to choose the words.
   B. The words were very difficult.
   C. There were more spelling words.
   D. The words came from the homework.

2. Why did Mrs. Jewls want Rondi to write on the board?
   A. Mrs. Jewls wanted the students to take turns.
   B. Mrs. Jewls thought Rondi had nice handwriting.
   C. Mrs. Jewls did not know how to spell a word.
   D. Mrs. Jewls was too tired from teaching all day.

3. What was one good thing about the Cloud of Doom?
   A. It made the weather cooler than usual.
   B. It made the students' nails grow more quickly.
   C. It helped Mrs. Jewls to teach the class about clouds.
   D. It helped the students to focus on their work.

4. Which of the following was NOT a rule in the library?
   A. No talking
   B. No somersaults
   C. No drinking
   D. No eating

5. How did Mrs. Surlaw organize the library?

   A. She put the books in fiction and nonfiction areas.

   B. She put the books in alphabetical order.

   C. She organized the books by their difficulty.

   D. She organized the books by their number of pages.

6. How did Jason know that Allison had already checked out a book?

   A. Allison was hugging the walrus.

   B. He could see the book in her bag.

   C. Allison had a piece of paper.

   D. Mrs. Surlaw told him.

7. Why did Jason choose a book that was 999 pages long?

   A. He heard from Allison that it was a good book.

   B. He wanted to use it to exercise his arms.

   C. He thought the book looked interesting.

   D. He wanted his book to be longer than Allison's.

Check Your Reading Speed

1분에 몇 단어를 읽는지 리딩 속도를 측정해 보세요.

$$\frac{548 \text{ words}}{\text{reading time (} \quad \text{) sec}} \times 60 = (\quad) \text{ WPM}$$

Build Your Vocabulary

point***
[pɔint]

n. (의도하는) 의미, 목적; (뾰족한) 끝; 의견; 요점; 점수; v. 가리키다
If you ask what the point of something is, or say that there is no point in it, you are indicating that a particular action has no purpose or would not be useful.

spell**
[spel]

v. 철자를 맞게 쓰다, 맞춤법에 맞게 글을 쓰다; (어떤 단어의) 철자를 말하다 (spelling n. 철자법, 맞춤법)
A spelling is the correct order of the letters in a word.

call on^{복습}

idiom (이름을 불러서) 학생에게 시키다; (사람을) 방문하다
If a teacher calls on students in a class, he or she asks them to answer a question or give their opinion.

pay attention^{복습}

idiom 주의를 기울이다; 관심을 갖다
If you pay attention to someone, you watch them, listen to them, or take notice of them.

blackboard^{복습}
[blǽkbɔ̀:rd]

n. 칠판
A blackboard is a dark-colored board that you can write on with chalk.

point out

idiom 지적하다, 언급하다; 알려주다
If you point out a fact or circumstance, you mention it in order to give someone information about it or make them notice it.

chirp*
[ʧə:rp]

v. 재잘거리다; (새나 곤충이) 짹짹거리다; n. 재잘거리는 소리; 짹짹 소리
If someone chirps, they say something in a lively and cheerful way.

arithmetic^{복습}
[əríθmətik]

n. 산수, 연산; 산술, 계산
Arithmetic is the part of mathematics that is concerned with the addition, subtraction, multiplication, and division of numbers.

slam^{복습}
[slæm]

v. 세게 치다, 놓다; 쾅 닫다; n. 쾅 하고 닫기; 쾅 하는 소리
If you slam something on, you put, move, or hit it against or onto a surface with great force.

scare**
[skɛər]

v. 겁주다, 놀라게 하다 (scared a. 무서워하는, 겁먹은)
If you are scared of someone or something, you are frightened of them.

nail^{복습}
[neil]

n. 손톱, 발톱; 못; v. 못으로 박다
Your nails are the thin hard parts that grow at the ends of your fingers and toes.

60

clipping ^{복습}
[klípiŋ]

n. 잘라 낸 조각, 오려 낸 것
Clippings are small pieces of something that have been cut from something larger.

clip[*]
[klip]

v. 깎다, 자르다; 핀으로 고정하다; n. 핀, 클립
If you clip something, you cut small pieces from it, especially in order to shape it.

storm^{**}
[stɔːrm]

n. 폭풍, 폭풍우; v. 쿵쾅대며 가다, 뛰쳐나가다; 기습하다
A storm is very bad weather, with heavy rain, strong winds, and often thunder and lightning.

crack^{**}
[kræk]

n. 찢어지는 듯한 소리; (무엇이 갈라져 생긴) 금;
v. 날카로운 소리를 내다; 갈라지다, 금이 가다
A crack is a sharp sound, like the sound of a piece of wood breaking.

thunder[*]
[θʌ́ndər]

n. 천둥, 우레; v. 천둥이 치다
Thunder is the loud noise that you hear from the sky after a flash of lightning, especially during a storm.

light^{***}
[lait]

v. (lit-lit) 불을 붙이다; (빛을) 비추다; n. 빛
If you light something such as a candle or fire, or if it lights, it starts burning.

settle down

idiom 진정되다; (조용히 한 곳에 자리 잡고) 정착하다
If a situation or a person that has been going through a lot of problems or changes settles down, they become calm.

chalk^{**}
[ʧɔːk]

n. 분필
Chalk is small sticks of soft white rock, used for writing or drawing with.

Check Your Reading Speed

1분에 몇 단어를 읽는지 리딩 속도를 측정해 보세요.

$$\frac{971 \text{ words}}{\text{reading time ( ) sec}} \times 60 = (\quad) \text{ WPM}$$

Build Your Vocabulary

librarian*
[laibréəriən]

n. (도서관의) 사서
A librarian is a person who is in charge of a library, which is a building where things such as books are kept for people to read, use, or borrow.

giant 복습
[dʒáiənt]

a. 거대한; 위대한; n. (이야기 속의) 거인
Something that is described as giant is much larger or more important than most others of its kind.

kindergarten 복습
[kíndərgàːrtn]

n. 유치원 (kindergartener n. 유치원생)
A kindergartener is a child who is in kindergarten, which is an informal kind of school for very young children, where they learn things by playing.

scare 복습
[skɛər]

v. 겁주다, 놀라게 하다 (scared a. 무서워하는, 겁먹은)
If you are scared of someone or something, you are frightened of them.

dare*
[dɛər]

v. 감히 ~하다, ~할 엄두를 내다; 부추기다; n. 모험, 도전
If you dare to do something, you become courageous enough to try to do it.

tusk
[tʌsk]

n. (코끼리 등의) 상아; (삽 등의) 뾰족한 끝
The tusks of an elephant, wild boar, or walrus are its two very long, curved, pointed teeth.

pillow 복습
[pílou]

n. 베개
A pillow is a rectangular cushion which you rest your head on when you are in bed.

yell*
[jel]

v. 고함치다, 소리 지르다; n. 고함, 외침
If you yell, you shout loudly, usually because you are excited, angry, or in pain.

somersault
[sʌ́mərsɔ̀ːlt]

n. 공중제비, 재주넘기; v. 공중제비를 하다
If someone or something does a somersault, they turn over completely in the air.

check out

idiom (도서관 등에서) 대출받다; (흥미로운 것을) 살펴보다
If you check out something such as a book or a video, you borrow it from a library.

wheel 복습
[hwiːl]

v. (바퀴 달린 것을) 밀다, 끌다; n. 바퀴; (자동차 등의) 핸들
If you wheel an object that has wheels somewhere, you push it along.

row**
[rou]

n. 열, 줄; v. 노를 젓다
A row of things or people is a number of them arranged in a line.

belong***
[bilɔ́:ŋ]

v. 제자리에 있다; ~에 속하다, ~의 소유물이다; 소속감을 느끼다
If a person or thing belongs in a particular place or situation, that is where they should be.

proper** ^{복습}
[prápər]

a. 적절한, 제대로 된; 올바른, 정당한
The proper thing is the one that is correct or most suitable.

rumble
[rʌmbl]

n. 우르릉거리는 소리; v. 우르릉거리는 소리를 내다
A rumble is a low continuous noise.

chirp ^{복습}
[ʧə:rp]

n. 재잘거리는 소리; 짹짹 소리; v. 재잘거리다; (새나 곤충이) 짹짹거리다
You can refer to a short, high-pitched sound as chirps.

shriek ^{복습}
[ʃri:k]

n. 꽥 하는 소리; 비명; v. 꽥 소리를 지르다; (날카롭게) 비명을 지르다
A shriek is a loud, high-pitched sound made because you are excited, frightened, or in pain.

shush
[ʃʌʃ]

v. 조용히 하라고 말하다; int. 쉿 (조용히 해)
If you shush someone, you tell them to be quiet by saying 'shush' or by putting your finger against your lips.

polite***
[pəláit]

a. 예의 바른, 공손한, 정중한; 예의상 (politely ad. 예의 바르게)
Someone who is polite has good manners and behaves in a way that is socially correct and not rude to other people.

greet ^{복습}
[gri:t]

v. 인사하다; 환영하다; 반응을 보이다
When you greet someone, you say 'hello' or shake hands with them.

scurry
[skə́:ri]

v. 종종걸음을 치다, 허둥지둥 가다
When people or small animals scurry somewhere, they move there quickly and hurriedly.

severe**
[sivíər]

a. 엄한; 극심한, 심각한; 가혹한
Someone who is severe behaves in a way that does not seem friendly or sympathetic, and is very strict or disapproving.

separate**
[sépərèit]

a. 별개의; 분리된; v. 분리하다, 나누다; 갈라지다
If you refer to separate things, you mean several different things, rather than just one thing.

alphabetical*
[ælfəbétikəl]

a. 알파벳순의
Alphabetical means arranged according to the normal order of the letters in the alphabet.

order***
[ɔ́:rdər]

n. 순서, ~순(順); 질서; 명령, 지시; v. 명령하다
If a set of things are arranged or done in a particular order, they are arranged or done so one thing follows another, often according to a particular factor such as importance.

skinny ^{복습}
[skíni]

a. (물건의) 폭이 좁은; 깡마른, 비쩍 여윈
A skinny object is narrow or slender.

mark ^{복습}
[ma:rk]

v. (표·기호 등으로) 표시하다; n. 표시, 부호; 자국, 흔적 (marker n. 표시)
A marker is an object which is used to show the position of something, or is used to help someone remember something.

all the way^{복습}	idiom 내내, 시종; 완전히 You can use all the way to emphasize that your remark applies to every part of a situation, activity, or period of time.
scowl [skaul]	v. 노려보다, 쏘아보다; n. 노려봄, 쏘아봄 When someone scowls, an angry or hostile expression appears on their face.
pretend*** [priténd]	v. ~인 척하다, ~인 것처럼 굴다; ~라고 가장하다 If you pretend that something is the case, you act in a way that is intended to make people believe that it is the case, although in fact it is not.
notice^{복습} [nóutis]	v. 알아채다, 인지하다; 주목하다, 관심을 기울이다; n. 신경 씀, 알아챔 If you notice something or someone, you become aware of them.
dash^{복습} [dæʃ]	v. 서둘러 가다; n. 황급히 달려감, 질주 If you dash somewhere, you run or go there quickly and suddenly.
aisle* [ail]	n. 통로 An aisle is a long narrow gap that people can walk along between rows of seats in a public building.
squeeze* [skwi:z]	v. (좁은 곳에) 밀어 넣다; (억지로) 비집고 들어가다; (꼭) 짜다; n. 짜기, 쥐기 If you squeeze a person or thing somewhere or if they squeeze there, they manage to get through or into a small space.
no way^{복습}	idiom 말도 안 돼; (강한 거절의 의미로) 절대로 안 돼, 싫어 You can say 'no way' for expressing surprise, or for telling someone that you do not believe them.
shrug^{복습} [ʃrʌg]	v. (두 손바닥을 위로 하고) 어깨를 으쓱하다; n. 어깨를 으쓱하기 If you shrug, you raise your shoulders to show that you are not interested in something or that you do not know or care about something.
bore^{복습} [bɔ:r]	v. 지루하게 하다 (boring a. 재미없는, 지루한) Someone or something boring is so dull and uninteresting that they make people tired and impatient.
bunch* [bʌntʃ]	n. (양·수가) 많음; 다발, 송이 A bunch of things is a number of things, especially a large number.
confidential* [kànfədénʃəl]	a. 비밀의, 기밀의 Information that is confidential is meant to be kept secret or private.
sigh^{복습} [sai]	v. 한숨을 쉬다, 한숨짓다; n. 한숨 When you sigh, you let out a deep breath, as a way of expressing feelings such as disappointment, tiredness, or pleasure.
lug [lʌg]	v. (무거운 것을 힘들게) 나르다, 끌다 If you lug a heavy or awkward object somewhere, you carry it there with difficulty.
thud [θʌd]	n. 쿵, 퍽, 툭 (무거운 것이 떨어질 때 나는 소리) A thud is a dull sound, such as that which a heavy object makes when it hits something soft.

64

plop
[plap]

v. 털썩 떨어뜨리다, 떨어지다; 털썩 주저앉다; n. 풍덩 하는 소리

If you plop something somewhere, you drop it there with a soft, gentle sound.

Chapters 13 & 14

1. Which of the following is NOT true about Sharie's umbrella?
   A. It had a smooth, curved wooden handle.
   B. It had some small holes that let the rain through.
   C. It made a nice sound when raindrops bounced on it.
   D. It had yellow polka dots on it.

2. Why didn't Sharie wave back to the other students?
   A. She was in too much of a hurry.
   B. She was mad at them.
   C. She did not see them wave.
   D. She was worried about falling.

3. How did Sharie get to her classroom?
   A. She asked other students to carry her.
   B. She came down from the roof.
   C. She ran up the stairs.
   D. She jumped through the window.

4. Why did Mr. K wear a paper bag on his head?

   A. He got the bag stuck on his head.

   B. He was trying to make the kids laugh.

   C. He wanted to keep his head warm.

   D. He thought he might encounter a student.

5. Why did Mr. K go to see Dr. P?

   A. Because he had a problem with one of the students

   B. Because his face was stuck in a strange position

   C. Because he wanted to help Dr. P

   D. Because he was worried about Dr. P

6. What did Dr. P ask Mr. K about?

   A. What kind of pet he had as a child

   B. What his parents were like when he was a child

   C. Where he went to school when he was a child

   D. What type of house he lived in as a child

7. Why did Dr. P feel satisfied when Mr. K left the office?

   A. He was offered a new job by Mr. K.

   B. He learned a lot of new information.

   C. He was able to help someone important.

   D. He got some new ideas for his book.

Check Your Reading Speed

1분에 몇 단어를 읽는지 리딩 속도를 측정해 보세요.

$$\frac{609 \text{ words}}{\text{reading time ( ) sec}} \times 60 = (\quad) \text{ WPM}$$

Build Your Vocabulary

stomp
[stamp]

v. 쿵쿵거리며 걷다, 발을 구르다
If you stomp somewhere, you walk there with very heavy steps.

puddle
[pʌdl]

n. (빗물 등의) 물웅덩이
A puddle is a small, shallow pool of liquid that has spread on the ground.

boot*
[buːt]

n. (pl.) 목이 긴 신발, 부츠; v. 세게 차다; (컴퓨터를) 부팅하다
Boots are shoes that cover your whole foot and the lower part of your leg.

stripe*
[straip]

n. 줄무늬
A stripe is a long line which is a different color from the areas next to it.

polka dot
[póulkə dàt]

n. 물방울무늬
Polka dot is a pattern consisting of an array of filled circles.

raindrop
[réindràp]

n. 빗방울
A raindrop is a single drop of rain.

bounce^{복습}
[bauns]

v. 튀다; 튀기다; n. 튐, 튀어 오름
When an object such as a ball bounces or when you bounce it, it moves upward from a surface or away from it immediately after hitting it.

smooth**
[smuːð]

a. 매끈한; 순조로운; 부드러운; v. 매끈하게 하다
A smooth surface has no roughness, lumps, or holes.

curve**
[kəːrv]

v. 곡선을 이루다, 곡선으로 나아가다; n. 커브, 곡선 (curved a. 곡선의)
A curved object has the shape of a curve or has a smoothly bending surface.

block***
[blak]

n. (도로로 나뉘는) 구역, 블록; 사각형 덩어리; v. 막다, 차단하다; 방해하다
A block in a town is an area of land with streets on all its sides.

clang^{복습}
[klæŋ]

v. 쨍그랑 하고 울리다; n. 쨍그랑 하는 소리
When a large metal object clangs, it makes a loud noise.

count^{복습}
[kaunt]

v. (수를) 세다; 계산에 넣다; n. (하나부터 순서대로 세는) 셈; 계산
When you count, you say all the numbers one after another up to a particular number.

glance[*]
[glæns]

v. 흘낏 보다; 대충 훑어보다; n. 흘낏 봄
If you glance at something or someone, you look at them very quickly and then look away again immediately.

sidewalk[*]
[sáidwɔːk]

n. (포장한) 보도, 인도
A sidewalk is a path with a hard surface by the side of a road.

stick out[복습]

idiom ~을 내밀다, 튀어나오게 하다
If you stick out part of your body, you extend it away from your body.

tilt[*]
[tilt]

v. 기울이다, (뒤로) 젖히다; (의견·상황 등이) 기울어지다; n. 기울어짐, 젖혀짐
If you tilt an object or if it tilts, it moves into a sloping position with one end or side higher than the other.

doom[복습]
[duːm]

n. 불운, 저주; 죽음, 파멸; v. 불행한 운명을 맞게 하다
Doom is a terrible future state or event which you cannot prevent.

include[복습]
[inklúːd]

v. 포함하다; ~을 (~에) 포함시키다
If one thing includes another thing, it has the other thing as one of its parts.

glare[복습]
[glɛər]

v. 노려보다; 환하다, 눈부시다; n. 노려봄; 환한 빛, 눈부심
If you glare at someone, you look at them with an angry expression on your face.

horrible[**]
[hɔ́ːrəbl]

a. 소름 끼치는, 무시무시한; 지긋지긋한, 끔찍한; 불쾌한
You can call something horrible when it causes you to feel great shock, fear, and disgust.

churn
[tʃəːrn]

v. (물·흙탕물 등이) 마구 휘돌다; 우유를 휘젓다; (속이) 뒤틀리다
If water, mud, or dust churns, or if something churns it, it moves about violently.

gust
[gʌst]

n. 세찬 바람, 돌풍; v. (갑자기) 몰아치다
A gust is a short, strong, sudden rush of wind.

tear[**]
[tɛər]

① v. (tore-torn) 뜯어내다; 찢어지다; 구멍을 뚫다; n. 찢어진 곳, 구멍 ② n. 눈물
To tear something from somewhere means to remove it roughly and violently.

horrify[복습]
[hɔ́ːrəfài]

v. 소름 끼치게 만들다 (horrified a. 겁에 질린, 충격받은)
If someone is horrified, they feel shocked or disgusted, usually because of something that they have seen or heard.

blacktop[복습]
[blǽktàp]

n. 아스팔트 도로; (포장에 쓰이는) 아스팔트; v. 아스팔트로 포장하다
Blacktop is a hard black substance which is used as a surface for roads, as well as a road covered with this substance.

chase[**]
[tʃeis]

v. 뒤쫓다, 추적하다; (돈·성공 등을) 좇다; n. 추적, 추격
If you chase someone or something, or chase after them, you run after them or follow them quickly in order to catch or reach them.

rack[*]
[ræk]

n. 받침대, 선반; v. (몹시) 괴롭히다
A rack is a frame or shelf, usually with bars or hooks, that is used for holding things or for hanging things on.

swoop
[swu:p]

v. (공기 중에서) 빠르게 움직이다; 급강하하다, 급습하다; n. 급강하; 급습
When something swoops, it moves very quickly and suddenly through the air.

grab^{복습}
[græb]

v. (와락·단단히) 붙잡다; ~을 잡으려고 하다; n. 와락 잡아채려고 함
If you grab something, you take it or pick it up suddenly and roughly.

let go

idiom (잡고 있던 것을) 놓다; (생각·태도 등을) 버리다
If you let go of something, you release your hold or grip of it.

definite^{복습}
[défənit]

a. 분명한, 뚜렷한; 확실한, 확고한 (definitely ad. 분명히, 틀림없이)
You use definitely to emphasize that something is the case, or to emphasize the strength of your intention or opinion.

slip^{복습}
[slip]

v. 미끄러지다; 슬며시 가다; (재빨리·슬며시) 놓다; n. 미끄러짐; (작은) 실수
If something slips, it slides out of place or out of your hand.

scary^{복습}
[skέəri]

a. 무서운, 겁나는
Something that is scary is rather frightening.

wave^{복습}
[weiv]

v. (손·팔을) 흔들다; 손짓하다; n. 파도, 물결; (손·팔·몸을) 흔들기
If you wave or wave your hand, you move your hand from side to side in the air, usually in order to say hello or goodbye to someone.

risk***
[risk]

v. ~의 위험을 무릅쓰다; 과감히 ~을 하다; 위태롭게 하다; n. 위험; 위험 요소
If you risk doing something, you do it, even though you know that it might have undesirable consequences.

alternative**
[ɔːltə́ːrnətiv]

n. 대안, 선택 가능한 것; a. 대체 가능한, 대안이 되는
If one thing is an alternative to another, the first can be found, used, or done instead of the second.

hang on

idiom 꽉 붙잡다; 잠깐 (기다려); (역경에도) 계속 버티다
If you hang on to something, you hold it very tightly, for example to stop it falling or to support yourself.

suck**
[sʌk]

v. (특정한 방향으로) 빨아들이다; (액체·공기 등을) 빨다; (입에 넣고 계속) 빨다
If something sucks a liquid, gas, or object in a particular direction, it draws it there with a powerful force.

horn^{복습}
[hɔːrn]

n. (차량의) 경적; (양·소 등의) 뿔
On a vehicle such as a car, the horn is the device that makes a loud noise as a signal or warning.

blare^{복습}
[blɛər]

v. (소리를) 요란하게 울리다; n. 요란한 소리
If something such as a siren or radio blares or if you blare it, it makes a loud, unpleasant noise.

sprawl
[sprɔːl]

v. 팔다리를 아무렇게나 벌리고 앉다, 대자로 눕다; 제멋대로 퍼져 나가다
If you sprawl somewhere, you sit or lie down with your legs and arms spread out in a careless way.

absent**
[ǽbsənt]

a. 결석한, 결근한; 없는; v. 결석하다, 결근하다
If someone or something is absent from a place or situation where they should be or where they usually are, they are not there.

Check Your Reading Speed

1분에 몇 단어를 읽는지 리딩 속도를 측정해 보세요.

$$\frac{919 \text{ words}}{\text{reading time ( ) sec}} \times 60 = (\quad) \text{ WPM}$$

Build Your Vocabulary

strict**
[strikt]

a. (규칙 등이) 엄한; 엄격한; 엄밀한
A strict rule or order is very clear and precise or severe and must always be obeyed completely.

confidential^{복습}
[kànfədénʃəl]

a. 비밀의, 기밀의 (confidentiality n. 비밀성, 기밀성)
Confidentiality is a situation in which you expect someone to keep information secret.

embarrass**
[imbǽrəs]

v. 당황스럽게 하다; 곤란하게 하다 (embarrassment n. 당황, 곤란)
Embarrassment is a feeling of being nervous or ashamed because of what people know or think about you.

involve**
[inválv]

v. (상황·사건·활동이 사람을) 관련시키다; 포함하다, 수반하다 (involved a. 관련된)
If you are involved in a situation or activity, you are taking part in it or have a strong connection with it.

omit*
[oumít]

v. 빠뜨리다, 누락시키다
If you omit something, you do not include it in an activity or piece of work, deliberately or accidentally.

brat
[bræt]

n. 버릇없는 녀석
If you call someone, especially a child, a brat, you mean that he or she behaves badly or annoys you.

just in case

idiom (혹시라도) ~할 경우에 대비해서
If you do something in case or just in case a particular thing happens, you do it because that thing might happen.

encounter*
[inkáuntər]

v. 마주치다; 맞닥뜨리다, 부딪히다; n. 만남, 접촉
If you encounter someone, you meet them, usually unexpectedly.

stray**
[strei]

a. 길을 잃은; 한쪽으로 샌, 빗나간; v. 길을 벗어나다; 옆길로 새다
Stray people or animals are lost and not in their expected or intended place.

trip***
[trip]

v. 발을 헛디디다; 실수하게 하다; n. 여행
If you trip when you are walking, you knock your foot against something and fall or nearly fall.

landing*
[lǽndiŋ]

n. 층계참; 착륙
In a house or other building, a landing is an area of floor that joins two sets of stairs.

get to one's feet

idiom 일어서다; 일어나다
If you get to your feet, you stand up.

limp*
[limp]

v. 다리를 절다, 절뚝거리다; a. 기운이 없는, 축 처진
If a person or animal limps, they walk with difficulty or in an uneven way because one of their legs or feet is hurt.

eyebrow^{복습}
[áibràu]

n. 눈썹
Your eyebrows are the lines of hair which grow above your eyes.

constant*
[kánstənt]

a. 변함없는; 끊임없는; 거듭되는
You use constant to describe something that happens all the time or is always there.

expression^{복습}
[ikspréʃən]

n. 표정; 표현, 표출
Your expression is the way that your face looks at a particular moment. It shows what you are thinking or feeling.

knock^{복습}
[nak]

v. (문 등을) 두드리다; n. 문 두드리는 소리
If you knock on something such as a door or window, you hit it, usually several times, to attract someone's attention.

straight face
[stréit fèis]

n. 무표정한 얼굴
If you keep a straight face, you do not laugh or smile, although you find something funny.

stroke^{복습}
[strouk]

v. 쓰다듬다, 어루만지다; 달래다; n. (손으로) 쓰다듬기; (글씨나 그림의) 획
If you stroke someone or something, you move your hand slowly and gently over them.

beard^{복습}
[biərd]

n. (턱)수염
A man's beard is the hair that grows on his chin and cheeks.

remove^{복습}
[rimú:v]

v. (옷 등을) 벗다; 없애다; 치우다; 옮기다; 떼다
If you remove clothing, you take it off.

regain*
[rigéin]

v. 되찾다, 회복하다; 되돌아오다
If you regain something that you have lost, you get it back again.

composure
[kəmpóuʒər]

n. (마음의) 평정
Composure is the appearance or feeling of calm and the ability to control your feelings.

rub^{복습}
[rʌb]

v. (손·손수건 등을 대고) 문지르다; (두 손 등을) 맞비비다; n. 문지르기, 비비기
If you rub a part of your body, you move your hand or fingers backward and forward over it while pressing firmly.

stuck^{복습}
[stʌk]

v. 움직일 수 없는, 꼼짝 못하는; (불쾌한 상황에서) 빠져나갈 수 없는; (대답 등이) 막힌
If something is stuck in a particular position, it is fixed tightly in this position and is unable to move.

nod^{복습}
[nad]

v. (고개를) 끄덕이다; n. (고개를) 끄덕임
If you nod, you move your head downward and upward to show that you are answering 'yes' to a question, or to show agreement, understanding, or approval.

couch^{복습}
[kauʧ]

n. 소파, 긴 의자
A couch is a long, comfortable seat for two or three people.

poke^{복습}
[pouk]

v. (손가락 등으로) 쿡 찌르다; 쑥 내밀다; n. 찌르기, 쑤시기
If you poke someone or something, you quickly push them with your finger or with a sharp object.

puff out^{복습}

idiom (공기를 채워) 불룩하게 부풀리다 (puffed-out a. 부푼)
If you puff out your cheeks, you make them larger and rounder by filling them with air.

cheek^{복습}
[ʧiːk]

n. 뺨, 볼
Your cheeks are the sides of your face below your eyes.

tug^{복습}
[tʌg]

v. (세게) 잡아당기다; n. (갑자기 세게) 잡아당김
If you tug something or tug at it, you give it a quick and usually strong pull.

tip*
[tip]

n. (뾰족한) 끝; v. 기울이다, 젖히다
The tip of something long and narrow is the end of it.

tongue^{복습}
[tʌŋ]

n. 혀; 언어
Your tongue is the soft movable part inside your mouth which you use for tasting, eating, and speaking.

mutter^{복습}
[mʌ́tər]

v. 중얼거리다; 투덜거리다; n. 중얼거림
If you mutter, you speak very quietly so that you cannot easily be heard, often because you are complaining about something.

declare^{복습}
[diklέər]

v. 분명히 말하다; 선언하다, 공표하다
If you declare something, you state something clearly and definitely.

bonk
[baːŋk]

v. (~의) 머리를 툭 때리다; (~에) 머리를 툭 부딪치다 n. (~에) 머리를 부딪치기
When you bonk someone, you hit them gently on the head.

exclaim^{복습}
[ikskléim]

v. 소리치다, 외치다
If you exclaim, you cry out suddenly in surprise, strong emotion, or pain.

bite*
[bait]

v. (bit-bitten) (이빨로) 물다, 베어 물다; n. 물기; 한 입; (짐승·곤충에게) 물린 상처
If you bite something, you use your teeth to cut into it, for example in order to eat it or break it.

thumb

through

idiom (책 등을) 휙휙 넘겨 보다
If you thumb through a book or magazine, you turn the pages of it quickly and read only small parts.

sticky*
[stíki]

a. 끈적거리는, 끈적끈적한; 달라붙는
A sticky substance is soft, or thick and liquid, and can stick to other things.

pet*
[pet]

n. 반려동물; v. (동물·아이를 다정하게) 어루만지다
A pet is an animal that you keep in your home to give you company and pleasure.

trickle
[trikl]

v. (액체가 가늘게) 흐르다; 천천히 가다; n. (물)방울; 소량
When a liquid trickles, or when you trickle it, it flows slowly in a thin stream.

zdrip* [drip]
v. 방울방울 흐르다; (액체를) 뚝뚝 흘리다;
n. (작은 액체) 방울; (액체가) 뚝뚝 떨어짐
When liquid drips somewhere, or you drip it somewhere, it falls in individual small drops.

progress** [prágres]
n. 진전; 진척; 나아감; v. 진전을 보이다; (앞으로) 나아가다
Progress is the process of gradually improving or getting nearer to achieving or completing something.

scoot [sku:t]
v. 휙 움직이다; 서둘러 가다
To scoot means to make someone or something move a short distance by pulling or pushing it.

lean** [li:n]
v. 기울이다, (몸을) 숙이다; ~에 기대다; a. 군살이 없는, 호리호리한
When you lean in a particular direction, you bend your body in that direction.

stare^{복습} [stɛər]
v. 빤히 쳐다보다, 응시하다; n. 빤히 쳐다보기, 응시
If you stare at someone or something, you look at them for a long time.

attach* [ətǽʧ]
v. 붙이다, 첨부하다; 연관되다 (attached a. 부착된, 첨부된)
If you attach something to an object, you join it or fasten it to the object.

swing^{복습} [swiŋ]
v. (전후·좌우로) 흔들(리)다; 휙 움직이다; n. 흔들기; 휘두르기
If something swings or if you swing it, it moves repeatedly backward and forward or from side to side from a fixed point.

back and forth^{복습} [bæk ən fɔ́:rθ]
ad. 앞뒤(좌우)로; 여기저기에, 왔다 갔다
If someone or something moves back and forth, they repeatedly move in one direction and then in the opposite direction.

barely* [bέərli]
ad. 간신히, 가까스로; 거의 ~ 아니게
You use barely to say that something is done in a way that is just possible but only with difficulty.

yard^{복습} [ja:rd]
n. 마당, 뜰; (학교의) 운동장; 정원 (backyard n. 뒷마당; 뒤뜰)
A backyard is an area of land at the back of a house, with grass and plants growing in it.

bake** [beik]
v. (음식을) 굽다; 매우 뜨겁다
If you bake, you spend some time preparing and mixing together ingredients to make bread, cakes, pies, or other food which is cooked in the oven.

twitch [twiʧ]
v. 씰룩거리다, 경련하다; 홱 잡아채다; n. 씰룩거림, 경련
If something, especially a part of your body, twitches or if you twitch it, it makes a little jumping movement.

note^{복습} [nout]
v. 주목하다; 언급하다; n. 메모; 음, 음표; 편지, 쪽지
If you note a fact, you become aware of it.

breakthrough [bréikθrù:]
n. 돌파구
A breakthrough is an important development or achievement.

74

smash*
[smæʃ]

v. (세게) 부딪치다; 박살내다; 부서지다; n. 박살내기; 요란한 소리
If something smashes or is smashed against something solid, it moves very fast and with great force against it.

pop^{복습}
[pap]

v. 불쑥 움직이다; 불쑥 나타나다; 펑 하고 터뜨리다; 펑 하는 소리를 내다; n. 펑 하고 터지는 소리
If something pops, it moves suddenly and quickly, and usually unexpectedly.

snap^{복습}
[snæp]

v. 탁 하고 움직이다; 딱딱거리다; 톡 쏘다; 사진을 찍다; n. 찰칵 하는 소리
If you snap something into a particular position, or if it snaps into that position, it moves quickly into that position, with a sharp sound.

belong^{복습}
[bilɔ́ːŋ]

v. 제자리에 있다; ~에 속하다, ~의 소유물이다; 소속감을 느끼다
If a person or thing belongs in a particular place or situation, that is where they should be.

tissue*
[tíʃuː]

n. 화장지; (세포) 조직
A tissue is a piece of thin soft paper that you use to blow your nose.

wipe^{복습}
[waip]

v. (먼지 · 물기 등을) 닦다; 지우다; n. 닦기
If you wipe dirt or liquid from something, you remove it by using a cloth or your hand.

imaginary**
[imǽdʒənèri]

a. 상상에만 존재하는, 가상의
An imaginary person, place, or thing exists only in your mind or in a story, and not in real life.

straighten*
[streitn]

v. 똑바르게 하다; (자세를) 바로 하다
If you straighten something, you make it tidy or put it in its proper position.

suit**
[suːt]

n. 정장; (특정한 활동 때 입는) 옷; v. (~에게) 편리하다, 맞다; 어울리다
A man's suit consists of a jacket, trousers, and sometimes a waistcoat, all made from the same fabric.

assure*
[əʃúər]

v. 장담하다, 확언하다; 확인하다
If you assure someone that something is true or will happen, you tell them that it is definitely true or will definitely happen, often in order to make them less worried.

dignified
[dígnəfàid]

a. 위엄 있는, 품위 있는
If you say that someone or something is dignified, you mean they are calm, impressive, and deserve respect.

satisfied*
[sǽtisfàid]

a. 만족하는, 흡족해하는; 납득하는
If you are satisfied with something, you are happy because you have got what you wanted or needed.

swallow**
[swálou]

v. (음식 등을) 삼키다; 마른침을 삼키다; n. [동물] 제비
If you swallow something, you cause it to go from your mouth down into your stomach.

Chapters 15 & 16

1. What was happening the longer people spent beneath the Cloud of Doom?
   A. They started to get crabbier.
   B. They wanted to study the cloud.
   C. They began to feel excited.
   D. They could not sleep well.

2. What did the "Unbreakables" do every morning?
   A. They met by the flagpole and did a special handshake.
   B. They met by the flagpole and sang a special song.
   C. They met in the classroom and did a special handshake.
   D. They met in the classroom and sang a special song.

3. What did Deedee do that Ron thought was gross?
   A. She ate the feetball when it was cold.
   B. She drank some feetsauce from a cup.
   C. She ate the heel of the feetball first.
   D. She dipped the feetball in sauce.

4. Why did Deedee shout and pull her hair?
   A. She found out that her friends said something mean about her.
   B. She could not get back into the building when she needed to.
   C. She suddenly realized that she was missing her homework.
   D. She was mad that her friends were playing three-square.

5. Why was Jason's book report late?
   A. He could not work because he was sick.
   B. He was reading a very long book.
   C. He decided to change his book.
   D. He was very slow at writing.

6. What did Jason think about the book's author?
   A. He thought that she was not very good at writing books.
   B. He thought that she always wrote books that had 999 pages.
   C. He thought that maybe she quit writing in the middle of the book.
   D. He thought that maybe she would be a very popular author.

7. What did Jason do during recess while everyone else played?
   A. He helped to clean the classroom.
   B. He read his 999-page book.
   C. He tried to memorize parts of the book.
   D. He followed Rondi and Allison around.

Check Your Reading Speed

1분에 몇 단어를 읽는지 리딩 속도를 측정해 보세요.

$$\frac{782 \text{ words}}{\text{reading time ( ) sec}} \times 60 = (\quad) \text{ WPM}$$

Build Your Vocabulary

pick on	idiom (부당하게) ~을 괴롭히다 If you pick on someone, you treat them badly or unfairly, especially repeatedly.
anxious*** [ǽŋkʃəs]	a. 불안해하는, 염려하는; 불안해 보이는; 간절히 바라는 If you are anxious, you are nervous or worried about something.
loom* [lu:m]	v. (무섭게) 흐릿하게 보이다; (일이) 곧 닥칠 것처럼 보이다 If something looms over you, it appears as a large or unclear shape, often in a frightening way.
nail^{복습} [neil]	n. 손톱, 발톱; 못; v. 못으로 박다 Your nails are the thin hard parts that grow at the ends of your fingers and toes.
crabby [krǽbi]	a. 괴팍한, 심술궂은 Someone who is crabby is bad-tempered and unpleasant to people.
flagpole^{복습} [flǽgpoul]	n. 깃대 A flagpole is a tall pole on which a flag can be displayed.
lock^{복습} [lak]	v. 고정하다; (자물쇠로) 잠그다; n. 자물쇠 If you lock something in a particular position or if it locks there, it is held or fitted firmly in that position.
thumb** [θʌm]	n. 엄지손가락; v. 엄지손가락으로 건드리다 Your thumb is the short thick part on the side of your hand next to your four fingers.
pinky^{복습} [píŋki]	n. 새끼손가락 Your pinky is the smallest finger on your hand.
hold one's nose	idiom (냄새가 고약해서) 코를 쥐다 When you hold your nose, you squeeze your nostrils with your fingers in order to avoid inhaling an unpleasant smell.
stink [stiŋk]	v. (고약한) 냄새가 나다; 아무 쓸모없다; n. 악취 To stink means to smell extremely unpleasant.
cafeteria^{복습} [kæfətíəriə]	n. (학교·회사 등의) 구내식당; 카페테리아 A cafeteria is a lunchroom or dining hall, as in a factory, office, or school, where food is often served from counters.

tray[*]
[trei]

n. 쟁반
A tray is a flat piece of wood, plastic, or metal, which usually has raised edges and which is used for carrying things, especially food and drinks.

plate[**]
[pleit]

n. 한 접시 (분량의 음식); 접시, 그릇
A plate of food is the amount of it on the plate, which is a round or oval flat dish that is used to hold food.

top[***]
[tap]

v. (다른 것의) 위에 놓다; 능가하다; 더 높다; n. 맨 위, 꼭대기; 팽이
If something is topped with something, it has that thing as its highest part.

spill[*]
[spil]

v. 흘리다, 쏟다; n. 유출; 흘린 액체
If a liquid spills or if you spill it, it accidentally flows over the edge of a container.

due[***]
[djuː]

a. ~하기로 되어 있는, ~할 예정인; ~을 받을 자격이 있는; n. 당연한 권리
If something is due at a particular time, it is expected to happen, be done, or arrive at that time.

swish
[swiʃ]

v. 휙 소리를 내며 움직이다; n. 휙 하는 소리
If something swishes or if you swish it, it moves quickly through the air, making a soft sound.

heel[**]
[hiːl]

n. 발뒤꿈치; (신발의) 굽; v. 한쪽으로 기울다
Your heel is the back part of your foot, just below your ankle.

gross[복습]
[grous]

a. 역겨운; 아주 무례한
If you describe something as gross, you think it is very unpleasant.

accuse[*]
[əkjúːz]

v. 비난하다, 혐의를 제기하다
If you accuse someone of doing something wrong or dishonest, you say or tell them that you believe that they did it.

wipe[복습]
[waip]

v. (먼지 · 물기 등을) 닦다; 지우다; n. 닦기
If you wipe dirt or liquid from something, you remove it by using a cloth or your hand.

complain[복습]
[kəmpléin]

v. 불평하다, 항의하다
If you complain about a situation, you say that you are not satisfied with it.

stinky
[stíŋki]

a. 악취가 나는; 지독한, 역겨운
If something is stinky, it smells extremely unpleasant.

dump[복습]
[dʌmp]

v. 버리다; (아무렇게나) 내려놓다; n. (쓰레기) 폐기장
If you dump something somewhere, you get rid of it because you do not want or need it.

trash[*]
[træʃ]

n. 쓰레기; v. 부수다, 엉망으로 만들다; (필요 없는 것을) 버리다
Trash consists of unwanted things or waste material such as used paper, empty containers and bottles, and waste food.

lunchroom
[lʌ́nʧruːm]

n. (학교 · 회사 등의) 구내식당
A lunchroom is the room in a school or company where you buy and eat your lunch.

horror*
[hɔ́ːrər]

n. 공포(감), 경악
Horror is a feeling of great shock, fear, and worry caused by something extremely unpleasant.

counter
[káuntər]

n. (주방의) 조리대; (식당 등의) 카운터, 기다란 대; (은행·상점 등의) 계산대
A counter is a long table, board, or cabinet top in a kitchen that is used to serve or prepare food.

rag*
[ræg]

n. 해진 천 (dishrag n. 행주)
A dishrag is a cloth used for washing dishes, pans, and flatware.

rush^{복습}
[rʌʃ]

v. 급히 움직이다, 서두르다; n. 분주함; 혼잡
If you rush somewhere, you go there quickly.

hopeful**
[hóupfəl]

a. 희망에 찬, 기대하는; 희망을 주는 (hopefully ad. 희망을 가지고)
If you are hopeful, you are fairly confident that something that you want to happen will happen.

out of breath

idiom 숨을 헐떡이며, 숨이 차서
If you are out of breath, you are breathing very quickly and with difficulty because you have been doing something energetic.

dumpster
[dʌ́mpstər]

n. 대형 쓰레기통
A dumpster is a large metal container for holding rubbish.

upside down^{복습}
[ʌ̀psaid dáun]

ad. (아래위가) 거꾸로
If something has been turned upside down, it has been turned around so that the part that is usually lowest is above the part that is usually highest.

bury**
[béri]

v. (보이지 않게) 묻다; (감정·실수 등을) 감추다
If an object is buried in something, the object is covered by something so that it can't be found.

wrinkle*
[riŋkl]

v. 주름이 생기다; (얼굴에) 주름을 잡다, 찡그리다; n. 주름
(wrinkled a. 주름진, 구겨진)
Cloth or paper that is wrinkled has a lot of small accidental folds on it.

soggy
[sági]

a. 질척한, 질척거리는
Something that is soggy is unpleasantly wet.

dig**
[dig]

v. (dug-dug) (무엇을 찾기 위해) 뒤지다; (구멍을) 파다; 찔러 넣다;
n. 쿡 찌르기; 발굴
If you dig into something such as a deep container, you put your hand in it to search for something.

strand*
[strænd]

n. 가닥, 올, 줄; v. 오도 가도 못 하게 하다, 발을 묶다
A strand of something such as hair, wire, or thread is a single thin piece of it.

drippy
[drípi]

a. 방울방울 떨어지는, 액체 상태의; 감상적인
If you describe something as drippy, you mean that liquid falls from it in individual small drops.

carton*
[kaːrtn]

n. (음식이나 음료를 담는) 곽; 상자
A carton is a plastic or cardboard container in which food or drink is sold.

core[*]
[kɔːr]

n. (사과 같은 과일의) 속; (사물의) 중심부; 핵심
The core of a fruit is the central part of it.

slice[*]
[slais]

n. (얇게 썬) 조각; 부분, 몫; v. 자르다; 베다
A slice of bread, meat, fruit, or other food is a thin piece that has been cut from a larger piece.

rustle[*]
[rʌsl]

v. 바스락거리다; n. 바스락거리는 소리
When something thin and dry rustles or when you rustle it, it makes soft sounds as it moves.

hooray
[huréi]

int. 만세
People sometimes shout 'hooray!' when they are very happy and excited about something.

relief[**]
[rilíːf]

n. 안도, 안심; (고통·불안 등의) 경감
If you feel a sense of relief, you feel happy because something unpleasant has not happened or is no longer happening.

ultimate[복습]
[ʌ́ltəmət]

a. 궁극적인, 최종적인; 최고의, 최상의; n. 극치
You use ultimate to describe the final result or aim of a long series of events.

Check Your Reading Speed

1분에 몇 단어를 읽는지 리딩 속도를 측정해 보세요.

$$\frac{391 \text{ words}}{\text{reading time ( ) sec}} \times 60 = (\quad) \text{ WPM}$$

Build Your Vocabulary

assign^{복습}
[əsáin]

v. (일·책임 등을) 맡기다; 선임하다, 파견하다 (assignment n. 과제, 임무)
An assignment is a task or piece of work that you are given to do, especially as part of your job or studies.

the pit of one's stomach

idiom (강한 감정을 나타내는 표현에서) 명치, 가슴
If you have a feeling in the pit of your stomach, you have a tight or sick feeling in your stomach, usually because you are afraid or anxious.

lug^{복습}
[lʌg]

v. (무거운 것을 힘들게) 나르다, 끌다
If you lug a heavy or awkward object somewhere, you carry it there with difficulty.

mark^{복습}
[maːrk]

n. 표시, 부호; 자국, 흔적; v. (표·기호 등으로) 표시하다 (bookmark n. 책갈피)
A bookmark is a narrow piece of card or leather that you put between the pages of a book so that you can find a particular page easily.

giggle^{복습}
[gigl]

v. 킥킥거리다, 피식 웃다; n. 킥킥거림, 피식 웃음
If someone giggles, they laugh in a childlike way, because they are amused, nervous, or embarrassed.

figure^{복습}
[fígjər]

v. 생각하다; 중요하다; n. (멀리서 흐릿하게 보이는) 사람; 수치; (중요한) 인물
If you figure that something is the case, you think or guess that it is the case.

notice^{복습}
[nóutis]

v. 알아채다, 인지하다; 주목하다, 관심을 기울이다; n. 신경 씀, 알아챔
If you notice something or someone, you become aware of them.

stay up

idiom (평상시보다 더 늦게까지) 안 자다
If you stay up, you do not go to bed.

goofy
[gúːfi]

a. 바보 같은, 얼빠진
If you describe someone or something as goofy, you think they are rather silly or ridiculous.

recess^{복습}
[risés]

n. (학교의) 쉬는 시간; (의회·위원회 등의) 휴회 기간
A recess is a break between classes at a school.

glance^{복습}
[glæns]

v. 흘낏 보다; 대충 훑어보다; n. 흘낏 봄
If you glance at something or someone, you look at them very quickly and then look away again immediately.

no way ^{복습}

idiom (강한 거절의 의미로) 절대로 안 돼, 싫어; 말도 안 돼
You can say 'no way' for expressing surprise, or for telling someone that you do not believe them.

Chapters 17 & 18

1. Why did the students stare at Mr. Kidswatter?
   A. They thought he was not at school that day.
   B. They noticed that he was making a strange face.
   C. It was the first time he had been inside their classroom.
   D. It was a surprise that he brought something for Mrs. Jewls.

2. What did Mr. Kidswatter want one of the students to do on Friday?
   A. He wanted someone to clean his office.
   B. He wanted someone to take a test.
   C. He wanted someone to meet a new student.
   D. He wanted someone to bang the gong.

3. Why did Stephen feel nervous?
   A. He was worried about showing his report to Mr. Kidswatter.
   B. He did not study for the upcoming test.
   C. He said something rude to Mr. Kidswatter.
   D. He could not make a mistake with the gong.

4. Why did Dr. Pickle have a mirror in his office?
   A. He received the mirror as a gift from a student.
   B. He thought that the mirror would bring him good luck.
   C. He asked visitors to his office to look in the mirror.
   D. He often checked his beard in the mirror.

5. What made Dr. Pickle wake up?
   A. He heard someone knocking on the door.
   B. He set an alarm on his phone.
   C. He heard the sound of a car horn.
   D. He asked a student to wake him up.

6. What did Dr. Pickle figure out about the Doofus Face?
   A. That it may make the students feel scared
   B. That it goes away by itself after a few hours
   C. That it shifts to the person who stares at it
   D. That it was happening to all of the students

7. What did Dr. Pickle do with the bust of Sigmund Freud?
   A. He smashed the mirror with it.
   B. He took it to his home.
   C. He polished it with some cleaner.
   D. He showed it to Mr. Kidswatter.

Check Your Reading Speed

1분에 몇 단어를 읽는지 리딩 속도를 측정해 보세요.

$$\frac{683 \text{ words}}{\text{reading time ( ) sec}} \times 60 = (\quad) \text{ WPM}$$

Build Your Vocabulary

principal 복습
[prínsəpəl]

n. 교장; 학장, 총장; a. 주요한, 주된
A principal is a teacher who is in charge of a school.

cabbage*
[kǽbidʒ]

n. 양배추
A cabbage is a round vegetable with white, green or purple leaves that is usually eaten cooked.

turn out

idiom ~인 것으로 드러나다; 모습을 드러내다; (전기·난방기를) 끄다
If something turns out a particular way, it happens in that way.

switch 복습
[switʃ]

v. 바꾸다, 전환하다; n. 스위치
If you switch two or more things, you replace one with another.

move on

idiom (새로운 일·주제로) 넘어가다
To move on to something means to start doing or discussing something new.

somewhat*
[sʌ́mhwʌt]

ad. 어느 정도, 약간, 다소
You use somewhat to indicate that something is the case to a limited extent or degree.

barely 복습
[béərli]

ad. 간신히, 가까스로; 거의 ~ 아니게
You use barely to say that something is done in a way that is just possible but only with difficulty.

swing 복습
[swiŋ]

v. (swung-swung) 휙 움직이다; (전후·좌우로) 흔들(리)다; n. 흔들기; 휘두르기
If something swings in a particular direction or if you swing it in that direction, it moves quickly in that direction with a smooth, curving movement.

bang 복습
[bæŋ]

v. 쾅 하고 치다; 쾅 하고 닫다; n. 쾅 하는 소리
If something bangs, it makes a sudden loud noise, once or several times.

clear one's throat

idiom 목을 가다듬다; 헛기침하다
If you clear your throat, you cough once in order to make it easier to speak or to attract people's attention.

wave 복습
[weiv]

v. (손·팔을) 흔들다; 손짓하다; n. 파도, 물결; (손·팔·몸을) 흔들기
If you wave or wave your hand, you move your hand from side to side in the air, usually in order to say hello or goodbye to someone.

conductor[*]
[kəndʌ́ktər]

n. (합창·합주의) 지휘자; (버스나 기차의) 안내원
A conductor is a person who stands in front of an orchestra or choir and directs its performance.

unison
[júːnisn]

n. 조화, 화합, 일치 (in unison idiom 일제히)
If two or more people do something in unison, they do it together at the same time.

container[*]
[kəntéinər]

n. 용기, 그릇; (화물 수송용) 컨테이너
A container is something such as a box or bottle that is used to hold or store things in.

stack[*]
[stæk]

v. (깔끔하게 정돈하여) 쌓다; n. 무더기, 더미
If you stack a number of things, you arrange them in neat piles.

weird 복습
[wiərd]

a. 기이한, 기묘한; 기괴한, 섬뜩한
If you describe something or someone as weird, you mean that they are strange.

donate 복습
[dóuneit]

v. 기부하다, 기증하다; 헌혈하다
If you donate something to a charity or other organization, you give it to them.

curl^{**}
[kəːrl]

v. (동그렇게) 감다, (몸을) 웅크리다; 곱슬곱슬하다; n. 곱슬곱슬한 머리카락
If your toes, fingers, or other parts of your body curl, or if you curl them, they form a curved or round shape.

examine^{***}
[igzǽmin]

v. 면밀히 살피다; 조사하다, 검토하다; 검사하다; 시험을 실시하다
If you examine something, you look at it carefully.

figure 복습
[fígjər]

v. 생각하다; 중요하다; n. (멀리서 흐릿하게 보이는) 사람; 수치; (중요한) 인물
If you figure that something is the case, you think or guess that it is the case.

willing^{**}
[wíliŋ]

a. 기꺼이 하는, 자발적인; 꺼리지 않는
If someone is willing to do something, they are fairly happy about doing it and will do it if they are asked or required to do it.

shoot^{***}
[ʃuːt]

v. (shot-shot) 휙 움직이다; (총 등을) 쏘다; 슛을 하다; n. 촬영
If someone or something shoots in a particular direction, they move in that direction quickly and suddenly.

beg 복습
[beg]

v. 간청하다, 애원하다; 구걸하다
If you beg someone to do something, you ask them very anxiously or eagerly to do it.

stretch 복습
[stretʃ]

v. (팔·다리를) 뻗다; 기지개를 켜다; 펼쳐지다; n. (길게) 뻗은 구간; 기간
If you stretch your arm or leg, you move it away from your body in order to reach something.

urge 복습
[əːrdʒ]

v. 재촉하다; 충고하다, 설득하려 하다; n. (강한) 욕구, 충동
If you urge someone to do something, you try hard to persuade them to do it.

double 복습
[dʌbl]

v. 두 배로 만들다; a. 두 배의, 갑절의; 이중의; n. 두 배, 갑절
When something doubles or when you double it, it becomes twice as great in number, amount, or size.

boom[*]
[bu:m]

v. 굵은 목소리로 말하다; 쾅 하는 소리를 내다; n. 쾅, 탕 하는 소리
When something such as someone's voice, a cannon, or a big drum booms, it makes a loud, deep sound that lasts for several seconds.

groan^{복습}
[groun]

v. 신음 소리를 내다; 끙끙거리다; n. 신음; 끙 하는 소리
If you groan, you make a long, low sound because you are in pain, or because you are upset or unhappy about something.

meek[*]
[mi:k]

a. 온순한, 온화한 (meekly ad. 온순하게)
If you describe a person as meek, you think that they are gentle and quiet, and likely to do what other people say.

stride[*]
[straid]

v. (strode-stridden) 성큼성큼 걷다; n. 걸음; 걸음걸이
If you stride somewhere, you walk there with quick, long steps.

lean^{복습}
[li:n]

v. 기울이다, (몸을) 숙이다; ~에 기대다; a. 군살이 없는, 호리호리한
When you lean in a particular direction, you bend your body in that direction.

exact^{복습}
[igzǽkt]

a. 정확한, 정밀한; 꼼꼼한, 빈틈없는 (exactly ad. 정확히, 꼭)
You use exactly before an amount, number, or position to emphasize that it is no more, no less, or no different from what you are stating.

straighten^{복습}
[streitn]

v. (자세를) 바로 하다; 똑바르게 하다
If you are standing in a relaxed or slightly bent position and then you straighten, you make your back or body straight and upright.

chest^{**}
[ʧest]

n. 가슴, 흉부; (나무로 만든) 상자
Your chest is the top part of the front of your body where your ribs, lungs, and heart are.

crowd^{**}
[kraud]

v. 모이다, 붐비다; 가득 메우다; 바싹 붙어 서다; n. 사람들, 군중
When people crowd around someone or something, they gather closely together around them.

blow^{복습}
[blou]

v. (기회를) 날리다; (입으로) 불다; (호각 · 악기 등을) 불다; n. 세게 때림
If you blow a chance or attempt to do something, you make a mistake which wastes the chance or causes the attempt to fail.

Check Your Reading Speed

1분에 몇 단어를 읽는지 리딩 속도를 측정해 보세요.

$$\frac{551 \text{ words}}{\text{reading time (\quad) sec}} \times 60 = (\quad) \text{ WPM}$$

Build Your Vocabulary

bust*
[bʌst]

n. 흉상, 반신상; v. 부수다, 고장 내다; 급습하다
A bust is a statue of the head and shoulders of a person.

statue*
[stǽtʃuː]

n. 조각상
A statue is a large sculpture of a person or an animal, made of stone or metal.

psychologist*
[saikálədʒist]

n. 심리학자
A psychologist is a person who studies the human mind and tries to explain why people behave in the way that they do.

beard^{복습}
[biərd]

n. (턱)수염
A man's beard is the hair that grows on his chin and cheeks.

handheld
[hǽndhèld]

a. 손에 들고 쓰는; 손바닥 크기의; n. 소형 기기
A handheld device such as a camera or a computer is small and light enough to be used while you are holding it.

trim*
[trim]

v. 다듬다, 손질하다; n. 다듬기, 약간 자르기; a. 잘 가꾼, 깔끔한
If you trim something, you cut off small amounts of it in order to make it look neater and tidier.

cheek^{복습}
[tʃiːk]

n. 뺨, 볼
Your cheeks are the sides of your face below your eyes.

puff out^{복습}

idiom (공기를 채워) 불룩하게 부풀리다
If you puff out your cheeks, you make them larger and rounder by filling them with air.

tongue^{복습}
[tʌŋ]

n. 혀; 언어
Your tongue is the soft movable part inside your mouth which you use for tasting, eating, and speaking.

stick out^{복습}

idiom ~을 내밀다, 튀어나오게 하다
If you stick out part of your body, you extend it away from your body.

eyebrow^{복습}
[áibràu]

n. 눈썹
Your eyebrows are the lines of hair which grow above your eyes.

doofus^{복습}
[dúːfəs]

n. 멍청이, 얼간이
If you call someone a doofus, you think they are foolish and stupid.

count^{복습}
[kaunt]

n. (하나부터 순서대로 세는) 셈; 계산; v. (수를) 세다; 계산에 넣다
A count is an act of saying numbers in order, up to a particular number.

plop^{복습}
[plap]

v. 털썩 떨어지다, 떨어뜨리다; 털썩 주저앉다; n. 풍당 하는 소리
If something plops somewhere, it drops there with a soft, gentle sound.

patient^{복습}
[péiʃənt]

n. 환자; a. 인내심 있는
A patient is a person who is receiving medical treatment from a
doctor or hospital.

horn^{복습}
[hɔːrn]

n. (차량의) 경적; (양·소 등의) 뿔
On a vehicle such as a car, the horn is the device that makes a loud
noise as a signal or warning.

blare^{복습}
[blɛər]

v. (소리를) 요란하게 울리다; n. 요란한 소리
If something such as a siren or radio blares or if you blare it, it
makes a loud, unpleasant noise.

hypnotize
[hípnətàiz]

v. 최면을 걸다; 혼을 빼놓다, 홀리다
If someone hypnotizes you, they put you into a state in which you
seem to be asleep but can still see, hear, or respond to things said
to you.

shift*
[ʃift]

v. 옮기다, 이동하다; 바뀌다, 달라지다; n. 변화; 교대 근무 (시간)
If something shifts, it moves from one place to another.

stare^{복습}
[stɛər]

v. 빤히 쳐다보다, 응시하다; n. 빤히 쳐다보기, 응시
If you stare at someone or something, you look at them for a long
time.

psychiatry
[saikáiətri]

n. 정신 의학
Psychiatry is the branch of medicine concerned with the treatment
of mental illness.

glimpse*
[glimps]

n. 잠깐 봄; 짧은 경험; v. 언뜻 보다; 깨닫다, 이해하다
If you get a glimpse of someone or something, you see them very
briefly and not very well.

hideous*
[hídiəs]

a. 흉측한, 흉물스러운, 끔찍한
If you say that someone or something is hideous, you mean that
they are very ugly or unattractive.

fame*
[feim]

n. 명성
If you achieve fame, you become very well-known.

worth^{복습}
[wəːrθ]

a. ~해 볼 만한, ~할 가치가 있는; (금전 등의 면에서) ~의 가치가 있는; n. 가치, 값어치
If something is worth a particular action, or if an action is worth
doing, it is considered to be important enough for that action.

stuck^{복습}
[stʌk]

a. 움직일 수 없는, 꼼짝 못하는; (불쾌한 상황에서) 빠져나갈 수 없는; (대답 등이) 막힌
If something is stuck in a particular position, it is fixed tightly in this
position and is unable to move.

bronze*
[branz]

n. 청동
Bronze is a yellowish-brown metal which is a mixture of copper and tin.

flip*
[flip]

v. 확 뒤집(히)다; (손가락으로) 툭 던지다; n. 툭 던지기
If something flips over, or if you flip it over or into a different
position, it moves or is moved into a different position.

slam ^{복습}
[slæm]

v. 세게 치다, 놓다; 쾅 닫다; n. 쾅 하고 닫기; 쾅 하는 소리
If you slam something on, you put, move, or hit it against or onto a surface with great force.

shatter*
[ʃǽtər]

v. 산산이 부서지다; 산산조각 내다; 엄청난 충격을 주다
If something shatters or is shattered, it breaks into a lot of small pieces.

dizzy*
[dízi]

a. 어지러운
If you feel dizzy, you feel that you are losing your balance and are about to fall.

confuse**
[kənfjúːz]

v. (사람을) 혼란시키다; (주제를) 혼란스럽게 하다 (confused a. 혼란스러워하는)
If you are confused, you do not know exactly what is happening or what to do.

exclaim ^{복습}
[ikskléim]

v. 소리치다, 외치다
If you exclaim, you cry out suddenly in surprise, strong emotion, or pain.

Chapters 19 & 20

1. Why was Stephen doing push-downs in the playground?

   A. He was showing Louis how to do push-downs.

   B. He wanted to win a push-down contest.

   C. He was trying to impress some of his friends.

   D. He wanted to get stronger in order to bang the gong.

2. Why did Mr. Kidswatter point at Stephen to bang the gong?

   A. He meant to point at Dana, but she bent down.

   B. He was glad that Stephen said he was the best principal.

   C. He tried to point to Mrs. Jewls, but Stephen stood up.

   D. He thought Stephen was the strongest student in the class.

3. Why was Stephen worried after talking to Louis?

   A. Louis gave him the idea of dropping the mallet on his foot.

   B. Louis said Stephen had to do a hundred more push-downs.

   C. Louis wanted to change the person who would bang the gong.

   D. Louis told Stephen he was doing push-downs the wrong way.

4. What did Jason do to make Mrs. Jewls horrified?

    A. He lost his paper clip on the way to school.

    B. He let his paper clip get bent into the wrong shape.

    C. He gave his paper clip to another student.

    D. He said that he did not like paper clips.

5. What was the first thing Mrs. Jewls did when she and Jason got to the closet?

    A. She picked up a red key and a green key.

    B. She removed the chains from the door.

    C. She turned the padlock dial to open the lock.

    D. She made the clamps snap open.

6. What did Jason think Mrs. Jewls was going to do?

    A. Send him to Mr. Kidswatter

    B. Call the fire department

    C. Make him carry a heavy book

    D. Lock him in the closet

7. What did Jason see inside the closet?

    A. He saw Mrs. Jewls's books.

    B. He saw some other students.

    C. He saw a scary monster.

    D. He saw a box of paper clips.

Check Your Reading Speed

1분에 몇 단어를 읽는지 리딩 속도를 측정해 보세요.

$$\frac{652 \text{ words}}{\text{reading time ( ) sec}} \times 60 = (\quad) \text{ WPM}$$

Build Your Vocabulary

playground^{복습}
[pléigràund]

n. (학교의) 운동장; 놀이터
A playground is a piece of land, at school or in a public area, where children can play.

surround**
[səráund]

v. 둘러싸다, 에워싸다; 포위하다
If a person or thing is surrounded by something, that thing is situated all around them.

classmate*
[klǽsmeit]

n. 급우, 반 친구
Your classmates are students who are in the same class as you at school or college.

grunt*
[grʌnt]

v. 끙 앓는 소리를 내다; 툴툴거리다; n. (사람이) 끙 하는 소리
If you grunt, you make a short, low sound instead of speaking, usually because of anger or pain.

blacktop^{복습}
[blǽktàp]

n. 아스팔트 도로; (포장에 쓰이는) 아스팔트; v. 아스팔트로 포장하다
Blacktop is a hard black substance which is used as a surface for roads, as well as a road covered with this substance.

might*
[mait]

n. (강력한) 힘, 권력; 세력 (with all one's might idiom 전력을 다하여, 힘껏)
If you do something with all your might, you do it using all your strength and energy.

encourage**
[inkə́:ridʒ]

v. 격려하다, 용기를 북돋우다; 부추기다
If you encourage someone, you give them confidence, for example by letting them know that what they are doing is good and telling them that they should continue to do it.

yard^{복습}
[ja:rd]

n. (학교의) 운동장; 마당, 뜰; 정원
A yard is a flat area of concrete or stone that is next to a building and often has a wall around it.

whistle^{복습}
[hwisl]

n. 호각, 호루라기; 휘파람 (소리); v. 호루라기를 불다; 휘파람을 불다
A whistle is a small metal tube which you blow in order to produce a loud sound and attract someone's attention.

make one's way^{복습}

idiom 나아가다, 가다
When you make your way somewhere, you walk or travel there.

correct^{복습}
[kərékt]

v. 바로잡다, 정정하다; a. 맞는, 정확한; 적절한, 옳은
If you correct someone, you say something which you think is more accurate or appropriate than what they have just said.

opposite ^{복습}
[ápəzit]

a. (정)반대의; 건너편의; 맞은편의; n. 반대(되는 것)
Opposite is used to describe things of the same kind which are completely different in a particular way.

kneel *
[niːl]

v. 무릎을 꿇다
When you kneel, you bend your legs so that your knees are touching the ground.

pat ^{복습}
[pæt]

v. 쓰다듬다, 토닥거리다; n. 쓰다듬기, 토닥거리기
If you pat something or someone, you tap them lightly, usually with your hand held flat.

bet *
[bet]

v. 틀림없다, 분명하다; 돈을 걸다; n. 내기; 짐작
You use expressions such as 'I bet,' 'I'll bet,' and 'you can bet' to indicate that you are sure something is true.

eyebrow ^{복습}
[áibràu]

n. 눈썹
Your eyebrows are the lines of hair which grow above your eyes.

mustache ^{복습}
[mʌ́stæʃ]

n. 콧수염
A man's mustache is the hair that grows on his upper lip.

twitch ^{복습}
[twitʃ]

v. 씰룩거리다, 경련하다; 홱 잡아채다; n. 씰룩거림, 경련
If something, especially a part of your body, twitches or if you twitch it, it makes a little jumping movement.

mutter ^{복습}
[mʌ́tər]

v. 중얼거리다; 투덜거리다; n. 중얼거림
If you mutter, you speak very quietly so that you cannot easily be heard, often because you are complaining about something.

never mind

idiom (중요하지 않으니까) 신경 쓰지 마; 걱정하지 마
You can say 'never mind' to tell someone that they need not do something or worry about something, because it is not important or because you will do it yourself.

solid ^{복습}
[sálid]

a. (다른 물질이 섞이지 않고) 순수한; 단단한; 고체의; n. 고체, 고형물
If an object is made of solid gold or solid wood, for example, it is made of gold or wood all the way through, rather than just on the outside.

iron ^{복습}
[áiərn]

n. 철, 쇠; 철분; 다리미
Iron is an element which usually takes the form of a hard, dark grey metal. It is used to make steel, and also forms part of many tools, buildings, and vehicles.

gasp ^{복습}
[gæsp]

v. (숨이 막히는 듯) 헉 소리를 내다; 숨이 턱 막히다; n. (숨이 막히는 듯) 헉 하는 소리
When you gasp, you take a short quick breath through your mouth, especially when you are surprised, shocked, or in pain.

donate ^{복습}
[dóuneit]

v. 기부하다, 기증하다; 헌혈하다
If you donate something to a charity or other organization, you give it to them.

nail ^{복습}
[neil]

n. 손톱, 발톱; 못; v. 못으로 박다
Your nails are the thin hard parts that grow at the ends of your fingers and toes.

examine ^{복습}
[igzǽmin]

v. 면밀히 살피다; 조사하다, 검토하다; 검사하다; 시험을 실시하다
If you examine something, you look at it carefully.

brat ^{복습}
[bræt]

n. 버릇없는 녀석
If you call someone, especially a child, a brat, you mean that he or she behaves badly or annoys you.

awful **
[ɔ́ːfəl]

a. 끔찍한, 지독한; (정도가) 대단한
If you say that someone or something is awful, you dislike that person or thing or you think that they are not very good.

boom ^{복습}
[buːm]

v. 굵은 목소리로 말하다; 쾅 하는 소리를 내다; n. 쾅, 탕 하는 소리
When something such as someone's voice, a cannon, or a big drum booms, it makes a loud, deep sound that lasts for several seconds.

mosquito *
[məskíːtou]

n. 모기
Mosquitos are small flying insects which bite people and animals in order to suck their blood.

bite ^{복습}
[bait]

n. (짐승·곤충에게) 물린 상처; 물기; 한 입; v. (이빨로) 물다, 베어 물다
A bite is an injury or a mark on your body where an animal, snake, or small insect has bitten you.

ankle *
[ǽŋkl]

n. 발목
Your ankle is the joint where your foot joins your leg.

bend ^{복습}
[bend]

v. (bent-bent) (몸이나 머리를) 굽히다, 숙이다; (무엇을) 구부리다; n. 굽이, 굽은 곳
When you bend, you move the top part of your body downward and forward.

scratch *
[skrætʃ]

v. (가려운 데를) 긁다; 할퀴다; n. 긁힌 자국
If you scratch yourself, you rub your fingernails against your skin because it is itching.

doom ^{복습}
[duːm]

v. 불행한 운명을 맞게 하다; n. 불운, 저주; 죽음, 파멸
If you are doomed to a particular state, something unpleasant is certain to happen, and you can do nothing to prevent it.

moan ^{복습}
[moun]

v. 투덜거리다, 불평하다; 신음하다; n. 투덜거림, 불평; 신음
To moan means to complain or speak in a way which shows that you are very unhappy.

terrible *
[térəbl]

a. (나쁜 정도가) 극심한, 엄청난; 끔찍한, 소름 끼치는; 형편없는
You use terrible to emphasize the great extent or degree of something.

point out ^{복습}

idiom 지적하다, 언급하다; 알려주다
If you point out a fact or circumstance, you mention it in order to give someone information about it or make them notice it.

million ^{복습}
[míljən]

n. 100만; a. 수많은
A million or one million is the number 1,000,000.

mansion *
[mǽnʃən]

n. 대저택
A mansion is a very large house.

96

sniff ^{복습}
[snif]

v. 코를 훌쩍이다; 냄새를 맡다; n. 냄새 맡기; 콧방귀 뀌기
When you sniff, you breathe in air through your nose hard enough to make a sound, for example, when you are trying not to cry.

sigh ^{복습}
[sai]

v. 한숨을 쉬다, 한숨짓다; n. 한숨
When you sigh, you let out a deep breath, as a way of expressing feelings such as disappointment, tiredness, or pleasure.

roll**
[roul]

v. 돌다, 돌아서다; 구르다, 굴러가다; n. 통, 두루마리; 명부, 명단
If you are lying down and you roll over, you turn your body so that a different part of you is facing upward.

confuse ^{복습}
[kənfjúːz]

v. (사람을) 혼란시키다; (주제를) 혼란스럽게 하다 (confused a. 혼란스러워하는)
If you are confused, you do not know exactly what is happening or what to do.

collapse*
[kəlǽps]

v. 주저앉다, 드러눕다; 붕괴되다, 무너지다; n. (건물의) 붕괴
If you collapse, you suddenly faint or fall down because you are very ill or weak.

Check Your Reading Speed

1분에 몇 단어를 읽는지 리딩 속도를 측정해 보세요.

$$\frac{977 \text{ words}}{\text{reading time ( ) sec}} \times 60 = (\text{ }) \text{ WPM}$$

Build Your Vocabulary

closet^{복습}
[klázit]

n. 벽장
A closet is a piece of furniture with doors at the front and shelves inside, which is used for storing things.

make it^{복습}

idiom 가다; 성공하다, 해내다
If you make it to somewhere, you succeed in reaching there.

awake^{복습}
[əwéik]

v. (awoke-awoken) 깨다, 깨우다; (감정을) 불러일으키다; a. 잠들지 않은, 깨어 있는
When you awake or when something awakes you, you wake up.

giggle^{복습}
[gigl]

v. 킥킥거리다, 피식 웃다; n. 킥킥거림, 피식 웃음
If someone giggles, they laugh in a childlike way, because they are amused, nervous, or embarrassed.

bend^{복습}
[bend]

v. (bent-bent) (무엇을) 구부리다; (몸이나 머리를) 굽히다, 숙이다; n. 굽이, 굽은 곳
If you bend something that is flat or straight, you use force to make it curved or to put an angle in it.

crook
[kruk]

v. 구부리다; n. 사기꾼 (crooked a. 구부러진)
If you describe something as crooked, especially something that is usually straight, you mean that it is bent or twisted.

horrify^{복습}
[hɔ́:rəfài]

v. 소름 끼치게 만들다 (horrified a. 충격받은, 겁에 질린)
If someone is horrified, they feel shocked or disgusted, usually because of something that they have seen or heard.

gasp^{복습}
[gæsp]

v. (숨이 막히는 듯) 헉 소리를 내다; 숨이 턱 막히다; n. (숨이 막히는 듯) 헉 하는 소리
When you gasp, you take a short quick breath through your mouth, especially when you are surprised, shocked, or in pain.

grab^{복습}
[græb]

v. (와락·단단히) 붙잡다; ~을 잡으려고 하다; n. 와락 잡아채려고 함
If you grab something, you take it or pick it up suddenly and roughly.

yank
[jæŋk]

v. 홱 잡아당기다; n. 홱 잡아당기기
If you yank someone or something somewhere, you pull them there suddenly and with a lot of force.

whimper
[hwímpər]

v. 훌쩍이다; n. (사람이) 훌쩍거림
If someone whimpers, they make quiet unhappy or frightened sounds, as if they are about to start crying.

whisper^{복습}
[hwíspər]

n. 속삭임, 소곤거리는 소리; v. 속삭이다, 소곤거리다, 귓속말을 하다
A whisper is a very quiet way of saying something so that other people cannot hear you.

slam ^{복습}
[slæm]

v. 쾅 닫다; 세게 치다, 놓다; n. 쾅 하고 닫기; 쾅 하는 소리
If you slam a door or window or if it slams, it shuts noisily and with great force.

drag*
[dræg]

v. 끌다, 끌고 가다; 힘들게 움직이다; n. 끌기, 당기기; 장애물
If someone drags you somewhere, they pull you there, or force you to go there by physically threatening you.

sign ^{복습}
[sain]

n. 표지판, 간판; 징후, 조짐; v. 서명하다; (손으로) 신호를 보내다
A sign is a piece of wood, metal, or plastic with words or pictures on it.

fire department
[fáiər dipà:rtmənt]

n. 소방서, 소방대
The fire department is an organization which has the job of putting out fires.

dial*
[dáiəl]

n. (시계·계기 등의) 문자반; v. 전화를 걸다
A dial is a round control on a piece of equipment that you turn to change something such as the temperature or sound.

combination**
[kàmbənéiʃən]

n. (숫자나 글자를 조합한 일련의) 번호; 조합, 결합; 연합
The combination of a lock is a set of letters or numbers in a particular order that can be used to open it.

lock ^{복습}
[lak]

n. 자물쇠; v. (자물쇠로) 잠그다; 고정하다
The lock on something such as a door or a drawer is the device which is used to keep it shut and prevent other people from opening it.

wrap ^{복습}
[ræp]

v. (무엇의 둘레를) 두르다; (포장지 등으로) 싸다, 포장하다; n. 포장지
(unwrap v. 벗기다)
When you unwrap something, you take off the paper, plastic, or other covering that is around it.

toss ^{복습}
[tɔ:s]

v. (가볍게·아무렇게나) 던지다; n. (고개를) 홱 젖히기
If you toss something somewhere, you throw it there lightly, often in a rather careless way.

clang ^{복습}
[klæŋ]

v. 쨍그랑 하고 울리다; n. 쨍그랑 하는 소리
When a large metal object clangs, it makes a loud noise.

steel ^{복습}
[sti:l]

n. 강철; v. (~에 대비해서) 마음을 단단히 먹다
Steel is a very strong metal which is made mainly from iron.

clamp ^{복습}
[klæmp]

n. 죄는 기구, 죔쇠; v. (죄는 기구로) 고정시키다; 꽉 물다
A clamp is a device that holds two things firmly together.

block ^{복습}
[blak]

v. 막다, 차단하다; 방해하다; n. 사각형 덩어리; (도로로 나뉘는) 구역, 블록
To block a road, channel, or pipe means to put an object across it or in it so that nothing can pass through it or along it.

snap ^{복습}
[snæp]

v. 탁 하고 움직이다; 딱딱거리다, 톡 쏘다; 사진을 찍다; n. 찰칵 하는 소리
If you snap something into a particular position, or if it snaps into that position, it moves quickly into that position, with a sharp sound.

clank
[klæŋk]

n. 철커덕 하는 소리; v. 철커덕 하는 소리가 나다
A clank is a loud, sharp sound or series of sounds, as is made by pieces of metal being struck together.

echo ^{복습}
[ékou]

v. (소리가) 울리다, 메아리치다; 그대로 따라 하다; n. (소리의) 울림, 메아리
If a sound echoes, it is reflected off a surface and can be heard again after the original sound has stopped.

amaze ^{복습}
[əméiz]

v. (대단히) 놀라게 하다 (amazed a. 놀란)
If you are amazed, you are very surprised.

slide *
[slaid]

v. (slid-slid/slidden) 슬그머니 움직이다; 미끄러지다; n. 떨어짐; 미끄러짐
When something slides somewhere or when you slide it there, it moves there smoothly over or against something.

compartment *
[kəmpáːrtmənt]

n. (물건 보관용) 칸; 객실
A compartment is one of the separate parts of an object that is used for keeping things in.

remove ^{복습}
[rimúːv]

v. 옮기다; 없애다; 치우다; 떼다; (옷 등을) 벗다
If you remove something from a place, you take it away.

precise ^{복습}
[prisáis]

a. 정확한, 정밀한; 엄밀한, 꼼꼼한 (precisely ad. 정확히)
Something that is precise is exact and accurate in all its details.

trigger *
[trígər]

v. (장치를) 작동시키다; 촉발시키다; n. (총의) 방아쇠
To trigger a machine or piece of equipment means to make it start to work.

siren
[sáiərən]

n. (신호·경보 등을 나타내는) 사이렌
A siren is a warning device which makes a long, loud noise. Most fire engines, ambulances, and police cars have sirens.

hold one's breath

idiom 숨을 죽이다
If you say that someone is holding their breath, you mean that they are waiting anxiously or excitedly for something to happen.

click *
[klik]

v. 찰칵 하는 소리를 내다; 이해가 되다; n. 찰칵 하는 소리
If something clicks or if you click it, it makes a short, sharp sound.

horrible ^{복습}
[hɔ́ːrəbl]

a. 소름 끼치는, 무시무시한; 지긋지긋한, 끔찍한; 불쾌한
You can call something horrible when it causes you to feel great shock, fear, and disgust.

plead *
[pliːd]

v. 애원하다
If you plead with someone to do something, you ask them in an intense, emotional way to do it.

on purpose ^{복습}

idiom 고의로, 일부러
If you do something on purpose, you do it intentionally.

slip ^{복습}
[slip]

v. 미끄러지다; 슬며시 가다; (재빨리·슬며시) 놓다; n. (작은) 실수; 미끄러짐
When something slips, it passes out of your mind or memory.

blabber
[blǽbər]

v. 횡설수설하다
If someone blabbers, they talk in a confused or excited way.

tag *
[tæg]

n. 꼬리표; v. 꼬리표를 붙이다 (price tag n. 가격표)
In a store, a price tag is a small piece of card or paper attached to an article for sale with the price written on it.

100

flap[*]
[flæp]

n. (납작한) 덮개; 퍼덕거림; v. 퍼덕거리다
A flap of cloth or other material is a flat piece of it that is fixed along one edge, especially used for covering or closing something.

color-code
[kʌ́lər-kòud]

v. (알기 쉽게) 색칠하여 구분하다
Things that are color-coded use colors to represent different features or functions.

grunt^{복습}
[grʌnt]

v. 끙 앓는 소리를 내다; 툴툴거리다; n. (사람이) 끙 하는 소리
If you grunt, you make a short, low sound instead of speaking, usually because of anger or pain.

spin^{**}
[spin]

v. (spun-spun) 돌리다, 회전시키다; (빙빙) 돌다, 회전하다; n. 회전, 돌기
If something spins or if you spin it, it turns quickly around a central point.

secure[*]
[sikjúər]

v. (단단히) 고정시키다; 얻어 내다; a. 안심하는; 안전한
If you secure an object, you fasten it firmly to another object.

Chapters 21 & 22

1. How did Stephen know that he had eaten the pepper-only pizza?

   A. He saw an empty plate in front of him.

   B. He was thirsty, and his tongue and lips felt hot.

   C. He was told about it by Miss Mush.

   D. He had a full feeling in his stomach.

2. Why did Stephen raise his hand when Mr. Kidswatter was asking for volunteers?

   A. He wanted to ask Mr. Kidswatter a question.

   B. All of the other students were raising their hands too.

   C. He thought Mr. Kidswatter was asking about something else.

   D. It was Stephen's dream to ring the gong someday.

3. Why didn't the students have instruments for music class?

   A. They were not back from being cleaned yet.

   B. Some of the students took them home.

   C. They were broken in the last class.

   D. Some of the other classes were using them.

4. Which of the following is NOT a way that students made sounds for the music class?
   A. Humming songs
   B. Flicking a cheek
   C. Blowing a nose
   D. Twiddling lips

5. What did Louis give to Stephen before he banged the gong?
   A. Some goggles
   B. Some gloves
   C. Some cotton balls
   D. Some headphones

6. What happened on Stephen's first swing of the gong?
   A. He dropped the mallet.
   B. He fell down on the floor.
   C. He accidentally hit Louis.
   D. He missed the gong completely.

7. What did Mrs. Jewls's students do when they heard the gong?
   A. They made a gong sound.
   B. They ran out of the classroom.
   C. They clapped their hands.
   D. They whooped and hollered.

Check Your Reading Speed

1분에 몇 단어를 읽는지 리딩 속도를 측정해 보세요.

$$\frac{579 \text{ words}}{\text{reading time ( ) sec}} \times 60 = (\quad) \text{ WPM}$$

Build Your Vocabulary

expel*
[ikspél]
v. 퇴학시키다; (어느 국가로부터) 쫓아내다, 추방하다
If someone is expelled from a school or organization, they are officially told to leave because they have behaved badly.

trip^{복습}
[trip]
v. 발을 헛디디다; 실수하게 하다; n. 여행
If you trip when you are walking, you knock your foot against something and fall or nearly fall.

yell^{복습}
[jel]
v. 고함치다, 소리 지르다; n. 고함, 외침
If you yell, you shout loudly, usually because you are excited, angry, or in pain.

blink^{복습}
[blíŋk]
v. 눈을 깜박이다; (불빛이) 깜박거리다; n. 눈을 깜박거림
When you blink or when you blink your eyes, you shut your eyes and very quickly open them again.

make sense
idiom 이해가 되다; 타당하다; 이해하기 쉽다
If something makes sense, you can understand it.

pepper**
[pépər]
n. 피망; 후추; v. 후추를 치다
A pepper is a hollow fruit, usually red, green, or yellow, with a spicy flavor, used to give flavor to food.

slice^{복습}
[slais]
n. (얇게 썬) 조각; 부분, 몫; v. 자르다; 베다
A slice of bread, meat, fruit, or other food is a thin piece that has been cut from a larger piece.

clue*
[kluː]
n. (문제 해결의) 실마리, 증거; (범행의) 단서
A clue is an object or piece of information that helps someone solve a crime or mystery.

thirsty*
[θɔ́ːrsti]
a. 목이 마른, 갈증이 나는; (~을) 갈망하는
If you are thirsty, you feel a need to drink something.

tongue^{복습}
[tʌŋ]
n. 혀; 언어
Your tongue is the soft movable part inside your mouth which you use for tasting, eating, and speaking.

have cold feet
idiom 겁먹다, 초조해지다, 주눅이 들다
If you have cold feet, you suddenly feel nervous about doing something that you have planned or agreed to do.

block^{복습}
[blak]
n. 사각형 덩어리; (도로로 나뉘는) 구역, 블록; v. 막다, 차단하다; 방해하다
A block of a substance is a large rectangular piece of it.

104

no wonder

idiom ~하는 것도 당연하다, ~할 만도 하다; (별로) 놀랄 일이 아니다
If you say 'no wonder,' you mean that something is not surprising.

freeze^{**}
[fri:z]

v. (두려움 등으로 몸이) 얼어붙다; 얼다; 얼리다; n. 동결; 한파 (frozen a. 얼어붙은)
If you describe someone as frozen, you mean that their body is fixed in a particular position, for example because they are very worried or afraid.

instrument^{**}
[ínstrəmənt]

n. 악기; 기구, 도구
A musical instrument is an object such as a piano, guitar, or flute, which you play in order to produce music.

announce^{복습}
[ənáuns]

v. 발표하다, 알리다; (공공장소에서) 방송으로 알리다
If you announce something, you tell people about it publicly or officially.

bang^{복습}
[bæŋ]

v. 쾅 하고 치다; 쾅 하고 닫다; n. 쾅 하는 소리
If you bang on something or if you bang it, you hit it hard, making a loud noise.

blow one's nose

idiom 코를 풀다
When you blow your nose, you force air out of it through your nostrils in order to clear it.

twiddle
[twidl]

v. 만지작거리다, 가지고 놀다
If you twiddle something, you twist it or turn it quickly with your fingers.

puff out^{복습}

idiom (공기를 채워) 불룩하게 부풀리다
If you puff out your cheeks, you make them larger and rounder by filling them with air.

pop^{복습}
[pap]

v. 펑 하고 터뜨리다; 펑 하는 소리를 내다; 불쑥 움직이다; 불쑥 나타나다;
n. 펑 하고 터지는 소리
If you pop something, you make it burst with a short explosive sound.

flick
[flik]

n. 획 움직임; v. (손가락 등으로) 튀기다; (버튼·스위치를) 탁 누르다
A flick of a part of your body is a small, sudden, quick movement or hit with it.

whistle^{복습}
[hwisl]

v. 휘파람을 불다; 호루라기를 불다; n. 휘파람 (소리); 호각, 호루라기
When you whistle or when you whistle a tune, you make a series of musical notes by forcing your breath out between your lips, or your teeth.

stand on one's head^{복습}

idiom 물구나무를 서다
If you stand on your head, you balance upside down with the top of your head and your hands on the ground.

jingle^{복습}
[dʒíŋgl]

v. 짤랑짤랑 소리를 내다; n. 딸랑딸랑 울리는 소리
When something jingles or when you jingle it, it makes a gentle ringing noise, like small bells.

pigtail
[pígtèil]

n. (하나 또는 두 갈래로) 땋은 머리
If someone has a pigtail or pigtails, their hair is plaited or braided into one or two lengths.

shriek[복습]
[ʃriːk]

v. 꽥 소리를 지르다; (날카롭게) 비명을 지르다; n. 꽥 하는 소리; 비명
If you shriek something, you shout it in a loud, high-pitched voice.

squeal
[skwiːl]

v. 꽤액 하는 소리를 내다; n. 끼익 하는 소리
If someone or something squeals, they make a long, high-pitched sound.

squawk
[skwɔːk]

v. 꽥꽥거리다, 시끄럽게 떠들다; (크게) 꽥꽥 울다
If a person squawks, they complain loudly, often in a high-pitched, harsh tone.

depend on

idiom ~에 달려 있다; ~에게 기대다, 의존하다 (depending on idiom ~에 따라)
You use 'depending on' when you are saying that something varies according to the circumstances mentioned.

instant[복습]
[ínstənt]

a. 즉각적인; n. 순간, 아주 짧은 동안 (instantly ad. 즉각, 즉시)
You use instant to describe something that happens immediately.

be carried away

idiom ~에 열중하다; 흥분하다
If you are carried away, you are so excited and enthusiastic about something that you lose control of your feelings and may behave in a silly way or without thinking.

notice[복습]
[nóutis]

v. 알아채다, 인지하다; 주목하다, 관심을 기울이다; n. 신경 씀, 알아챔
If you notice something or someone, you become aware of them.

position[★★]
[pəzíʃən]

n. 자세; 위치; 자리; v. ~의 자리를 잡다
When someone or something is in a particular position, they are sitting, lying, or arranged in that way.

buddy[*]
[bʌ́di]

n. 친구
A buddy is a close friend, usually a male friend of a man.

Check Your Reading Speed

1분에 몇 단어를 읽는지 리딩 속도를 측정해 보세요.

$$\frac{608 \text{ words}}{\text{reading time ( ) sec}} \times 60 = (\quad) \text{ WPM}$$

Build Your Vocabulary

spot[**]
[spat]

v. 발견하다, 찾다, 알아채다; n. (특정한) 곳; (작은) 점
If you spot something or someone, you notice them.

vanish[*]
[vǽniʃ]

v. (갑자기) 사라지다; 없어지다
If someone or something vanishes, they disappear suddenly or in a way that cannot be explained.

wheel^{복습}
[hwi:l]

v. (바퀴 달린 것을) 밀다, 끌다; n. 바퀴; (자동차 등의) 핸들
If you wheel an object that has wheels somewhere, you push it along.

on time

idiom 시간을 어기지 않고, 정각에
If you are on time, you are there at the expected time.

gigantic[*]
[dʒaigǽntik]

a. 거대한
If you describe something as gigantic, you are emphasizing that it is extremely large in size, amount, or degree.

dot^{복습}
[dat]

n. 점; v. 점을 찍다; 여기저기 흩어져 있다
A dot is a very small round mark or spot.

iron^{복습}
[áiərn]

n. 철, 쇠; 철분; 다리미
Iron is an element which usually takes the form of a hard, dark grey metal. It is used to make steel, and also forms part of many tools, buildings, and vehicles.

hook^{복습}
[huk]

n. (갈)고리, 걸이; v. ~에 걸다; 갈고리로 잠그다
A hook is a bent piece of metal or plastic that is used for catching or holding things, or for hanging things up.

nod^{복습}
[nad]

v. (고개를) 끄덕이다; n. (고개를) 끄덕임
If you nod, you move your head downward and upward to show that you are answering 'yes' to a question, or to show agreement, understanding, or approval.

confident[**]
[kánfədənt]

a. 자신감 있는, 대담한; 확신하는 (confidently ad. 자신 있게)
If a person or their manner is confident, they feel sure about their own abilities, qualities, or ideas.

bang^{복습}
[bæŋ]

v. 쾅 하고 치다; 쾅 하고 닫다; n. 쾅 하는 소리
If you bang on something or if you bang it, you hit it hard, making a loud noise.

principal^{복습}
[prínsəpəl]

n. 교장; 학장, 총장; a. 주요한, 주된
A principal is a teacher who is in charge of a school.

cotton^{복습}
[katn]

n. 솜; 면직물; 목화; a. 면으로 된
Cotton is a soft, white, downy substance consisting of the hairs or fibers attached to the seeds of particular plants.

stuff^{복습}
[stʌf]

v. (재빨리) 쑤셔 넣다; (빽빽이) 채워 넣다; n. 일, 것; 물건
If you stuff something somewhere, you push it there quickly and roughly.

wobble
[wabl]

v. (불안정하게) 흔들리다; 뒤뚱거리며 가다; n. 흔들림, 떨림
If something or someone wobbles, they make small movements from side to side, for example because they are unsteady.

countdown^{복습}
[káuntdaun]

n. 카운트다운; (중요한 행사의) 초읽기
A countdown is the counting aloud of numbers in reverse order before something happens, for example before a spacecraft is launched.

tighten[*]
[taitn]

v. (단단히) 조이다, 조여지다; (더) 팽팽해지다; 더 엄격하게 하다
If you tighten your grip on something, or if your grip tightens, you hold the thing more firmly or securely.

grip^{복습}
[grip]

n. 꽉 붙잡음; 통제, 지배; v. 꽉 잡다, 움켜잡다
A grip is a firm, strong hold on something.

groan^{복습}
[groun]

v. 신음 소리를 내다; 끙끙거리다; n. 신음; 끙 하는 소리
If you groan, you make a long, low sound because you are in pain, or because you are upset or unhappy about something.

stagger[*]
[stǽgər]

v. 비틀거리다, 휘청거리며 가다; 깜짝 놀라게 하다
If you stagger, you walk very unsteadily, for example because you are ill or drunk.

balance^{**}
[bǽləns]

n. (몸의) 균형; 평형; v. 균형을 유지하다
Balance is the ability to remain steady when you are standing up.

concentrate^{**}
[kánsəntrèit]

v. (정신을) 집중하다, 전념하다; n. 농축물
If you concentrate on something, you give all your attention to it.

swing^{복습}
[swiŋ]

v. (swung-swung) 획 움직이다; (전후·좌우로) 흔들(리)다; n. 흔들기; 휘두르기
If something swings in a particular direction or if you swing it in that direction, it moves quickly in that direction with a smooth, curving movement.

might^{복습}
[mait]

n. (강력한) 힘, 권력; 세력 (with all one's might idiom 전력을 다하여, 힘껏)
If you do something with all your might, you do it using all your strength and energy.

weight^{**}
[weit]

n. 무게, 체중
The weight of a person or thing is how heavy they are, measured in units such as kilograms, pounds, or tons.

echo^{복습}
[ékou]

v. (소리가) 울리다, 메아리치다; 그대로 따라 하다; n. (소리의) 울림, 메아리
If a sound echoes, it is reflected off a surface and can be heard again after the original sound has stopped.

skull[*]
[skʌl]

n. 두개골, 해골
Your skull is the bony part of your head which encloses your brain.

rattle^{복습}
[rǽtl]

v. 덜거덕거리게 하다; 덜거덕거리다; 당황하게 하다; n. 덜거덕거리는 소리
When something rattles or when you rattle it, it makes short sharp knocking sounds because it is being shaken or it keeps hitting against something hard.

all the way^{복습}

idiom 내내, 시종; 완전히
You use all the way to emphasize how long a distance is.

yell^{복습}
[jel]

v. 고함치다, 소리 지르다; n. 고함, 외침
If you yell, you shout loudly, usually because you are excited, angry, or in pain.

whoop
[hu:p]

v. 와 하고 함성을 지르다; n. 와 하는 함성
If you whoop, you shout loudly in a very happy or excited way.

holler
[hάlər]

v. 소리지르다, 고함치다
If you holler, you shout loudly.

frame^{복습}
[freim]

n. (가구·건물·차량 등의) 뼈대; 틀, 액자; v. 틀에 넣다, 테를 두르다
The frame of an object such as a piece of furniture, vehicle, or other object is the structure or main supporting parts of it.

frustrate*
[frΛstreit]

v. 좌절감을 주다, 불만스럽게 하다; 방해하다 (frustrated a. 좌절감을 느끼는)
IIf you are frustrated, you feel annoyed or angry because you are unable to do what you want.

plain^{복습}
[plein]

ad. 분명히, 완전히; a. 평범한; 솔직한; n. (pl.) 평원, 평지
You can use plain before an adjective in order to emphasize it.

strike*
[straik]

v. (struck-struck/stricken) (세게) 치다, 부딪치다; 갑자기 떠오르다; n. 치기; 파업
If something that is falling or moving strikes something else, it hits that thing hard or with force.

bounce^{복습}
[bauns]

v. 튀다; 튀기다; n. 튐, 튀어 오름
If sound or light bounces off a surface or is bounced off it, it reaches the surface and is reflected back.

back and forth^{복습}
[bæk ən fɔ́:rθ]

ad. 앞뒤(좌우)로; 여기저기에, 왔다 갔다
If someone or something moves back and forth, they repeatedly move in one direction and then in the opposite direction.

vibrate*
[vάibreit]

v. 진동하다, (가늘게) 떨다 (vibration n. 진동, 떨림)
Vibration means a very small, fast, and continuous shaking movement.

Chapters 23 & 24

1. Which of the following is NOT something the students blamed on the Cloud of Doom?
   A. Changing answers in the arithmetic test
   B. Pulling someone else's pigtails
   C. Arriving to class late
   D. Losing some homework assignments

2. What did Terrence do with his test?
   A. He put it in the trash basket.
   B. He gave it back to Mrs. Jewls.
   C. He kicked it out the window.
   D. He kept it in his backpack.

3. What did Benjamin think was unfair?
   A. Mrs. Jewls started the test one day early.
   B. Mrs. Jewls would not let the students to go to recess.
   C. Mrs. Jewls made the students stay late.
   D. Mrs. Jewls gave the students more homework.

4. What was happening to the Cloud of Doom?
   A. It was growing bigger and more powerful.
   B. It was drifting closer to the school.
   C. It was making too much noise for the students.
   D. It was dropping a lot of rain on the playground.

5. What is true about the Ultimate Test?
   A. It would last for more than one day.
   B. It was given to all of the classes.
   C. It had one hundred questions.
   D. It could be taken again if needed.

6. Why did Joy do well on written spelling tests?
   A. She got the answers from Mrs. Jewls before the test.
   B. She had memorized every word in the dictionary.
   C. She wrote squiggles that looked like more than one letter.
   D. She asked other students for help.

7. Why was Ron mad about the spelling bee?
   A. He thought Maurecia should be the winner.
   B. He could not hear the word Mrs. Jewls said.
   C. He did not have time to study for it.
   D. He got eliminated on a made-up word.

Check Your Reading Speed

1분에 몇 단어를 읽는지 리딩 속도를 측정해 보세요.

$$\frac{689 \text{ words}}{\text{reading time ( ) sec}} \times 60 = (\text{ }) \text{ WPM}$$

Build Your Vocabulary

blame[**]
[bleim]
v. ~을 탓하다, ~때문으로 보다; n. 책임; 탓
If you blame a person or thing for something bad, you believe or say that they are responsible for it or that they caused it.

arithmetic[복습]
[əríθmətik]
n. 산수, 연산; 산술, 계산
Arithmetic is the part of mathematics that is concerned with the addition, subtraction, multiplication, and division of numbers.

awful[복습]
[ɔ́:fəl]
a. 끔찍한, 지독한; (정도가) 대단한
If you say that someone or something is awful, you dislike that person or thing or you think that they are not very good.

complain[복습]
[kəmpléin]
v. 불평하다, 항의하다
If you complain about a situation, you say that you are not satisfied with it.

doom[복습]
[du:m]
n. 불운, 저주; 죽음, 파멸; v. 불행한 운명을 맞게 하다
Doom is a terrible future state or event which you cannot prevent.

stroke[복습]
[strouk]
n. (글씨나 그림의) 획; (손으로) 쓰다듬기; v. 쓰다듬다, 어루만지다; 달래다
The strokes of a pen or brush are the movements or marks that you make with it when you are writing or painting.

swing[복습]
[swiŋ]
v. (swung-swung) 휙 움직이다; (전후·좌우로) 흔들(리)다; n. 흔들기; 휘두르기
If something swings in a particular direction or if you swing it in that direction, it moves quickly in that direction with a smooth, curving movement.

discipline[복습]
[dísəplin]
n. 규율, 훈육; 단련법, 수련법
Discipline is the practice of making people obey rules or standards of behavior, and punishing them when they do not.

on time[복습]
idiom 시간을 어기지 않고, 정각에
If you are on time, you are there at the expected time.

pigtail[복습]
[pígtèil]
n. (하나 또는 두 갈래로) 땋은 머리
If someone has a pigtail or pigtails, their hair is plaited or braided into one or two lengths.

accuse[복습]
[əkjú:z]
v. 비난하다, 혐의를 제기하다
If you accuse someone of doing something wrong or dishonest, you say or tell them that you believe that they did it.

demand ^{복습}
[dimǽnd]

v. 강력히 묻다, 따지다; 요구하다; n. 요구 (사항)
If you demand something such as information or action, you ask for it in a very forceful way.

shrug ^{복습}
[ʃrʌg]

v. (두 손바닥을 위로 하고) 어깨를 으쓱하다; n. 어깨를 으쓱하기
If you shrug, you raise your shoulders to show that you are not interested in something or that you do not know or care about something.

fist ^{복습}
[fist]

n. 주먹
Your hand is referred to as your fist when you have bent your fingers in toward the palm.

bug**
[bʌg]

n. 벌레, 작은 곤충
A bug is an insect or similar small creature.

sniff ^{복습}
[snif]

v. 냄새를 맡다; 코를 훌쩍이다; n. 냄새 맡기; 콧방귀 뀌기
If you sniff something or sniff at it, you smell it by taking air in through your nose.

glare ^{복습}
[glɛər]

v. 노려보다; 환하다, 눈부시다; n. 노려봄; 환한 빛, 눈부심
If you glare at someone, you look at them with an angry expression on your face.

crumple
[krʌmpl]

v. 구기다; 구겨지다; (얼굴이) 일그러지다
If you crumple something such as paper or cloth, or if it crumples, it is squashed and becomes full of untidy creases and folds.

trash ^{복습}
[træʃ]

n. 쓰레기; v. 부수다, 엉망으로 만들다; (필요 없는 것을) 버리다
Trash consists of unwanted things or waste material such as used paper, empty containers and bottles, and waste food.

stare ^{복습}
[stɛər]

v. 빤히 쳐다보다, 응시하다; n. 빤히 쳐다보기, 응시
If you stare at someone or something, you look at them for a long time.

sail**
[seil]

v. 미끄러지듯 나아가다; 항해하다; n. 돛; 항해
If a person or thing sails somewhere, they move there smoothly and fairly quickly.

spill ^{복습}
[spil]

v. 흘리다, 쏟다; n. 유출; 흘린 액체
If the contents of a bag, box, or other container spill or are spilled, they come out of the container onto a surface.

declare ^{복습}
[diklέər]

v. 선언하다, 공표하다; 분명히 말하다
If you declare something, you state officially and formally that it exists or is the case.

exclaim ^{복습}
[ikskléim]

v. 소리치다, 외치다
If you exclaim, you cry out suddenly in surprise, strong emotion, or pain.

know better

idiom (~할 정도로) 어리석지는 않다
If someone knows better than to do something, they are old enough or experienced enough to know it is the wrong thing to do.

get it

idiom 이해하다
To get it means to understand an argument or the person making it.

responsibility^{복습}
[rispànsəbílət̬i]

n. 책임, 책무
If you have responsibility for something or someone, or if they are your responsibility, it is your job or duty to deal with them and to take decisions relating to them.

double^{복습}
[dʌbl]

v. 두 배로 만들다; a. 두 배의, 갑절의; 이중의; n. 두 배, 갑절
When something doubles or when you double it, it becomes twice as great in number, amount, or size.

blackboard^{복습}
[blǽkbɔ̀ːrd]

n. 칠판
A blackboard is a dark-colored board that you can write on with chalk.

ultimate^{복습}
[ʌ́ltəmət]

a. 궁극적인, 최종적인; 최고의, 최상의; n. 극치
You use ultimate to describe the final result or aim of a long series of events.

complete*
[kəmplíːt]

v. 완료하다, 끝마치다; a. 모든 것이 갖춰진, 완전한; 완벽한
If you complete something, you finish doing, making, or producing it.

groan^{복습}
[groun]

n. 신음; 끙 하는 소리; v. 신음 소리를 내다; 끙끙거리다
A groan is a long low sound that a person makes, especially when they are in pain or unhappy.

broom*
[bruːm]

n. 비, 빗자루
A broom is a kind of brush with a long handle. You use a broom for sweeping the floor.

sweep**
[swiːp]

v. (빗자루로) 쓸다; (빗자루나 손으로) 털다; n. 쓸기, 비질하기
If you sweep an area of floor or ground, you push dirt or garbage off it using a brush with a long handle.

moan^{복습}
[moun]

n. 투덜거림, 불평; 신음; v. 투덜거리다, 불평하다; 신음하다
A moan is a complaint about something.

scratch^{복습}
[skræʧ]

v. (가려운 데를) 긁다; 할퀴다; n. 긁힌 자국
If you scratch yourself, you rub your fingernails against your skin because it is itching.

make one's way^{복습}

idiom 나아가다, 가다
When you make your way somewhere, you walk or travel there.

churn^{복습}
[ʧɔːrn]

v. (물·흙탕물 등이) 마구 휘돌다; 우유를 휘젓다; (속이) 뒤틀리다
If water, mud, or dust churns, or if something churns it, it moves about violently.

hardly^{복습}
[háːrdli]

ad. 거의 ~ 아니다; 거의 ~할 수가 없다; 막 ~하자마자
You use hardly to modify a statement when you want to emphasize that it is only a small amount or detail which makes it true, and that therefore it is best to consider the opposite statement as being true.

lightning*
[láitniŋ]

n. 번개; a. 번개 같은, 아주 빠른
Lightning is the very bright flashes of light in the sky that happen during thunderstorms.

flash**
[flæʃ]

v. 번쩍이다, (잠깐) 비치다; 비추다; n. 섬광, 번쩍임
If a light flashes or if you flash a light, it shines with a sudden bright light, especially as quick, regular flashes of light.

thunder ^{복습}
[θándər]

n. 천둥, 우레; v. 천둥이 치다
Thunder is the loud noise that you hear from the sky after a flash of lightning, especially during a storm.

boom ^{복습}
[bu:m]

v. 쾅 하는 소리를 내다; 굵은 목소리로 말하다; n. 쾅, 탕 하는 소리
When something such as someone's voice, a cannon, or a big drum booms, it makes a loud, deep sound that lasts for several seconds.

Check Your Reading Speed

1분에 몇 단어를 읽는지 리딩 속도를 측정해 보세요.

$$\frac{643 \text{ words}}{\text{reading time ( ) sec}} \times 60 = (\quad) \text{ WPM}$$

Build Your Vocabulary

flagpole복습
[flǽgpoul]

n. 깃대
A flagpole is a tall pole on which a flag can be displayed.

kindergarten복습
[kíndərgà:rtn]

n. 유치원
A kindergarten is an informal kind of school for very young children, where they learn things by playing.

memorize*
[méməràiz]

v. 암기하다
If you memorize something, you learn it so that you can remember it exactly.

dictionary**
[díkʃənèri]

n. 사전
A dictionary is a book in which the words and phrases of a language are listed alphabetically, together with their meanings or their translations in another language.

spell복습
[spel]

v. (어떤 단어의) 철자를 말하다; 철자를 맞게 쓰다, 맞춤법에 맞게 글을 쓰다
When you spell a word, you write or speak each letter in the word in the correct order.

point out복습

idiom 지적하다, 언급하다; 알려주다
If you point out a fact or circumstance, you mention it in order to give someone information about it or make them notice it.

lock복습
[lak]

v. 고정하다; (자물쇠로) 잠그다; n. 자물쇠
If you lock something in a particular position or if it locks there, it is held or fitted firmly in that position.

thumb복습
[θʌm]

n. 엄지손가락; v. 엄지손가락으로 건드리다
Your thumb is the short thick part on the side of your hand next to your four fingers.

pinky복습
[píŋki]

n. 새끼손가락
Your pinky is the smallest finger on your hand.

glance복습
[glæns]

v. 흘낏 보다; 대충 훑어보다; n. 흘낏 봄
If you glance at something or someone, you look at them very quickly and then look away again immediately.

greet복습
[gri:t]

v. 인사하다; 환영하다; 반응을 보이다
When you greet someone, you say 'hello' or shake hands with them.

last복습
[læst]

v. (특정한 시간 동안) 계속되다; ad. 맨 끝에, 마지막에
If an event, situation, or problem lasts for a particular length of time, it continues to exist or happen for that length of time.

major^{★★}
[méidʒər]

a. 주요한, 중대한; 심각한; n. (대학생의) 전공
You use major when you want to describe something that is more important, serious, or significant than other things in a group or situation.

fudge
[fʌdʒ]

v. 얼버무리다, 얼렁뚱땅 넘어가다; n. 얼버무림; (사탕의 일종인) 퍼지
If you fudge something, you avoid making a clear and definite decision, distinction, or statement about it.

squiggle
[skwigl]

n. 갈겨 쓴 글씨; (글자·그림 등에서) 구불구불한 선
A squiggle is a line, for example in somebody's handwriting, that is drawn or written in a careless way with curves and waves in it.

doubt^{★★★}
[daut]

n. 의심, 의혹; v. 확신하지 못하다, 의심하다
If you have doubt or doubts about something, you feel uncertain about it and do not know whether it is true or possible.

curious^{복습}
[kjúəriəs]

a. 호기심이 많은; 궁금한; 별난
Someone who is curious wants to find out about something.

squawk^{복습}
[skwɔ:k]

v. 꽥꽥거리다, 시끄럽게 떠들다; (크게) 꽥꽥 울다
If a person squawks, they complain loudly, often in a high-pitched, harsh tone.

confidential^{복습}
[kànfədénʃəl]

a. 비밀의, 기밀의
Information that is confidential is meant to be kept secret or private.

dilly-dally^{복습}
[díli-dæli]

v. 꾸물거리다, 미적거리다
If you dilly-dally, you waste time, especially by being slow, or by not being able to do something, go somewhere, or make a decision.

leave out

idiom ~을 빼다, 배제시키다
If you leave someone or something out of an activity, collection, discussion, or group, you do not include them in it.

protest^{★★}
[próutest]

v. 항의하다, 이의를 제기하다; n. 항의
If you protest against something or about something, you say or show publicly that you object to it.

stuck^{복습}
[stʌk]

a. (대답 등이) 막힌; 움직일 수 없는, 꼼짝 못하는; (불쾌한 상황에서) 빠져나갈 수 없는
If you get stuck when you are trying to do something, you are unable to continue doing it because it is too difficult.

eliminate[★]
[ilímənèit]

v. 탈락시키다; 없애다, 제거하다
When a person or team is eliminated from a competition, they are defeated and so stop participating in the competition.

spectacle^{복습}
[spéktəkl]

n. (기이한·놀라운) 모습, 상황; 장관, 광경; 구경거리; (pl.) 안경
A spectacle is a strange or interesting sight.

skeptical^{복습}
[sképtikəl]

a. 의심 많은, 회의적인
If you are skeptical about something, you have doubts about it.

murmur[★]
[mɔ́:rmər]

n. 속삭임, 소곤거림; v. 중얼거리다, 속삭이다, 소곤거리다
A murmur is something that is said but can hardly be heard.

vacuum [복습]
[vǽkjuəm]

n. 진공청소기; 진공; v. 진공청소기로 청소하다
A vacuum or a vacuum cleaner is an electric machine that sucks up dust and dirt from carpets.

definition*
[dèfəníʃən]

n. 정의; 의미; 선명도
A definition is a statement giving the meaning of a word or expression, especially in a dictionary.

count [복습]
[kaunt]

v. (수를) 세다; 계산에 넣다; n. (하나부터 순서대로 세는) 셈; 계산
When you count, you say all the numbers one after another up to a particular number.

correct [복습]
[kərékt]

a. 맞는, 정확한; 적절한, 옳은; v. 바로잡다, 정정하다 (correctly ad. 바르게, 정확하게)
If something is correct, it is in accordance with the facts and has no mistakes.

include [복습]
[inklúːd]

v. 포함하다; ~을 (~에) 포함시키다
If one thing includes another thing, it has the other thing as one of its parts.

give one's best shot

idiom 최선을 다하다
If you give something your best shot, you do it as well as you possibly can.

cheat**
[ʧiːt]

v. 속이다, 사기 치다; (시험·경기 등에서) 부정행위를 하다
If someone cheats you, they trick or deceive you so that you do not get or keep something you have a right to have.

made-up
[méid-ʌp]

a. 만들어 낸, 지어낸, 가짜의
A made-up word, name, or story is invented, rather than really existing or being true.

118

1. Why was it difficult for Deedee to jump rope?
    A. Because her legs felt sore from too much jumping
    B. Because she was scared of getting hit by the rope
    C. Because she did not get enough sleep the night before
    D. Because one of her legs was longer than the other

2. Why did the other students rush up to Joy?
    A. They wanted to show her the prize.
    B. They thought that she was hurt.
    C. She asked them to help her get off the ground.
    D. She had set a world record for Jump Rope Arithmetic.

3. Which of the following is NOT true about Maurecia?
    A. She earned more points than Joy.
    B. She made a mistake on an easy one.
    C. She did not like jumping rope very much.
    D. She had jumped for almost an hour.

4. Why were the students already worn out before the Stairway Quiz?

    A. They had practiced running up the stairs in the morning.

    B. They had done other parts of the test that day.

    C. They had cleaned up their classroom before the quiz.

    D. They had run around the school looking for Louis.

5. What was Deedee's special talent?

    A. She could go up and down stairs very quickly.

    B. She could remember the answers to questions easily.

    C. She could blow a whistle very loudly.

    D. She could carry a lot of things carefully.

6. Why did Deedee have to go back to the tenth floor?

    A. She forgot to answer the question on the tenth floor.

    B. She dropped something as she was running.

    C. She got the answer to a question wrong.

    D. She pushed another student out of her way.

7. What was Maurecia doing when she came out of the school?

    A. She was waving at her friends.

    B. She was shaking hands with reporters.

    C. She was taking pictures of the playground.

    D. She was carrying a big trophy.

Check Your Reading Speed

1분에 몇 단어를 읽는지 리딩 속도를 측정해 보세요.

$$\frac{676 \text{ words}}{\text{reading time ( ) sec}} \times 60 = (\quad) \text{ WPM}$$

Build Your Vocabulary

arithmetic ^{복습}
[əríθmətik]

n. 산수, 연산; 산술, 계산
Arithmetic is the part of mathematics that is concerned with the addition, subtraction, multiplication, and division of numbers.

major ^{복습}
[méidʒər]

a. 주요한, 중대한; 심각한; n. (대학생의) 전공
You use major when you want to describe something that is more important, serious, or significant than other things in a group or situation.

trip ^{복습}
[trip]

v. 발을 헛디디다; 실수하게 하다; n. 여행
If you trip when you are walking, you knock your foot against something and fall or nearly fall.

talent ^{복습}
[tǽlənt]

n. (타고난) 재능, 재주; 재능 있는 사람
Talent is the natural ability to do something well.

upside-down
[ʌ̀psaid-dáun]

a. (아래위가) 거꾸로 된, 뒤집힌
If something is upside-down, it has been turned around so that the part that is usually lowest is above the part that is usually highest.

jingle ^{복습}
[dʒíŋgl]

v. 짤랑짤랑 소리를 내다; n. 딸랑딸랑 울리는 소리
When something jingles or when you jingle it, it makes a gentle ringing noise, like small bells.

times ^{복습}
[taimz]

prep. ~으로 곱한
You use times in arithmetic to link numbers or amounts that are multiplied together to reach a total.

skip[*]
[skip]

v. 깡충깡충 뛰다; (일을) 거르다; n. 깡충깡충 뛰기
When someone skips, they jump up and down over a rope which they or two other people are holding at each end and turning round and round.

rattle off

idiom (기억하고 있는 내용을) 줄줄 말하다
If you rattle off something, you say it quickly or easily from memory.

substitute[*]
[sʌ́bstətjùːt]

n. 대신하는 사람; 대체물; v. 대신하다, 교체되다 (substitute teacher n. 대체 교사)
A substitute teacher is a teacher whose job is to take the place of other teachers at different schools when they are unable to be there.

divide ^{복습}
[diváid]

v. (수를) 나누다; (묶음을) 나누다; (여러 부분들로) 나누다, 가르다
If you divide a larger number by a smaller number or divide a smaller number into a larger number, you calculate how many times the smaller number can fit exactly into the larger number.

tie[**]
[tai]

v. 동점을 이루다; (끈이나 매듭으로) 묶다; n. 끈; (강한) 유대
If two people tie in a competition or game or if they tie with each other, they have the same number of points or the same degree of success.

chant[*]
[ʧænt]

v. 구호를 외치다; 되풀이하여 말하다; n. (연이어 외치는) 구호
If you chant something or if you chant, you repeat the same words over and over again.

twirl
[twəːrl]

v. 빙빙 돌리다, 빠르게 돌다; n. 회전
If you twirl something or if it twirls, it turns around and around with a smooth, fairly fast movement.

whoop[복습]
[huːp]

v. 와 하고 함성을 지르다; n. 와 하는 함성
If you whoop, you shout loudly in a very happy or excited way.

holler[복습]
[hάlər]

v. 소리지르다, 고함치다
If you holler, you shout loudly.

sprawl[복습]
[sprɔːl]

v. 팔다리를 아무렇게나 벌리고 앉다, 대자로 눕다; 제멋대로 퍼져 나가다
If you sprawl somewhere, you sit or lie down with your legs and arms spread out in a careless way.

blacktop[복습]
[blǽktàp]

n. 아스팔트 도로; (포장에 쓰이는) 아스팔트; v. 아스팔트로 포장하다
Blacktop is a hard black substance which is used as a surface for roads, as well as a road covered with this substance.

classmate[복습]
[klǽsmeit]

n. 급우, 반 친구
Your classmates are students who are in the same class as you at school or college.

rush[복습]
[rʌʃ]

v. 급히 움직이다, 서두르다; n. 분주함; 혼잡
If you rush somewhere, you go there quickly.

hold one's breath[복습]

idiom 숨을 죽이다
If you say that someone is holding their breath, you mean that they are waiting anxiously or excitedly for something to happen.

solid[복습]
[sάlid]

a. (다른 물질이 섞이지 않고) 순수한; 단단한; 고체의; n. 고체, 고형물
If an object is made of solid gold or solid wood, for example, it is made of gold or wood all the way through, rather than just on the outside.

trophy[*]
[tróufi]

n. 트로피, 우승컵; 전리품
A trophy is a prize, for example a silver cup, that is given to the winner of a competition or race.

daydream[*]
[déidrìm]

n. 백일몽, 공상; v. 공상에 잠기다
A daydream is a series of pleasant thoughts, usually about things that you would like to happen.

surround[복습]
[səráund]

v. 둘러싸다, 에워싸다; 포위하다
If a person or thing is surrounded by something, that thing is situated all around them.

poke[복습]
[pouk]

v. (손가락 등으로) 쿡 찌르다; 쑥 내밀다; n. 찌르기, 쑤시기
If you poke someone or something, you quickly push them with your finger or with a sharp object.

bitter^{**}
[bítər]

a. 쓰라린, 비통한; 격렬한 (bitterly ad. 쓰라리게, 비통하게)
You use bitterly when you are describing an attitude which involves strong, unpleasant emotions such as anger or dislike.

Check Your Reading Speed

1분에 몇 단어를 읽는지 리딩 속도를 측정해 보세요.

$$\frac{1{,}090 \text{ words}}{\text{reading time (} \quad \text{) sec}} \times 60 = (\quad) \text{ WPM}$$

Build Your Vocabulary

stairway
[stérwèi]

n. (건물 내·외부에 있는 일련의) 계단
A stairway is a staircase or a flight of steps, inside or outside a building.

worn out
[wɔːrn áut]

a. 매우 지친; 닳고 닳은
Someone who is worn out is extremely tired after hard work or a difficult or unpleasant experience.

crawl**
[krɔːl]

n. 기어가기, 서행; v. 기어가다; 기다, 몹시 느리게 가다
A crawl is the act of moving forward on your hands and knees.

handwriting*
[hǽndràitiŋ]

n. 손으로 쓰기; (개인의) 필적
Your handwriting is the writing that is done with a pen or pencil, not printed or typed.

imitate**
[ímətèit]

v. 흉내내다; 모방하다, 본뜨다 (imitation n. 흉내 내기)
Imitation means an act of copying someone's actions, words, or behavior, often in order to make people laugh.

upside-down***ᵇᵒᵏˢᵘᵖ
[Ʌpsaid-dáun]

a. (아래위가) 거꾸로 된, 뒤집힌
If something is upside-down, it has been turned around so that the part that is usually lowest is above the part that is usually highest.

blindfold
[bláindfòuld]

v. (눈가리개로) 눈을 가리다; n. 눈가리개 (blindfolded a. 눈가리개를 한)
If you blindfold someone, you tie a strip of cloth over their eyes so that they cannot see.

stamina
[stǽmənə]

n. 체력, 지구력
Stamina is the physical or mental energy needed to do a tiring activity for a long time.

obvious**
[ábviəs]

a. 분명한, 명백한; 너무 빤한
If something is obvious, it is easy to see or understand.

advantage**
[ædvǽntidʒ]

n. (누구에게) 유리한 점, 이점, 장점
An advantage is something that puts you in a better position than other people.

yardᵇᵒᵏˢᵘᵖ
[jaːrd]

n. (학교의) 운동장; 마당, 뜰; 정원
A yard is a flat area of concrete or stone that is next to a building and often has a wall around it.

blow ^{복습}
[blou]

v. (blew-blown) (호각·악기 등을) 불다; (입으로) 불다; (기회를) 날리다; n. 세게 때림
When a whistle or horn blows or someone blows it, they make a sound by blowing into it.

whistle ^{복습}
[hwisl]

n. 호각, 호루라기; 휘파람 (소리); v. 호루라기를 불다; 휘파람을 불다
A whistle is a small metal tube which you blow in order to produce a loud sound and attract someone's attention.

pump *
[pʌmp]

v. (아래위로 빠르게) 흔들다; (거세게) 솟구치다; 펌프로 공기를 넣다; n. 펌프
If something pumps, it moves quickly up and down or in and out.

elbow **
[élbou]

n. 팔꿈치; v. (팔꿈치로) 밀치다
Your elbow is the part of your arm where the upper and lower halves are joined.

flail
[fleil]

v. 마구 움직이다, (팔다리를) 마구 흔들다
If your arms or legs flail or if you flail them about, they wave about in an energetic but uncontrolled way.

pack *
[pæk]

n. 무리; 꾸러미; v. (짐을) 싸다; (사람·물건으로) 가득 채우다
You can refer to a group of people who go around together as a pack.

besides ^{복습}
[bisáidz]

prep. ~외에; ad. 게다가, 뿐만 아니라
Besides means other than someone or something.

even ^{복습}
[í:vən]

a. 고른; 평평한; 균등한; 짝수의; ad. ~조차; 훨씬 (uneven a. 고르지 않은)
Something that is uneven is not regular or consistent.

skinny ^{복습}
[skíni]

a. 깡마른, 비쩍 여윈; (물건의) 폭이 좁은
A skinny person is extremely thin, often in a way that you find unattractive.

squeeze ^{복습}
[skwi:z]

v. (억지로) 비집고 들어가다; (좁은 곳에) 밀어 넣다; (꼭) 짜다; n. 짜기, 쥐기
If you squeeze a person or thing somewhere or if they squeeze there, they manage to get through or into a small space.

mustache ^{복습}
[mʌ́stæʃ]

n. 콧수염
A man's mustache is the hair that grows on his upper lip.

landing ^{복습}
[lǽndiŋ]

n. 층계참; 착륙
In a house or other building, a landing is an area of floor that joins two sets of stairs.

stump *
[stʌmp]

v. 당황하게 하다; 쿵쿵거리며 걷다; n. (나무의) 그루터기 (stumped a. 당황한)
If you are stumped by a question or problem, you cannot think of any solution or answer to it.

charge **
[ʧa:rdʒ]

v. 급히 가다, 달려가다; (요금·값을) 청구하다; n. 요금
If you charge toward someone or something, you move quickly and aggressively toward them.

rub ^{복습}
[rʌb]

v. (손·손수건 등을 대고) 문지르다; (두 손 등을) 맞비비다; n. 문지르기, 비비기
If you rub a part of your body, you move your hand or fingers backward and forward over it while pressing firmly.

126

beard 복습
[biərd]

n. (턱)수염
A man's beard is the hair that grows on his chin and cheeks.

distant**
[dístənt]

a. 먼, (멀리) 떨어져 있는; 다정하지 않은
Distant means very far away.

footstep*
[fútstèp]

n. 발소리; 발자국
A footstep is the sound or mark that is made by someone walking each time their foot touches the ground.

interrupt**
[ìntərʌ́pt]

v. (말·행동을) 방해하다; 중단시키다
When you interrupt someone, you stop them in the midst of doing or saying something.

inspiration**
[ìnspəréiʃən]

n. 영감; 고취, 고무
Inspiration is a feeling of enthusiasm you get from someone or something, which gives you new and creative ideas.

correct 복습
[kərékt]

a. 맞는, 정확한; 적절한, 옳은; v. 바로잡다, 정정하다
If something is correct, it is in accordance with the facts and has no mistakes.

librarian 복습
[laibréəriən]

n. (도서관의) 사서
A librarian is a person who is in charge of a library, which is a building where things such as books are kept for people to read, use, or borrow.

spell 복습
[spel]

v. (어떤 단어의) 철자를 말하다; 철자를 맞게 쓰다, 맞춤법에 맞게 글을 쓰다
When you spell a word, you write or speak each letter in the word in the correct order.

point 복습
[pɔint]

n. (뾰족한) 끝; 의견; 요점; (의도하는) 의미; 목적; 점수; v. 가리키다
The point of something such as a pin, needle, or knife is the thin, sharp end of it.

blur
[blə:r]

v. 흐릿해지다; 모호해지다; n. 흐릿한 형체; (기억이) 희미한 것
If something such as a memory or an idea has blurred, or if something has blurred it, it is no longer clear in your mind.

all the way 복습

idiom 내내, 시종; 완전히
You use all the way to emphasize how long a distance is.

greet 복습
[gri:t]

v. 인사하다; 환영하다; 반응을 보이다
When you greet someone, you say 'hello' or shake hands with them.

cabbage 복습
[kǽbidʒ]

n. 양배추
A cabbage is a round vegetable with white, green or purple leaves that is usually eaten cooked.

stripe 복습
[straip]

n. 줄무늬
A stripe is a long line which is a different color from the areas next to it.

nail 복습
[neil]

n. 손톱, 발톱; 못; v. 못으로 박다
Your nails are the thin hard parts that grow at the ends of your fingers and toes.

recite[*]
[risáit]

v. (열거하듯) 죽 말하다; 암송하다
If you recite something such as a list, you say it aloud.

alphabet^{**}
[ǽlfəbèt]

n. 알파벳
An alphabet is a set of letters usually presented in a fixed order which is used for writing the words of a particular language or group of languages.

concentrate^{복습}
[kánsəntrèit]

v. (정신을) 집중하다, 전념하다; n. 농축물
If you concentrate on something, you give all your attention to it.

figure out^{복습}

idiom (생각한 끝에) ~을 이해하다; (양·비용을) 계산하다
If you figure out someone or something, you come to understand them by thinking carefully.

alongside[*]
[əlɔ́ːŋsáid]

prep. ~ 옆에, 나란히; ~와 함께; ~와 동시에
If one thing is alongside another thing, the first thing is next to the second.

just in case^{복습}

idiom (혹시라도) ~할 경우에 대비해서
If you do something in case or just in case a particular thing happens, you do it because that thing might happen.

turn on the jets

idiom 전력을 다해 달리다
If you turn on the jets, you move as fast as humanly possible.

leap[*]
[liːp]

v. (높이·길게) 뛰다, 뛰어오르다; n. 높이 뛰기, 도약
If you leap, you jump high in the air or jump a long distance.

practically^{**}
[prǽktikəli]

ad. 사실상, 거의; 현실적으로, 실제로
Practically means almost, but not completely or exactly.

shoot^{복습}
[ʃuːt]

v. (shot-shot) 휙 움직이다; (총 등을) 쏘다; 슛을 하다; n. 촬영
If someone or something shoots in a particular direction, they move in that direction quickly and suddenly.

dirt^{복습}
[dəːrt]

n. 흙; 먼지, 때
You can refer to the earth on the ground as dirt, especially when it is dusty.

pound[*]
[paund]

v. (가슴이) 쿵쿵 뛰다; 치다, 두드리다; n. (화폐 단위·무게 단위) 파운드
If your heart is pounding, it is beating with an unusually strong and fast rhythm, usually because you are afraid.

confuse^{복습}
[kənfjúːz]

v. (사람을) 혼란시키다; (주제를) 혼란스럽게 하다 (confused a. 혼란스러워하는)
If you are confused, you do not know exactly what is happening or what to do.

trudge^{복습}
[trʌdʒ]

v. 터덜터덜 걷다; 느릿느릿 걷다; n. 터덜터덜 걷기
If you trudge somewhere, you walk there slowly and with heavy steps, especially because you are tired or unhappy.

snap^{복습}
[snæp]

v. 사진을 찍다; 탁 하고 움직이다; 딱딱거리다, 톡 쏘다; n. 찰칵 하는 소리
If you snap a picture, you take a photograph of someone or something.

giant^{복습}
[dʒáiənt]

a. 거대한; 위대한; n. (이야기 속의) 거인
Something that is described as giant is much larger or more important than most others of its kind.

128

trophy ^{복습}
[tróufi]

n. 트로피, 우승컵; 전리품
A trophy is a prize, for example a silver cup, that is given to the winner of a competition or race.

lock ^{복습}
[lak]

v. 고정하다; (자물쇠로) 잠그다; n. 자물쇠
If you lock something in a particular position or if it locks there, it is held or fitted firmly in that position.

thumb ^{복습}
[θʌm]

n. 엄지손가락; v. 엄지손가락으로 건드리다
Your thumb is the short thick part on the side of your hand next to your four fingers.

Chapters 27 & 28

1. Why couldn't Mrs. Jewls concentrate on her book?
   A. She kept thinking about her lesson plan.
   B. She was too worried about the students.
   C. The bell was making a kachooga booping sound.
   D. The students were shouting at each other.

2. Why didn't the students scream when the lights went out?
   A. They did not notice.
   B. They were too afraid.
   C. Mrs. Jewls told them not to.
   D. Mrs. Jewls warned them about it.

3. How did Benjamin and Rondi know the situation was serious?
   A. Mrs. Jewls cried in front of the students.
   B. Mrs. Jewls wanted to leave the paper clips behind.
   C. They heard an announcement from Mr. Kidswatter.
   D. They saw students from other classes on the staircase.

4. Where did the students from Mrs. Jewls's class go?
   A. Down to the school's cafeteria
   B. Down to the first floor of the school
   C. Into the closet that wasn't there
   D. Into the classroom of the lady with a long fingernail

5. What was unusual about the way Miss Zarves taught history?

   A. She did not give tests to the students.

   B. She sometimes made other teachers teach her class.

   C. She let the students decide whom to learn about.

   D. She taught about people who were not famous.

6. Why did Myron have trouble reading the papers from Miss Zarves?

   A. He forgot his glasses at home.

   B. The letters were too small.

   C. The writing was in Chinese.

   D. The room was too dark.

7. How did the students get back to the stairway?

   A. Myron clipped Miss Zarves's fingernail.

   B. Myron found a secret door.

   C. The students followed Mrs. Jewls.

   D. The students waited for Miss Zarves to fall asleep.

Check Your Reading Speed

1분에 몇 단어를 읽는지 리딩 속도를 측정해 보세요.

$$\frac{661 \text{ words}}{\text{reading time ( ) sec}} \times 60 = (\quad) \text{ WPM}$$

Build Your Vocabulary

ultimate^{복습} [ʌ́ltəmət]	a. 궁극적인, 최종적인; 최고의, 최상의; n. 극치 You use ultimate to describe the final result or aim of a long series of events.
kindergarten^{복습} [kíndərgà:rtn]	n. 유치원 A kindergarten is an informal kind of school for very young children, where they learn things by playing.
talent^{복습} [tǽlənt]	n. (타고난) 재능, 재주; 재능 있는 사람 Talent is the natural ability to do something well.
clipping^{복습} [klípiŋ]	n. 잘라 낸 조각, 오려 낸 것 Clippings are small pieces of something that have been cut from something larger.
bucket^{복습} [bʌ́kit]	n. 양동이, 들통 A bucket is a round metal or plastic container with a handle attached to its sides.
startle* [sta:rtl]	v. 깜짝 놀라게 하다 (startled a. 놀란) If you are startled, you are slightly shocked or frightened because of a sudden surprise.
chalk^{복습} [tʃɔ:k]	n. 분필 Chalk is small sticks of soft white rock, used for writing or drawing with.
closet^{복습} [klázit]	n. 벽장 A closet is a piece of furniture with doors at the front and shelves inside, which is used for storing things.
toss^{복습} [tɔ:s]	v. (가볍게·아무렇게나) 던지다; n. (고개를) 홱 젖히기 If you toss something somewhere, you throw it there lightly, often in a rather careless way.
supply** [səplái]	n. (pl.) 공급품, 비품; 공급(량); v. 공급하다 You can use supplies to refer to food, equipment, and other essential things that people need, especially when these are provided in large quantities.
remove^{복습} [rimú:v]	v. 옮기다; 없애다; 치우다; 떼다; (옷 등을) 벗다 If you remove something from a place, you take it away.
dust* [dʌst]	n. (흙)먼지; v. 먼지를 털다 Dust is very small dry particles of earth or sand.

concentrate 복습
[kánsəntrèit]
v. (정신을) 집중하다, 전념하다; n. 농축물
If you concentrate on something, you give all your attention to it.

boom 복습
[bu:m]
n. 쾅, 탕 하는 소리; v. 굵은 목소리로 말하다; 쾅 하는 소리를 내다
A boom is a deep loud sound that continues for some time, for example the noise of thunder or an explosion.

scare 복습
[skɛər]
v. 겁주다, 놀라게 하다 (scared a. 무서워하는, 겁먹은)
If you are scared of someone or something, you are frightened of them.

light 복습
[lait]
v. (lit-lit) 불을 붙이다; (빛을) 비추다; n. 빛
If you light something such as a candle or fire, or if it lights, it starts burning.

flicker
[flíkər]
v. (불·빛 등이) 깜박거리다; 스치다; 움직거리다; n. (빛의) 깜박거림
If a light or flame flickers, it shines unsteadily.

blow 복습
[blou]
v. (blew-blown) (입으로) 불다; (호각·악기 등을) 불다; (기회를) 날리다; n. 세게 때림
If you blow, you send out a stream of air from your mouth.

leave off
idiom 중단하다
If you leave off something, you stop doing it.

run for one's life
idiom (필사적으로) 도망치다, 간신히 도망가다
If you run for your life, you run away to save your life.

doom 복습
[du:m]
n. 불운, 저주; 죽음, 파멸; v. 불행한 운명을 맞게 하다
Doom is a terrible future state or event which you cannot prevent.

block 복습
[blak]
v. 막다, 차단하다; 방해하다; n. 사각형 덩어리; (도로로 나뉘는) 구역, 블록
To block a road, channel, or pipe means to put an object across it or in it so that nothing can pass through it or along it.

glare 복습
[glɛər]
v. 노려보다; 환하다, 눈부시다; n. 노려봄; 환한 빛, 눈부심
If you glare at someone, you look at them with an angry expression on your face.

budge
[bʌdʒ]
v. 약간 움직이다, 꼼짝하다; 의견을 바꾸다
If someone or something will not budge, they will not move.

urge 복습
[əːrdʒ]
v. 재촉하다; 충고하다, 설득하려 하다; n. (강한) 욕구, 충동
If you urge someone to do something, you try hard to persuade them to do it.

siren 복습
[sáiərən]
n. (신호·경보 등을 나타내는) 사이렌
A siren is a warning device which makes a long, loud noise. Most fire engines, ambulances, and police cars have sirens.

wail
[weil]
v. (길고 높은) 소리를 내다; 울부짖다, 통곡하다
If something such as a siren or an alarm wails, it makes a long, loud, high-pitched sound.

steel 복습
[sti:l]
n. 강철; v. (~에 대비해서) 마음을 단단히 먹다
Steel is a very strong metal which is made mainly from iron.

shatter [복습]
[ʃǽtər]

v. 산산이 부서지다; 산산조각 내다; 엄청난 충격을 주다
If something shatters or is shattered, it breaks into a lot of small pieces.

strew
[struː]

v. (strewed-strewed/strewn) 흩다, 흩뿌리다; 흩어지다
To strew things somewhere, or to strew a place with things, means to scatter them there.

staircase[*]
[stéərkèis]

n. (건물 내부에 난간으로 죽 이어져 있는) 계단
A staircase is a set of stairs inside a building.

grab [복습]
[græb]

v. (와락·단단히) 붙잡다; ~을 잡으려고 하다; n. 와락 잡아채려고 함
If you grab something, you take it or pick it up suddenly and roughly.

pigtail [복습]
[pígtèil]

n. (하나 또는 두 갈래로) 땋은 머리
If someone has a pigtail or pigtails, their hair is plaited or braided into one or two lengths.

demand [복습]
[dimǽnd]

v. 강력히 묻다, 따지다; 요구하다; n. 요구 (사항)
If you demand something such as information or action, you ask for it in a very forceful way.

gust [복습]
[gʌst]

n. 세찬 바람, 돌풍; v. (갑자기) 몰아치다
A gust is a short, strong, sudden rush of wind.

exclaim [복습]
[ikskléim]

v. 소리치다, 외치다
If you exclaim, you cry out suddenly in surprise, strong emotion, or pain.

doorway[*]
[dóːrwèi]

n. 출입구
A doorway is a space in a wall where a door opens and closes.

beckon
[békən]

v. (오라고) 손짓하다; 아주 매력적으로 보이다
If you beckon to someone, you signal to them to come to you.

pinky [복습]
[píŋki]

n. 새끼손가락
Your pinky is the smallest finger on your hand.

Check Your Reading Speed

1분에 몇 단어를 읽는지 리딩 속도를 측정해 보세요.

$$\frac{937 \text{ words}}{\text{reading time (   ) sec}} \times 60 = (\quad) \text{ WPM}$$

Build Your Vocabulary

moth*
[mɔːθ]

n. [곤충] 나방
A moth is an insect like a butterfly which usually flies around at night.

file*
[fail]

v. 줄지어 가다; (문서 등을) 보관하다; n. 파일, 서류철; (컴퓨터) 파일
If people file somewhere, they walk there in a line.

make do

idiom 견디다, 만족하다
If you make do with something, you manage with the things that you have, even though this is not really enough.

bump^{복습}
[bʌmp]

v. 마주치다; 부딪치다; 덜컹거리며 가다; n. 쿵, 탁 (부딪치는 소리)
If you bump into someone you know, you meet them unexpectedly.

lounge^{복습}
[laundʒ]

n. (호텔·클럽 등의) 휴게실; (공항 등의) 대합실; v. 느긋하게 있다
In a hotel, club, or other public place, a lounge is a room where people can sit and relax.

neat**
[niːt]

a. 정돈된, 단정한; 뛰어난, 훌륭한
A neat place, thing, or person is tidy and smart, and has everything in the correct place.

trim^{복습}
[trim]

a. 잘 가꾼, 깔끔한; v. 다듬다, 손질하다; n. 다듬기, 약간 자르기
Something that is trim is neat and attractive.

silky
[sílki]

a. 비단 같은; 보드라운, 광택 있는
If something has a silky texture, it is smooth, soft, and shiny, like silk.

orderly*
[ɔ́ːrdərli]

a. 정돈된, 정연한; 질서 있는, 평화로운
Something that is orderly is arranged or organized in a neat, careful, logical way.

adorable
[ədɔ́ːrəbl]

a. 사랑스러운
If you say that someone or something is adorable, you are emphasizing that they are very attractive and you feel great affection for them.

considerable**
[kənsídərəbl]

a. 상당한, 많은 (considerably ad. 상당히, 많이)
Considerable means great in amount or degree.

tear^{복습}
[tɛər]

① v. (tore-torn) 찢어지다; 뜯어내다; 구멍을 뚫다; n. 찢어진 곳, 구멍 ② n. 눈물
If you tear paper, cloth, or another material, or if it tears, you pull it into two pieces or you pull it so that a hole appears in it.

strain**
[strein]

v. 안간힘을 쓰다; 무리하게 사용하다; 한계에 이르게 하다; n. 부담; 압박
If you strain to do something, you make a great effort to do it when it is difficult to do.

fade*
[feid]

v. (색깔이) 바래다, 희미해지다; 서서히 사라지다 (faded a. 색이 바랜)
When a colored object fades or when the light fades it, it gradually becomes paler.

trash^{복습}
[træʃ]

n. 쓰레기; v. 부수다, 엉망으로 만들다; (필요 없는 것을) 버리다
Trash consists of unwanted things or waste material such as used paper, empty containers and bottles, and waste food.

shrug^{복습}
[ʃrʌg]

v. (두 손바닥을 위로 하고) 어깨를 으쓱하다; n. 어깨를 으쓱하기
If you shrug, you raise your shoulders to show that you are not interested in something or that you do not know or care about something.

stare^{복습}
[stɛər]

v. 빤히 쳐다보다, 응시하다; n. 빤히 쳐다보기, 응시
If you stare at someone or something, you look at them for a long time.

accuse^{복습}
[əkjúːz]

v. 비난하다, 혐의를 제기하다
If you accuse someone of doing something wrong or dishonest, you say or tell them that you believe that they did it.

hesitate^{복습}
[hézətèit]

v. 망설이다, 주저하다; 거리끼다 (hesitation n. 주저, 망설임)
Hesitation is an unwillingness to do something, or a delay in doing it, because you are uncertain, worried, or embarrassed about it.

portion*
[pɔ́ːrʃən]

n. 부분, 일부; 1인분; 몫; v. 나누다
A portion of something is a part of it.

ultimate^{복습}
[ʌ́ltəmət]

a. 궁극적인, 최종적인; 최고의, 최상의; n. 극치
You use ultimate to describe the final result or aim of a long series of events.

giggle^{복습}
[gigl]

v. 킥킥거리다, 피식 웃다; n. 킥킥거림, 피식 웃음
If someone giggles, they laugh in a childlike way, because they are amused, nervous, or embarrassed.

ignore**
[ignɔ́ːr]

v. 무시하다; (사람을) 못 본 척하다
If you ignore someone or something, you pay no attention to them.

closet^{복습}
[klázit]

n. 벽장
A closet is a piece of furniture with doors at the front and shelves inside, which is used for storing things.

stack^{복습}
[stæk]

n. 무더기, 더미; v. (깔끔하게 정돈하여) 쌓다
A stack of things is a pile of them.

helpless*
[hélplis]

a. 무력한, 속수무책인 (helplessly ad. 무력하게)
If you are helpless, you do not have the strength or power to do anything useful or to control or protect yourself.

complain^{복습}
[kəmpléin]

v. 불평하다, 항의하다
If you complain about a situation, you say that you are not satisfied with it.

dictionary 복습
[díkʃənèri]
n. 사전
A dictionary is a book in which the words and phrases of a language are listed alphabetically, together with their meanings or their translations in another language.

fumble
[fʌmbl]
v. (손으로) 더듬거리다; (말을) 더듬거리다
If you fumble for something or fumble with something, you try and reach for it or hold it in a clumsy way.

sheet**
[ʃi:t]
n. (종이) 한 장; 침대에 깔거나 위로 덮는 얇은 천
A sheet of paper is a rectangular piece of paper.

glance 복습
[glæns]
v. 흘깃 보다; 대충 훑어보다; n. 흘깃 봄
If you glance at something or someone, you look at them very quickly and then look away again immediately.

spot 복습
[spat]
v. 발견하다, 찾다, 알아채다; n. (특정한) 곳; (작은) 점
If you spot something or someone, you notice them.

scissors 복습
[sízərz]
n. 가위
Scissors are a small cutting tool with two sharp blades that are screwed together.

make sense 복습
idiom 타당하다; 이해가 되다; 이해하기 쉽다
If a course of action makes sense, it seems sensible.

astonish*
[əstániʃ]
v. 깜짝 놀라게 하다 (astonished a. 깜짝 놀란)
If you are astonished by something, you are very surprised about it.

suggestion 복습
[səgdʒésʧən]
n. 제안, 의견; 암시
If you make a suggestion, you put forward an idea or plan for someone to think about.

notice 복습
[nóutis]
v. 알아채다, 인지하다; 주목하다, 관심을 기울이다; n. 신경 씀, 알아챔
If you notice something or someone, you become aware of them.

press 복습
[pres]
v. 누르다; (무엇에) 바짝 대다; 꾹 밀어 넣다; n. 언론
If you press something or press down on it, you push hard against it with your foot or hand.

snip 복습
[snip]
v. (가위로 싹둑) 자르다; n. 싹둑 자르기
If you snip something, you cut it quickly using sharp scissors.

sprawl 복습
[sprɔ:l]
v. 팔다리를 아무렇게나 벌리고 앉다, 대자로 눕다; 제멋대로 퍼져 나가다
If you sprawl somewhere, you sit or lie down with your legs and arms spread out in a careless way.

staircase 복습
[stéərkèis]
n. (건물 내부에 난간으로 죽 이어져 있는) 계단
A staircase is a set of stairs inside a building.

million 복습
[míljən]
n. 100만; a. 수많은
A million or one million is the number 1,000,000.

triumphant 복습
[traiʌ́mfənt]
a. 의기양양한; 크게 성공한, 큰 승리를 거둔 (triumphantly ad. 의기양양하게)
Someone who is triumphant has gained a victory or succeeded in something and feels very happy about it.

Chapters 29 & 30

1. What did the students have to do between the twenty-sixth and twenty-seventh floors?

   A. They had to lift the blackboard.

   B. They had to watch out for a skateboard.

   C. They had to climb over Mr. Kidswatter's desk.

   D. They had to answer Mr. Kidswatter's questions.

2. How did the playground look different after the storm?

   A. It was filled with school supplies.

   B. It was missing some equipment.

   C. It was covered in water.

   D. It was white because of the snow.

3. Why was recess so long on the day the storm ended?

   A. So that the students had a chance to get exercise

   B. So that the students could get some fresh air

   C. So that the teachers could call the parents

   D. So that the teachers had time to clean up

4. What was the most important thing about the stew that Miss Mush was making?

   A. The nutrition that it had

   B. The colors that it had

   C. The way that it tasted

   D. The cost of making it

5. Why did Miss Mush's stomach tighten?

   A. She felt pressure to make a delicious lunch.

   B. She was worried that she would be late.

   C. She got sick from eating the stew.

   D. She was nervous about meeting Mr. Kidswatter.

6. Why didn't Miss Mush want to put oranges in the stew?

   A. She really wanted to use carrots instead.

   B. She thought they would not taste good.

   C. She did not have any oranges in her kitchen.

   D. She thought they were an obvious choice.

7. What did Miss Mush do as she gave each student some stew?

   A. She told them the ingredients.

   B. She asked them how it tasted.

   C. She apologized to them.

   D. She congratulated them.

Check Your Reading Speed

1분에 몇 단어를 읽는지 리딩 속도를 측정해 보세요.

$$\frac{770 \text{ words}}{\text{reading time ( ) sec}} \times 60 = (\quad) \text{ WPM}$$

Build Your Vocabulary

storm ^{복습} [stɔ:rm]	n. 폭풍, 폭풍우; v. 쿵쾅대며 가다, 뛰쳐나가다; 기습하다 A storm is very bad weather, with heavy rain, strong winds, and often thunder and lightning.
boom ^{복습} [bu:m]	n. 쾅, 탕 하는 소리; v. 굵은 목소리로 말하다; 쾅 하는 소리를 내다 A boom is a deep loud sound that continues for some time, for example the noise of thunder or an explosion.
make one's way ^{복습}	idiom 나아가다, 가다 When you make your way somewhere, you walk or travel there.
strew ^{복습} [stru:]	v. (strewed-strewed/strewn) 흩다, 흩뿌리다; 흩어지다 To strew things somewhere, or to strew a place with things, means to scatter them there.
cafeteria ^{복습} [kæfətíəriə]	n. (학교·회사 등의) 구내식당; 카페테리아 A cafeteria is a lunchroom or dining hall, as in a factory, office, or school, where food is often served from counters.
tray ^{복습} [trei]	n. 쟁반 A tray is a flat piece of wood, plastic, or metal, which usually has raised edges and which is used for carrying things, especially food and drinks.
instrument ^{복습} [ínstrəmənt]	n. 악기; 기구, 도구 A musical instrument is an object such as a piano, guitar, or flute, which you play in order to produce music.
stuff ^{복습} [stʌf]	v. (빽빽이) 채워 넣다; (재빨리) 쑤셔 넣다; n. 일, 것; 물건 (stuffed animal n. (솜으로 채워 넣은) 봉제인형) Stuffed animals are toys that are made of cloth filled with a soft material and which look like animals.
bust ^{복습} [bʌst]	n. 흉상, 반신상; v. 부수다, 고장 내다; 급습하다 A bust is a statue of the head and shoulders of a person.
block ^{복습} [blak]	v. 막다, 차단하다; 방해하다; n. 사각형 덩어리; (도로로 나뉘는) 구역, 블록 To block a road, channel, or pipe means to put an object across it or in it so that nothing can pass through it or along it.
enormous ^{복습} [inɔ́:rməs]	a. 거대한, 막대한 Something that is enormous is extremely large in size or amount.

include^{복습}
[inklúːd]

v. 포함하다; ~을 (~에) 포함시키다
If one thing includes another thing, it has the other thing as one of its parts.

nail^{복습}
[neil]

n. 손톱, 발톱; 못; v. 못으로 박다
Your nails are the thin hard parts that grow at the ends of your fingers and toes.

bucket^{복습}
[bʌ́kit]

n. 양동이, 들통
A bucket is a round metal or plastic container with a handle attached to its sides.

unfortunate^{복습}
[ʌnfɔ́ːrʧənət]

a. 운이 없는, 불운한, 불행한 (unfortunately ad. 불행하게도, 유감스럽게도)
You can use unfortunately to introduce or refer to a statement when you consider that it is sad or disappointing, or when you want to express regret.

clipping^{복습}
[klípiŋ]

n. 잘라 낸 조각, 오려 낸 것
Clippings are small pieces of something that have been cut from something larger.

blackboard^{복습}
[blǽkbɔ̀ːrd]

n. 칠판
A blackboard is a dark-colored board that you can write on with chalk.

chalk^{복습}
[ʧɔːk]

n. 분필
Chalk is small sticks of soft white rock, used for writing or drawing with.

shuffle^{복습}
[ʃʌfl]

v. (게임을 하기 위해 카드를) 섞다; 발을 끌며 걷다; 이리저리 움직이다;
n. 느릿느릿 걷기
If you shuffle playing cards, you mix them up before you begin a game.

deck*
[dek]

n. (카드) 한 벌; (배의) 갑판
A deck of cards is a complete set of playing cards.

deal out

idiom 나누다, 분배하다, 돌리다
If you deal out playing cards, you give them out to the players in a game.

eventually**
[ivénʧuəli]

ad. 결국, 마침내
Eventually means at the end of a situation or process or as the final result of it.

chirp^{복습}
[ʧəːrp]

v. (새나 곤충이) 짹짹거리다; 재잘거리다; n. 짹짹 소리; 재잘거리는 소리
When a bird or an insect such as a cricket or grasshopper chirps, it makes short, high-pitched sounds.

yard^{복습}
[jaːrd]

n. (학교의) 운동장; 마당, 뜰; 정원
A yard is a flat area of concrete or stone that is next to a building and often has a wall around it.

shovel*
[ʃʌ́vəl]

v. 삽질하다, 삽으로 파다; n. 삽
If you shovel earth, coal, or snow, you lift and move it with a shovel which is a tool with a rounded blade and a long handle.

roof [복습]
[ru:f]

n. 지붕
The roof of a building is the covering on top of it that protects the people and things inside from the weather.

dump [복습]
[dʌmp]

v. (아무렇게나) 내려놓다; 버리다; n. (쓰레기) 폐기장
If you dump something somewhere, you put it or unload it there quickly and carelessly.

playground [복습]
[pléigràund]

n. (학교의) 운동장; 놀이터
A playground is a piece of land, at school or in a public area, where children can play.

sparkle*
[spa:rkl]

v. 반짝이다; n. 반짝거림, 광채
If something sparkles, it is clear and bright and shines with a lot of very small points of light.

pack [복습]
[pæk]

v. (사람·물건으로) 가득 채우다; (짐을) 싸다; n. 무리; 꾸러미
If people or things pack into a place or if they pack a place, there are so many of them that the place is full.

guardrail
[gá:rdrèil]

n. (계단의) 난간; (도로의) 가드레일
A guardrail is a railing that is placed along the edge of something such as a staircase, path, or boat, so that people can hold onto it or so that they do not fall over the edge.

slippery*
[slípəri]

a. 미끄러운, 미끈거리는; 약삭빠른
Something that is slippery is smooth, wet, or oily and is therefore difficult to walk on or to hold.

look out

idiom 조심해!
If you say or shout 'look out!' to someone, you are warning them that they are in danger.

reverse*
[rivə́:rs]

a. (정)반대의; v. (정반대로) 뒤바꾸다; n. (정)반대
Reverse means opposite to what you expect or to what has just been described.

opposite [복습]
[ápəzit]

n. 반대(되는 것); a. (정)반대의; 건너편의; 맞은편의
The opposite of someone or something is the person or thing that is most different from them.

charge [복습]
[tʃa:rdʒ]

v. 급히 가다, 달려가다; (요금·값을) 청구하다; n. 요금
If you charge toward someone or something, you move quickly and aggressively toward them.

slide [복습]
[slaid]

v. 미끄러지듯이 움직이다; 슬며시 넣다; n. 떨어짐; 미끄러짐
When something slides somewhere or when you slide it there, it moves there smoothly over or against something.

clump
[klʌmp]

n. 덩어리; 무리, 무더기; v. 무리를 짓다; 쿵쾅거리다
A clump can refer to a solid mass of something such as earth or mud.

smack*
[smæk]

v. 탁 소리가 나게 치다; 세게 부딪치다; n. 강타; ad. 정통으로
If you smack something somewhere, you put it or throw it there so that it makes a loud, sharp noise.

recess [복습]
[risés]

n. (학교의) 쉬는 시간; (의회·위원회 등의) 휴회 기간
A recess is a break between classes at a school.

142

stuck^{복습}
[stʌk]

a. (불쾌한 상황에서) 빠져나갈 수 없는; 움직일 수 없는, 꼼짝 못하는; (대답 등이) 막힌
If you are stuck in a boring or unpleasant situation, you are unable to change it or get away from it.

mess*
[mes]

n. (지저분하고) 엉망(진창)인 상태; (많은 문제로) 엉망인 상황; v. 엉망으로 만들다
If you say that something is a mess or in a mess, you think that it is in an untidy state.

predict^{복습}
[pridíkt]

v. 예측하다, 예견하다
If you predict an event, you say that it will happen.

race
[reis]

v. 급히 가다; 경주하다, 경쟁하다; n. 경주; 인종, 종족
If you race somewhere, you go there as quickly as possible.

declare^{복습}
[dikléər]

v. 선언하다, 공표하다; 분명히 말하다
If you declare something, you state officially and formally that it exists or is the case.

no way^{복습}

idiom 말도 안 돼; (강한 거절의 의미로) 절대로 안 돼, 싫어
You can say 'no way' for expressing surprise, or for telling someone that you do not believe them.

pigtail^{복습}
[pígtèil]

n. (하나 또는 두 갈래로) 땋은 머리
If someone has a pigtail or pigtails, their hair is plaited or braided into one or two lengths.

insist^{복습}
[insíst]

v. 고집하다, 주장하다, 우기다
If you insist that something is the case, you say so very firmly and refuse to say otherwise, even though other people do not believe you.

defense*
[diféns]

n. 변호, 옹호; 방어; 방어 시설
A defense is something that you say or write which supports ideas or actions that have been criticized or questioned.

flake*
[fleik]

n. (얇은) 조각; v. (조각조각) 벗겨지다
A flake is a small thin piece of something, especially one that has broken off a larger piece.

snowflake
[snóuflèik]

n. 눈송이
A snowflake is one of the soft, white bits of frozen water that fall as snow.

spectacle^{복습}
[spéktəkl]

n. (pl.) 안경; (기이한·놀라운) 모습, 상황; 장관, 광경; 구경거리
Glasses are sometimes referred to as spectacles.

prove**
[pru:v]

v. 입증하다, 증명하다; (~임이) 드러나다
If you prove that something is true, you show by means of argument or evidence that it is definitely true.

scowl^{복습}
[skaul]

v. 노려보다, 쏘아보다; n. 노려봄, 쏘아봄
When someone scowls, an angry or hostile expression appears on their face.

skeptical^{복습}
[sképtikəl]

a. 의심 많은, 회의적인
If you are skeptical about something, you have doubts about it.

spot^{복습}
[spat]

v. 발견하다, 찾다, 알아채다; n. (특정한) 곳; (작은) 점
If you spot something or someone, you notice them.

stick out^{복습}

idiom ~을 내밀다, 튀어나오게 하다
If something is sticking out from a surface or object, it extends up or away from it.

dot^{복습}
[dat]

n. 점; v. 점을 찍다; 여기저기 흩어져 있다
A dot is a very small round mark or spot.

budge^{복습}
[bʌdʒ]

v. 약간 움직이다, 꼼짝하다; 의견을 바꾸다
If someone or something will not budge, they will not move.

yank^{복습}
[jæŋk]

n. 홱 잡아당기기; v. 홱 잡아당기다
A yank is a quick forceful pull of something.

jerk[*]
[dʒəːrk]

v. 홱 움직이다; n. (갑자기 날카롭게) 홱 움직임; 얼간이
If you jerk something or someone in a particular direction, or they jerk in a particular direction, they move a short distance very suddenly and quickly.

slip^{복습}
[slip]

v. 미끄러지다; 슬며시 가다; (재빨리 · 슬며시) 놓다; n. (작은) 실수; 미끄러짐
If something slips, it slides out of place or out of your hand.

grip^{복습}
[grip]

n. 꽉 붙잡음; 통제, 지배; v. 꽉 잡다, 움켜잡다
A grip is a firm, strong hold on something.

flagpole^{복습}
[flǽgpoul]

n. 깃대
A flagpole is a tall pole on which a flag can be displayed.

puny
[pjúːni]

a. 보잘것없는, 별 볼일 없는; 작고 연약한
Someone or something that is puny is very small or weak.

reach out^{복습}

idiom (손 · 팔을) 뻗다; 접근하다, 연락하다; 추구하다, 노력하다
If you reach out, you move your arm and hand to take or touch something.

spin^{복습}
[spin]

v. (빙빙) 돌다, 회전하다; 돌리다, 회전시키다; n. 회전, 돌기
If something spins or if you spin it, it turns quickly around a central point.

curve^{복습}
[kəːrv]

v. 곡선을 이루다, 곡선으로 나아가다; n. 커브, 곡선 (curved a. 곡선의)
A curved object has the shape of a curve or has a smoothly bending surface.

hook^{복습}
[huk]

v. ~에 걸다; 갈고리로 잠그다; n. (갈)고리, 걸이
To hook means to fasten or hang something on something else using a hook which is a bent piece of metal or plastic.

whirl[*]
[hwəːrl]

v. 빙그르르 돌다; (마음 · 생각 등이) 혼란스럽다; n. 빙빙 돌기
If something or someone whirls around or if you whirl them around, they move around or turn around very quickly.

dizzy^{복습}
[dízi]

a. 어지러운 (dizzily ad. 어지럽게)
If you feel dizzy, you feel that you are losing your balance and are about to fall.

144

top ^{복습}
[tap]

n. 팽이; 맨 위, 꼭대기; v. (다른 것의) 위에 놓다; 능가하다; 더 높다
A top is a child's toy that turns around on a point when it is moved very quickly by hand or by a string.

rush ^{복습}
[rʌʃ]

n. 분주함; 혼잡; v. 급히 움직이다, 서두르다
A rush is a situation in which you need to go somewhere or do something very quickly.

Check Your Reading Speed

1분에 몇 단어를 읽는지 리딩 속도를 측정해 보세요.

$$\frac{\text{1,145 words}}{\text{reading time ( ) sec}} \times 60 = (\quad) \text{ WPM}$$

Build Your Vocabulary

stove*
[stouv]

n. (요리용 가스·전기) 레인지; 스토브, 난로
A stove is a piece of equipment which provides heat, either for cooking or for heating a room.

cafeteria^{복습}
[kæfətíəriə]

n. (학교·회사 등의) 구내식당; 카페테리아
A cafeteria is a lunchroom or dining hall, as in a factory, office, or school, where food is often served from counters.

enormous^{복습}
[inɔ́:rməs]

a. 거대한, 막대한
Something that is enormous is extremely large in size or amount.

pot**
[pat]

n. (둥글고 속이 깊은) 냄비, 솥; 병, 항아리
A pot is a deep round container used for cooking stews, soups, and other food.

blaze*
[bleiz]

v. 활활 타다; 눈부시게 빛나다; n. 불길, 활활 타는 불; 휘황찬란한 빛
(blazing a. 활활 타는)
When a fire blazes, it burns strongly and brightly.

squeaky
[skwí:ki]

a. 끼익 하는 소리가 나는
Something that is squeaky makes high-pitched sounds.

know better^{복습}

idiom (~할 정도로) 어리석지는 않다
If someone knows better than to do something, they are old enough or experienced enough to know it is the wrong thing to do.

interrupt^{복습}
[ìntərʌ́pt]

v. (말·행동을) 방해하다; 중단시키다
When you interrupt someone, you stop them in the midst of doing or saying something.

inspiration^{복습}
[ìnspəréiʃən]

n. 영감; 고취, 고무
Inspiration is a feeling of enthusiasm you get from someone or something, which gives you new and creative ideas.

rub^{복습}
[rʌb]

v. (손·손수건 등을 대고) 문지르다; (두 손 등을) 맞비비다; n. 문지르기, 비비기
If you rub a part of your body, you move your hand or fingers backward and forward over it while pressing firmly.

chin^{복습}
[tʃin]

n. 턱
Your chin is the part of your face that is below your mouth and above your neck.

storm^{복습}
[stɔ:rm]

n. 폭풍, 폭풍우; v. 쿵쾅대며 가다, 뛰쳐나가다; 기습하다
A storm is very bad weather, with heavy rain, strong winds, and often thunder and lightning.

146

doom ^{복습}
[duːm]

n. 불운, 저주; 죽음, 파멸; v. 불행한 운명을 맞게 하다
Doom is a terrible future state or event which you cannot prevent.

declare ^{복습}
[diklέər]

v. 분명히 말하다; 선언하다, 공표하다
If you declare something, you state something clearly and definitely.

brilliant *
[bríljənt]

a. 훌륭한, 멋진; 아주 밝은, 선명한, 눈부신
You can say that something is brilliant when you are very pleased about it or think that it is very good.

inventory
[ínvəntɔ̀ːri]

n. 재고(품); (특정 건물 내의) 물품 목록
An inventory is a supply or stock of something.

cabbage ^{복습}
[kǽbidʒ]

n. 양배추
A cabbage is a round vegetable with white, green or purple leaves that is usually eaten cooked.

pepper ^{복습}
[pépər]

n. 피망; 후추; v. 후추를 치다
A pepper is a hollow fruit, usually red, green, or yellow, with a spicy flavor, used to give flavor to food.

wave ^{복습}
[weiv]

v. (손·팔을) 흔들다; 손짓하다; n. 파도, 물결; (손·팔·몸을) 흔들기
If you wave something, you hold it up and move it rapidly from side to side.

toss ^{복습}
[tɔːs]

v. (가볍게·아무렇게나) 던지다; n. (고개를) 홱 젖히기
If you toss something somewhere, you throw it there lightly, often in a rather careless way.

shoot ^{복습}
[ʃuːt]

v. (shot-shot) 휙 움직이다; (총 등을) 쏘다; 슛을 하다; n. 촬영
If someone or something shoots in a particular direction, they move in that direction quickly and suddenly.

ingredient *
[ingríːdiənt]

n. 재료, 성분, 원료
Ingredients are the things that are used to make something, especially all the different foods you use when you are cooking a particular dish.

shield *
[ʃiːld]

v. 보호하다, 가리다; n. 방패; 보호 장치
If you shield your eyes, you put your hand above your eyes to protect them from direct sunlight or smoke.

see about

idiom ~을 준비하다, 처리하다
When you see about something, you arrange for it to be done or provided.

peel *
[piːl]

v. (과일·채소 등의) 껍질을 벗기다; 벗겨지다; n. (과일·채소의 두꺼운) 껍질
When you peel fruit or vegetables, you remove their skins.

remind ^{복습}
[rimáind]

v. 상기시키다, 다시 한번 알려 주다
If someone reminds you of a fact or event that you already know about, they say something which makes you think about it.

hiss *
[his]

v. 쉬익 하는 소리를 내다; (화난 어조로) 낮게 말하다; n. 쉿 하는 소리
To hiss means to make a sound like a long 's.'

steam^{**}
[sti:m]

n. 김, 증기; 추진력; v. 김을 내뿜다; 화내다, 발끈하다
Steam is the hot mist that forms when water boils.

nutrition
[nju:tríʃən]

n. 영양, 영양 공급
Nutrition is the process of giving or getting the right type of food for good health and growth.

stir[*]
[stə:r]

v. 젓다; 약간 움직이다; 자극하다; n. 젓기; 동요, 충격
If you stir a liquid or other substance, you move it around or mix it in a container using something such as a spoon.

definition^{복습}
[dèfəníʃən]

n. 선명도; 정의; 의미
Definition is the quality of being clear and distinct.

seed^{**}
[si:d]

n. 씨, 씨앗, 종자
A seed is the small, hard part of a plant from which a new plant grows.

hold one's nose^{복습}

idiom (냄새가 고약해서) 코를 쥐다
When you hold your nose, you squeeze your nostrils with your fingers in order to avoid inhaling an unpleasant smell.

sniff^{복습}
[snif]

v. 냄새를 맡다; 코를 훌쩍이다; n. 냄새 맡기; 콧방귀 뀌기
If you sniff something or sniff at it, you smell it by taking air in through your nose.

sole[*]
[soul]

n. (신발의) 바닥, 밑창; 발바닥; a. 유일한, 단 하나의; 혼자의
The sole of your foot or of a shoe or sock is the underneath surface of it.

lace[*]
[leis]

n. (구두 등의) 끈; 레이스; v. 끈으로 묶다
Laces are thin pieces of material that are put through special holes in some types of clothing, especially shoes.

rustle^{복습}
[rʌsl]

v. 바스락거리다; n. 바스락거리는 소리
When something thin and dry rustles or when you rustle it, it makes soft sounds as it moves.

serve^{복습}
[sə:rv]

v. (식당 등에서 음식을) 제공하다; 도움이 되다, 기여하다; n. (테니스 등에서) 서브
When you serve food and drink, you give people food and drink.

stomach^{복습}
[stʌ́mək]

n. 위(胃), 속; 복부, 배
Your stomach is the organ inside your body where food goes after it has been eaten and where it starts to be digested.

tighten^{복습}
[taitn]

v. (단단히) 조이다, 조여지다; (더) 팽팽해지다; 더 엄격하게 하다
If a part of your body tightens, the muscles in it become tense and stiff, for example, because you are angry or afraid.

announce^{복습}
[ənáuns]

v. (공공장소에서) 방송으로 알리다; 발표하다, 알리다 (announcement n. 발표)
An announcement is a statement made to the public or to the media that gives information about something that has happened or that will happen.

pressure[*]
[préʃər]

n. 압박, 스트레스; 압력; v. 강요하다; 압력을 가하다
If you are experiencing pressure, you feel that you must do a lot of tasks or make a lot of decisions in very little time, or that people expect a lot from you.

148

ladder ^{복습}
[lǽdər]

n. 사다리
A ladder is a piece of equipment used for climbing up something or down from something.

stare ^{복습}
[stɛər]

v. 빤히 쳐다보다, 응시하다; n. 빤히 쳐다보기, 응시
If you stare at someone or something, you look at them for a long time.

bubble*
[bʌbl]

v. 거품이 일다, 보글보글 끓다; n. 거품; 비누 방울
When a liquid bubbles, bubbles move in it, for example, because it is boiling or moving quickly.

soot
[sut]

n. 그을음, 검댕; v. 검댕으로 더럽히다
Soot is black powder which rises in the smoke from a fire and collects usually on the inside of chimneys.

sweat*
[swet]

n. 땀; 노력; v. 땀을 흘리다; 물기가 스며 나오다
Sweat is the salty colorless liquid which comes through your skin when you are hot, ill, or afraid.

obvious ^{복습}
[ábviəs]

a. 너무 빤한; 분명한, 명백한
If you describe something that someone says as obvious, you are being critical of it because you think it is unnecessary or shows lack of imagination.

strike ^{복습}
[straik]

v. (struck-struck/stricken) 갑자기 떠오르다; (세게) 치다, 부딪치다; n. 치기; 파업
If an idea or thought strikes you, it suddenly comes into your mind.

pumpkin ^{복습}
[pʌ́mpkin]

n. 호박
A pumpkin is a large, round, orange vegetable with a thick skin.

exclaim ^{복습}
[ikskléim]

v. 소리치다, 외치다
If you exclaim, you cry out suddenly in surprise, strong emotion, or pain.

giant ^{복습}
[dʒáiənt]

a. 거대한; 위대한; n. (이야기 속의) 거인
Something that is described as giant is much larger or more important than most others of its kind.

splash*
[splæʃ]

n. 첨벙 하는 소리; v. 첨벙거리다; 후두둑 떨어지다; (물 등을) 끼얹다
A splash is the sound made when something hits water or falls into it.

take turns

idiom ~을 교대로 하다
If two or more people take turns to do something, they do it one after the other several times, rather than doing it together.

creep*
[kri:p]

v. (crept-crept) 서서히 나타나다; 살금살금 움직이다; 기다
If an expression or color creeps into someone's face, it gradually appears there.

doubt ^{복습}
[daut]

n. 의심, 의혹; v. 확신하지 못하다, 의심하다 (self-doubt n. 자기 회의)
Self-doubt is a lack of confidence in yourself and your abilities.

verge
[vəːrdʒ]

n. 경계, 한계; 가장자리 (on the verge of idiom 막 ~하려는)
If you are on the verge of something, you are going to do it very soon or it is likely to happen or begin very soon.

descend*
[disénd]

v. 내려오다, 내려가다; (아래로) 경사지다
If you descend or if you descend a staircase, you move downward from a higher to a lower level.

fool*
[fu:l]

v. 속이다, 기만하다; n. 바보
If someone fools you, they deceive or trick you.

warn^{복습}
[wɔːrn]

v. 주의를 주다, 경고하다, 조심하라고 하다
If you warn someone about something such as a possible danger or problem, you tell them about it so that they are aware of it.

snap^{복습}
[snæp]

v. 딱딱거리다, 톡 쏘다; 탁 하고 움직이다; 사진을 찍다; n. 찰칵 하는 소리
If someone snaps at you, they speak to you in a sharp, unfriendly way.

shoulder to shoulder

idiom 서로 어깨를 맞대고; 힘을 모아, 협력하여
If people stand shoulder to shoulder, they stand side by side.

line up

idiom 한 줄로 서다
If people line up, they form a line, standing one behind the other or beside each other.

whisper^{복습}
[hwíspər]

v. 속삭이다, 소곤거리다, 귓속말을 하다; n. 속삭임, 소곤거리는 소리
When you whisper, you say something very quietly.

assure^{복습}
[əʃúər]

v. 장담하다, 확언하다; 확인하다
If you assure someone that something is true or will happen, you tell them that it is definitely true or will definitely happen, often in order to make them less worried.

apron*
[éiprən]

n. 앞치마
An apron is a piece of clothing that you put on over the front of your normal clothes and tie round your waist, especially when you are cooking.

splotch
[splatʃ]

v. 얼룩지게 하다, 더러워지게 하다; n. 얼룩
If something is splotched, it has large marks or spots that do not have a regular shape.

lumpy^{복습}
[lʌ́mpi]

a. 덩어리진, 울퉁불퉁한
Something that is lumpy contains or is covered with small solid pieces.

grayish
[gréiiʃ]

a. 회색을 띤
Grayish means slightly gray in color.

scoop
[sku:p]

v. (큰 숟갈 같은 것으로) 뜨다; 재빨리 들어올리다; n. 숟갈; 한 숟갈(의 양)
If you scoop something from a container, you remove it with something such as a spoon.

bowl**
[boul]

n. (우묵한) 그릇, 통; 한 그릇(의 양)
A bowl is a round container with a wide uncovered top.

polite^{복습}
[pəláit]

v. 예의 바른, 공손한, 정중한; 예의상의
Someone who is polite has good manners and behaves in a way that is socially correct and not rude to other people.

remove ^{복습}
[rimú:v]

v. 떼다; 없애다; 치우다; 옮기다; (옷 등을) 벗다
If you remove one thing from another thing, you take or extract the former from the latter.

count ^{복습}
[kaunt]

v. (수를) 세다; 계산에 넣다; n. (하나부터 순서대로 세는) 셈; 계산
If you count all the things in a group, you add them up in order to find how many there are.

point ^{복습}
[pɔint]

n. (뾰족한) 끝; 의견; 요점; (의도하는) 의미, 목적; 점수; v. 가리키다
The point of something such as a pin, needle, or knife is the thin, sharp end of it.

swirl ^{복습}
[swə:rl]

v. 빙빙 돌게 하다; 빙빙 돌다, 소용돌이치다; n. 소용돌이
If you swirl something liquid or flowing, or if it swirls, it moves round and round quickly.

muck
[mʌk]

n. 진흙, 진창; 배설물
Muck is dirt or some other unpleasant substance.

poke ^{복습}
[pouk]

v. (손가락 등으로) 쿡 찌르다; 쑥 내밀다; n. 찌르기, 쑤시기
If you poke someone or something, you quickly push them with your finger or with a sharp object.

solid ^{복습}
[sálid]

a. 단단한; 고체의; (다른 물질이 섞이지 않고) 순수한; n. 고체, 고형물
A substance that is solid is very hard or firm.

enthusiastic*
[inθù:ziǽstik]

a. 열렬한, 열광적인 (enthusiastically ad. 열광적으로)
If you are enthusiastic about something, you show how much you like or enjoy it by the way that you behave and talk.

swallow ^{복습}
[swálou]

v. (음식 등을) 삼키다; 마른침을 삼키다; n. [동물] 제비
If you swallow something, you cause it to go from your mouth down into your stomach.

opposite ^{복습}
[ápəzit]

n. 반대(되는 것); a. (정)반대의; 건너편의; 맞은편의
The opposite of someone or something is the person or thing that is most different from them.

stab*
[stæb]

v. (뾰족한 것으로) 찌르다; n. 찌르기; 찌르는 듯한 통증
If you stab something or stab at it, you push at it with your finger or with something pointed that you are holding.

gooey
[gú:i]

a. 부드럽고 끈적거리는
If you describe a food or other substance as gooey, you mean that it is very soft and sticky.

chew*
[ʧu:]

v. (음식을) 씹다
If you chew food or gum, you keep biting it and moving it around your mouth to taste the flavor of it. You do not swallow it.

describe ^{복습}
[diskráib]

v. (~이 어떠한지를) 말하다, 묘사하다
If you describe a person, object, event, or situation, you say what they are like or what happened.

bite ^{복습}
[bait]

n. 한 입; 물기; (짐승·곤충에게) 물린 상처; v. (이빨로) 물다, 베어 물다
A bite of food is the amount of food you take into your mouth when you bite it.

polka dot ^{복습}
[póulkə dàt]

n. 물방울무늬
Polka dot is a pattern consisting of an array of filled circles.

silly**
[síli]

a. 어리석은, 바보 같은; n. 바보
If you say that someone or something is silly, you mean that they are foolish, childish, or ridiculous.

stripe ^{복습}
[straip]

n. 줄무늬
A stripe is a long line which is a different color from the areas next to it.

outline*
[áutlàin]

n. 윤곽; v. 윤곽을 보여 주다; 개요를 서술하다
The outline of an object is the line which bounds its limits and shows its shape.

grab ^{복습}
[græb]

v. (와락·단단히) 붙잡다; ~을 잡으려고 하다; n. 와락 잡아채려고 함
If you grab something, you take it or pick it up suddenly and roughly.

roll ^{복습}
[roul]

v. 구르다, 굴러가다; 돌다, 돌아서다; n. 통, 두루마리; 명부, 명단
When something rolls or when you roll it, it moves along a surface, turning over many times.

sweaty
[swéti]

a. 땀투성이의, 땀에 젖은; 땀나게 하는
If parts of your body or your clothes are sweaty, they are soaked or covered with sweat.

sooty
[súti]

a. 그을음이 묻은; 거무튀튀한, 거무스름한
Something that is sooty is covered with soot, which is black powder from the smoke of a fire.

cheek ^{복습}
[ʧiːk]

n. 뺨, 볼
Your cheeks are the sides of your face below your eyes.

recipe**
[résəpi]

n. 조리법, 요리법; 방안
A recipe is a list of ingredients and a set of instructions that tell you how to cook something.

gaze*
[geiz]

v. (가만히) 응시하다, 바라보다; n. 응시, (눈여겨보는) 시선
If you gaze at someone or something, you look steadily at them for a long time.

lunchroom ^{복습}
[lánʧruːm]

n. (학교·회사 등의) 구내식당
A lunchroom is the room in a school or company where you buy and eat your lunch.

수고하셨습니다!

드디어 끝까지 다 읽으셨군요! 축하드립니다! 여러분은 이 책을 통해 총 22,390개의 단어를 읽으셨고, 800개 이상의 어휘와 표현들을 익히셨습니다. 이 책에 나온 어휘는 다른 원서를 읽을 때에도 빈번히 만날 수 있는 필수 어휘들입니다. 이 책을 읽었던 경험은 비슷한 수준의 다른 원서들을 읽을 때 큰 도움이 될 것입니다.

이제 자신의 상황에 맞게 원서를 반복해서 읽거나, 오디오북을 들어 볼 수 있습니다. 혹은 비슷한 수준의 다른 원서를 찾아 읽는 것도 좋습니다. 일단 원서를 완독한 뒤에 어떻게 계속 영어 공부를 이어갈 수 있을지, 도움말을 꼼꼼히 살펴보고 각자 상황에 맞게 적용해 보세요!

리딩(Reading)을 확실하게 다지고 싶다면? 반복해서 읽어 보세요!

리딩 실력을 탄탄하게 다지고 싶다면, 같은 원서를 2~3번 반복해서 읽을 것을 권합니다. 같은 책을 여러 번 읽으면 지루할 것 같지만, 꼭 그렇지도 않습니다. 반복해서 읽을 때 처음과 주안점을 다르게 두면, 전혀 다른 느낌으로 재미있게 읽을 수 있습니다.

처음 원서를 읽을 때는 생소한 단어들과 스토리로 인해 읽으면서 곧바로 이해하기가 매우 힘들 수 있습니다. 전체 맥락을 잡고 읽어도 약간 버거운 느낌이지요. 하지만 반복해서 읽기 시작하면 달라집니다. 일단 내용을 파악한 상황이기 때문에 문장 구조나 어휘의 활용에 더 집중하게 되고, 조금 더 깊이 있게 읽을 수 있습니다. 좋은 표현과 문장을 수집하고 메모할 만한 여유도 생기게 되지요. 어휘도 많이 익숙해졌기 때문에 리딩 속도에도 탄력이 붙습니다. 처음 읽을 때는 '내용'에서 재미를 느꼈다면, 반복해서 읽을 때에는 '영어'에서 재미를 느끼게 되는 것입니다. 따라서 리딩 실력을 더욱 확고하게 다지고자 한다면, 같은 책을 2~3회 정도 반복해서 읽을 것을 권해 드립니다.

리스닝(Listening) 실력을 늘리고 싶다면?
귀를 통해서 읽어 보세요!

많은 영어 학습자들이 '리스닝이 안 돼서 문제'라고 한탄합니다. 그리고 리스닝 실력을 늘리는 방법으로 무슨 뜻인지 몰라도 반복해서 듣는 '무작정 듣기'를 선택합니다. 하지만 뜻도 모르면서 무작정 듣는 일에는 엄청난 인내력이 필요합니다. 그래서 대부분 며칠 시도하다가 포기해 버리고 말지요.

따라서 모르는 내용을 무작정 듣는 것보다는 어느 정도 알고 있는 내용을 반복해서 듣는 것이 더 효과적인 듣기 방법입니다. 그리고 이런 방식의 듣기에 활용할 수 있는 가장 좋은 교재가 오디오북입니다.

리스닝 실력을 향상하고 싶다면, 이 책에서 제공하는 오디오북을 이용해서 듣는 연습을 해 보세요. 활용법은 간단합니다. 일단 책을 한 번 완독했다면, 오디오북을 통해 다시 들어 보는 것입니다. 휴대 기기에 넣어 시간이 날 때 틈틈이 듣는 것도 좋고, 책상에 앉아 눈으로는 텍스트를 보며 귀로 읽는 것도 좋습니다. 이미 읽었던 내용이라 이해하기가 훨씬 수월하고, 애매했던 발음들도 자연스럽게 교정할 수 있습니다. 또 성우의 목소리 연기를 듣다 보면 내용이 더욱 생동감 있게 다가와 이해도가 높아지는 효과도 거둘 수 있습니다.

반대로 듣기에 자신 있는 사람이라면, 책을 읽기 전에 처음부터 오디오북을 먼저 듣는 것도 좋은 방법입니다. 귀를 통해 책을 쭉 읽어 보고, 이후에 다시 눈으로 책을 읽으면서 잘 들리지 않았던 부분을 보충하는 것이지요.

중요한 것은 내용을 따라가면서, 내용에 푹 빠져서 반복해 들어야 한다는 것입니다. 이렇게 연습을 반복해서 눈으로 읽지 않은 책이라도 '귀를 통해' 읽을 수 있을 정도가 되면, 리스닝으로 고생하는 일은 거의 없을 것입니다.

왼쪽의 QR 코드를 스마트폰으로 인식하여
저자 루이스 새커가 직접 읽은 오디오북을 들어 보세요!
더불어 롱테일북스 홈페이지(www.longtailbooks.co.kr)에서도
오디오북 MP3 파일을 다운로드 받을 수 있습니다.

스피킹(Speaking)이 고민이라면? 소리 내어 읽어 보세요!

스피킹 역시 많은 학습자들이 고민하는 부분입니다. 스피킹이 고민이라면, 원서를 큰 소리로 읽는 낭독 훈련(Voice Reading)을 해 보세요!

'소리 내어 읽는 것이 말하기에 정말로 도움이 될까?'라고 의아한 생각이 들 수도 있습니다. 하지만 인간의 두뇌 입장에서 봤을 때, 성대 구조를 활용해서 '발화'한다는 점에서는 소리 내어 읽기와 말하기에 큰 차이가 없다고 합니다. 소리 내어 읽는 것은 '타인의 생각'을 전달하고, 직접 말하는 것은 '자신의 생각'을 전달한다는 차이가 있을 뿐, 머릿속에서 문장을 처리하고 조음기관(혀와 성대 등)을 움직여 의미를 만든다는 점에서 같은 과정인 것이지요. 따라서 소리 내어 읽는 연습을 꾸준히 하는 것은 스피킹 연습에 큰 도움이 됩니다.

소리 내어 읽기를 하는 방법은 간단합니다. 일단 오디오북을 들으면서 성우의 목소리를 최대한 따라 하며 같이 읽어 보세요. 발음뿐 아니라 억양, 어조, 느낌까지 완벽히 따라 한다고 생각하면서 소리 내어 읽습니다. 따라 읽는 것이 조금 익숙해지면, 옆의 누군가에게 이 책을 읽어 준다는 생각으로 소리 내어 계속 읽어 나갑니다. 한 번 눈과 귀로 읽었던 책이기 때문에 보다 수월하게 진행할 수 있고, 자연스럽게 어휘와 표현을 복습하는 효과도 거두게 됩니다. 또 이렇게 소리 내어 읽은 것을 녹음해서 들어 보면 스스로에게도 좋은 피드백이 됩니다.

최근 말하기가 강조되면서 소리 내어 읽기가 크게 각광을 받고 있기는 하지만, 그렇다고 소리 내어 읽기가 무조건 좋은 것만은 아닙니다. 책을 소리 내어 읽다 보면, 무의식적으로 속으로 발음을 하는 습관을 가지게 되어 리딩 속도 자체는 오히려 크게 떨어지는 현상이 발생할 수 있습니다. 따라서 빠른 리딩 속도가 중요한 수험생이나 상위권 학습자들에게는 소리 내어 읽기가 적절하지 않은 방법입니다. 효과가 좋다는 말만 믿고 무턱대고 따라 하기보다는 자신의 필요에 맞게 우선순위를 정하고 원서를 활용하는 것이 좋습니다.

라이팅(Writing)까지 욕심이 난다면? 요약하는 연습을 해 보세요!

원서를 라이팅 연습에 직접적으로 활용하는 데에는 한계가 있지만, 적절히 활용하면 원서도 유용한 라이팅 자료가 될 수 있습니다.

특히 책을 읽고 그 내용을 요약하는 연습은 큰 도움이 됩니다. 요약 훈련의 방식도 간단합니다. 원서를 읽고 그날 읽은 분량만큼 혹은 책을 다 읽고 전체 내용을 기반으로, 책 내용을 한번 요약하고 나의 느낌을 영어로 적어 보는 것입니다.

이때 그 책에 나왔던 단어와 표현을 최대한 활용하여 요약하는 것이 중요합니다. 영어 표현력은 결국 얼마나 다양한 어휘로 많은 표현을 해 보았느냐가 좌우하게 됩니다. 이런 면에서 내가 읽은 책을, 그 책에 나온 문장과 어휘로 다시 표현해 보는 것은 매우 효율적인 방법입니다. 책에 나온 어휘와 표현을 단순히 읽고 무슨 말인지 아는 정도가 아니라, 실제로 직접 활용해서 쓸 수 있을 만큼 확실하게 익히게 되는 것이지요. 여기에 첨삭까지 받을 수 있는 방법이 있다면 금상첨화입니다.

이러한 '표현하기' 연습은 스피킹 훈련에도 그대로 적용될 수 있습니다. 책을 읽고 그 내용을 3분 안에 다른 사람에게 영어로 말하는 연습을 해 보세요. 순발력과 표현력을 기르는 좋은 훈련이 될 것입니다.

꾸준히 원서를 읽고 싶다면? 뉴베리 수상작을 계속 읽어 보세요!

뉴베리 상이 세계 최고 권위의 아동 문학상인 만큼, 그 수상작들은 확실히 완성도를 검증받은 작품이라고 할 수 있습니다. 특히 '쉬운 어휘로 쓰인 깊이 있는 문장'으로 이루어졌다는 점이 영어 학습자들에게 큰 호응을 얻고 있습니다. 이렇게 '검증된 원서'를 꾸준히 읽는 것은 영어 실력 향상에 큰 도움이 됩니다.

아래에 수준별로 제시된 뉴베리 수상작 목록을 보며 적절한 책들을 찾아 계속 읽어 보세요. 꼭 뉴베리 수상작이 아니더라도 마음에 드는 작가의 다른 책을 읽어 보는 것 또한 아주 좋은 방법입니다.

•영어 초보자도 쉽게 읽을 만한 아주 쉬운 수준. 소리 내어 읽기에도 아주 적합.
Sarah, Plain and Tall*(Medal, 8,331단어), The Hundred Penny Box (Honor, 5,878단어), The Hundred Dresses*(Honor, 7,329단어), My Father's Dragon (Honor, 7,682단어), 26 Fairmount Avenue (Honor, 6,737단어)

• 중·고등학생 정도 영어 학습자라면 쉽게 읽을 수 있는 수준. 소리 내어 읽기에도 비교적 적합한 편.
Because of Winn-Dixie★(Honor, 22,123단어), What Jamie Saw (Honor, 17,203단어), Charlotte's Web (Honor, 31,938단어), Dear Mr. Henshaw (Medal, 18,145단어), Missing May (Medal, 17,509단어)

• 대학생 정도 영어 학습자라면 무난한 수준. 소리 내어 읽기에는 적합하지 않음.
Number The Stars★(Medal, 27,197단어), A Single Shard (Medal, 33,726단어), The Tale of Despereaux★(Medal, 32,375단어), Hatchet★(Medal, 42,328단어), Bridge to Terabithia (Medal, 32,888단어), A Fine White Dust (Honor, 19,022단어), Jennifer, Hecate, Macbeth, William McKinley and Me, Elizabeth (Honor, 23,266단어)

• 원서 완독 경험을 가진 학습자에게 적절한 수준. 소리 내어 읽기에는 적합하지 않음.
The Giver★(Medal, 43,617단어), From the Mixed-Up Files of Mrs. Basil E. Frankweiler (Medal, 30,906단어), The View from Saturday (Medal, 42,685단어), Holes★(Medal, 47,079단어), Criss Cross (Medal, 48,221단어), Walk Two Moons (Medal, 59,400단어), The Graveyard Book (Medal, 67,380단어)

뉴베리 수상작과 뉴베리 수상 작가의 좋은 작품을 엄선한 「뉴베리 컬렉션」에도 위 목록에 있는 도서 중 상당수가 포함될 예정입니다.

★「뉴베리 컬렉션」으로 이미 출간된 도서

어떤 책들이 출간되었는지 확인하려면, 지금 인터넷 서점에서
뉴베리 컬렉션을 검색해 보세요.

뉴베리 수상작을 동영상 강의로 만나 보세요!

영어원서 전문 동영상 강의 사이트 영서당(yseodang.com)에서는 뉴베리 컬렉션 『Wayside School』 시리즈, 『Holes』, 『Because of Winn-Dixie』, 『The Miraculous Journey of Edward Tulane』 등의 동영상 강의를 제공하고 있습니다. 뉴베리 수상작이라는 최고의 영어 교재와 EBS 출신 인기 강사가 만난 명강의! 지금 사이트를 방문해서 무료 샘플 강의를 들어 보세요!

'스피드 리딩 카페'를 통해 원서 읽기 습관을 길러 보세요!

일상에서 영어를 한마디도 쓰지 않는 비영어권 국가에서 살고 있는 우리가 영어 환경에 가장 쉽고, 편하고, 부담 없이 노출되는 방법은 바로 '영어원서 읽기'입니다. 언제 어디서든 원서를 붙잡고 읽기만 하면 곧바로 영어를 접하는 환경이 만들어지기 때문이지요. 하루에 20분씩만 꾸준히 읽는다면, 1년에 무려 120시간 동안 영어에 노출될 수 있습니다. 이러한 이유 때문에 영어 교육 전문가들이 영어원서 읽기를 추천하는 것이지요.

하지만 원서 읽기가 좋다는 것을 알아도 막상 꾸준히 읽는 것은 쉽지 않습니다. 그럴 때에는 13만 명 이상의 회원을 보유한 국내 최대 원서 읽기 동호회 〈스피드 리딩 카페〉(cafe.naver. com/readingtc)를 방문해 보세요.

원서별로 정리된 무료 PDF 단어장과 수준별 추천 원서 목록 등 유용한 자료는 물론, 뉴베리 수상작을 포함한 다양한 원서의 리뷰를 무료로 확인할 수 있습니다. 특히 함께 모여서 원서를 읽는 '북클럽'은 중간에 포기하지 않고 원서를 끝까지 읽는 습관을 기르는 데 큰 도움이 될 것입니다.

Chapters 1 & 2

1. B   But Wayside School is a thirty-story building, with one room on each floor. So for those who happen to be in Mrs. Jewls's class, way up on the thirtieth floor, they must be ready on first whoop.

2. C   Inside the principal's office, Mr. Kidswatter sat behind his enormous desk as he watched the clock. At the moment the second hand reached the number twelve, he shrieked into his microphone. "WHOOP-WHOOP! WHOOP-WHOOP! WHOOP-WHOOP!"

3. D   At the end of each day, Mr. Kidswatter would bang a giant gong with a large iron mallet. It was his favorite thing about being principal.

4. A   Todd had a sick feeling in his stomach, and it wasn't just the mac and cheese. In big letters, across the top of the blackboard, Mrs. Jewls had written: ULTIMATE TEST STARTS TOMORROW!

5. A   By the time Terrence got to school, he had already kicked ninety-nine different things.

6. C   "There's really one way to understand just how big a million is," said Mrs. Jewls. "And it's not by using arithmetic. We need to collect a million somethings."

7. D   "Mrs. Jewls!" called Rondi. "Terrence is cutting his toenail, right in class!" Some kids laughed. Some said, "Gross!"

Chapters 3 & 4

1. B   In truth, Kathy didn't know what D.J. was talking about. She just liked to argue. No matter what D.J. said, she always said the opposite. "Up!" D.J. said again. "Down!" Kathy instantly replied.

2. D   "Why are you crying?" asked Kathy. Dana showed her the book she'd been reading. *The Lost Giraffe.* "So?" asked Kathy. "The giraffe is lost," Dana sobbed.

3. C   "Stand on your head and drink a glass of water," Myron suggested. "Eat a lemon," said Jenny. "Hold your tongue while you say the Pledge of Allegiance," said Joy.

4. B   "I will count to five. And then you will fall into a deep, deep sleep." Dr. Pickle slowly counted. "One . . . two . . . BOO!" D.J. fell off the couch. "Well?" asked Dr. Pickle. D.J. got up. He waited a moment. "I think they're gone," he said.

5. B   Dana's picture showed a giraffe studying a map. She had drawn a large question mark over the giraffe's head. Her book report only had to be one page, but she had written two whole pages. *The Lost Giraffe* was her favorite book ever!

6. A   Mrs. Jewls slammed her hand on her desk. "Do you think paper clips grow on trees?" she asked. "I don't know," said Calvin. "I gave each one of you a paper clip at the beginning of the year. It was your responsibility to take care of it." She opened her desk drawer, took out her paper clip box, and opened it.

7. A   "I'm going to be a paper clip bender when I grow up," said Calvin. Mrs. Jewls smiled at Calvin. She had never been more proud of a student.

Chapters 5 & 6

1. C   Eric Ovens is kind, quiet, and 100 percent trustworthy. Sadly, that kind of person is often overlooked. But not today, he thought as he sat at his desk, patiently waiting for Mrs. Jewls to finish taking attendance. Today would be his day of glory! In his pocket was a plastic bag with eighty-three nail clippings!

2. B   Eric Fry had kept his hand in a fist all morning. Everyone thought he was just trying to be tough. Now he opened his fist and let forty nail clippings fall into the collection bucket.

3. B   "How did you get so many?" Mrs. Jewls asked him. Eric B. stopped dancing. "I went door-to-door, asking my neighbors," he said.

4. A   Eric Ovens wasn't the only one who had noticed that Kathy had become nice. Others, too, began to notice her odd behavior.

5. B   She entered the counselor's office. "That beard is really ugly. I guess your face must be even worse, huh?" Dr. Pickle didn't get angry. He just stroked his beard and said, "Very interesting." Kathy sniffed. "Smells like pickles," she commented. "Very interesting, indeed," the counselor said, and then asked her to sit down.

6. C   Unfortunately, there was no known cure for oppositosis. Other psychiatrists had tried to help their patients learn to be kind and think positively. Dr. Pickle knew that would never work on Kathy. He had his own theory, however. He could try to turn her opposites into double opposites.

7. C   "What's wrong with my homework?" asked Kathy. "It's written backward!" said Mrs. Jewls. "Every sentence. Every word. Every letter. Even the numbers are backward."

Chapters 7 & 8

1. A   And there, just outside his classroom door, was the most curious thing that Mac had ever seen. Next to the wall was some sort of giant closet. It hadn't been there before lunch. But that wasn't what made it curious. The closet was wrapped up in heavy chains, and locked with a giant padlock.

2. D   Mac sniffed, but all he could smell were chicken fingers. Behind the chains, and the steel bar, each door had its own lock. He could see two keyholes, one red and the other green. He put on his catcher's mask, just to be safe, and tried to open one door, then the other. They wouldn't budge.

3. D   Deedee read the signs aloud. "Keep back. Do not open doors. Danger." She tried one of the doors. "I think it's locked," said Mac. More kids made it up the stairs. Each one stopped at the closet, read the signs, and then tried to open the doors.

4. D   There were only twenty-eight kids in Mrs. Jewls's class, but Joy stretched both her arms high in the air. She fisgured it doubled her chance of being chosen. She waved them back and forth, and around in circles.

5. B   There was a safety railing around the edge, but it was for taller people. Mrs. Jewls was afraid her students could slip right under it.

6. A   "That one there is a cumulus cloud." Some of the students wrote it down in their notebooks. Bebe drew a picture of a sleeping giant. The cumulus cloud was his pillow. "And that's a cirrus cloud over there," said Mrs. Jewls. Bebe drew a picture of flying angels. Hundreds of white feathers had fallen from their wings and had swirled into a cloud.

7. C   "What kind of cloud is that one, Mrs. Jewls?" asked Benjamin. He was pointing at a dull, dark cloud way off in the distance. Mrs. Jewls gasped.

Chapters 9 & 10

1. D   Suddenly there was a loud BANG, and the next thing Louis knew, he was lying on the blacktop. He slowly sat up. He wiggled his fingers. He stuck out his tongue and moved it from side to side. He seemed to be okay. He stood up, still a little wobbly. Bits of green rubber were scattered across the playground. His air pump was on the other side of the dodgeball circle. The ball must have exploded from too much air, he realized.

2. A   He picked up a piece of green rubber. Then another. And another. There already weren't enough balls to go around. The school couldn't afford to lose another one. He'd have to sew it back together.

3. D   "The gong!" he remembered. He hurried to the principal's office, stuffing

cotton balls into his ears as he ran. "You're late, Louis," said Mr. Kidswatter, but Louis couldn't hear him.

4. B   "What if I pay for them?" asked Louis. Mr. Kidswatter laughed. "You? Where would you get that kind of money? Did you rob a bank?" "I have money," said Louis. "I've written some books about Wayside School." "And you got paid for that?" Mr. Kidswatter asked. Louis shrugged.

5. A   Everybody has a special talent. Bebe can draw. Joe can stand on his head and sing "Jingle Bells." But this story isn't about Bebe or Joe. It's about Dana. Dana can make funny faces.

6. A   Jenny, Leslie, and Dana liked Patches the best, because it was impossible to predict which way it would bounce.

7. B   Finally, Mr. Kidswatter turned away. "Cute kid," he said, and patted Dana on the head. He headed back to the building. Dana's face instantly popped back into place.

Chapters 11 & 12

1. A   In some classrooms, teachers choose the weekly spelling words. Not so in Mrs. Jewls's class. She lets her students pick.

2. C   This is why other teachers don't let their students choose the words. Mrs. Jewls couldn't spell *pistachios*. So she did what every teacher everywhere does in such situations. "That's an excellent word, Rondi," she said. "Would you like to come up and write it on the board?"

3. B   "And it hasn't been all bad," Mrs. Jewls continued. "We've been getting a whole lot more nail clippings." That was true. Ever since the Cloud of Doom appeared, everyone's fingernails and toenails had been growing a lot faster. They had to be clipped three or four times a week.

4. A   There were lots of rules in the library. No eating, no drinking, no yelling, no somersaults, and no hugging the walrus until after you checked out a book.

5. D   Some libraries have separate areas for fiction and nonfiction. Mrs. Surlaw didn't believe in that sort of thing. After all, who was she to decide what was true and what wasn't? She also didn't believe in alphabetical order. Her books were organized by number of pages. Skinny books were at one end of the library, and the fat ones were at the opposite end.

6. A   Jason had trouble squeezing his book back into place. By the time he did, he couldn't see Allison anywhere. He went from one end of the library to the other, searching between the aisles. When he finally saw her, she was hugging the walrus. That meant she had already checked out her book.

7. D   Still he couldn't be sure. Just to be safe, he chose a book with 510 pages. There was no way Allison chose a longer book than that! He started to bring it to Mrs. Surlaw. *But what if she did?* ··· Finally, Jason chose the last book, on the last shelf, at the very end of the library. He had to hold it with both hands as he lugged it to the checkout desk. The number on its last page was 999.

Chapters 13 & 14

1. B   Her umbrella was purple with green stripes. Or maybe it was green with purple stripes. She couldn't be sure. The whole thing was covered with yellow polka dots of various sizes. She liked listening to the raindrops bounce off of it. The harder it rained, the better the sound. She liked the feel of the smooth, curved wooden handle.

2. D   She could see inside the classroom windows as she went past them. Some of the kids waved at her. She couldn't wave back. She couldn't risk falling.

3. D   At the thirtieth floor, she could see her own desk, next to the window. The window was open. She closed her eyes, then jumped. A horn blared. When Sharie opened her eyes, she lay sprawled across the top of her desk.

4. D   Mr. K headed up the stairs. He wore a paper bag over his head. It was ten o'clock in the morning. All the little brats—as he liked to call them—should be in class, but he wore the paper bag just in case he encountered a stray one.

5. B   Mr. K removed the bag. "Yikes!" screamed Dr. P, throwing both his hands up in the air. He quickly regained his composure. "So, why did you come see me?" he asked as he rubbed his beard. Mr. K made an "uhhhh" noise as he pointed to his face. "Your face is stuck?" said Dr. P. Mr. K nodded.

6. A   He silently read to himself for a minute or two, then looked up and asked, "Did you have a pet when you were a child?" Mr. K nodded. Dr. P looked back at his book and read some more. "A cat?" Mr. K shook his head. "A dog?" He nodded.

7. C   Dr. P leaned back in his chair, with his hands behind his head. He felt very satisfied. It's not every day that he gets to help someone as important as Mr. K.

Chapters 15 & 16

1. A   For whatever reason, the longer everyone spent beneath the Cloud, the crabbier they got.

2. A   Maurecia, Joy, Deedee, and Ron were more than just best friends forever. Their friendship was so strong, they called themselves the "Unbreakables." Every morning, they met before school by the flagpole. They had a special four-handed handshake.

3. C   "You eat the heel first?" asked Maurecia. "So, what's wrong with that?" asked

Deedee. "It's gross!" said Ron. "You're supposed to start with the toes!"

4. C   Suddenly, her face filled with horror. "Oh, no!" she called out, and then pulled her hair with both hands. She didn't have her homework, or her history book! She turned and ran back into the building.

5. B   "Jason, is your book report ready yet?" Mrs. Jewls asked him each day he walked into class. "Sorry, Mrs. Jewls," he told her. "It's a really, really, really long book."

6. C   He wondered if anyone had ever read a book with 999 pages. Maybe the author never even finished writing it. Perhaps she quit after 300 pages, figuring nobody would ever get that far anyway.

7. B   The next day during recess, while everyone else played, Jason preferred to sit by himself with his book. He even liked the kissing parts, but had to keep glancing around, to make sure Allison and Rondi couldn't see what he was reading.

Chapters 17 & 18

1. C   Suddenly, the classroom door swung open and banged against the wall. Everyone turned to see Mr. Kidswatter. "Good morning, children," he said. They stared at him. He had never been inside their classroom before.

2. D   Mr. Kidswatter curled his fingers as he examined his nails. "No, I'm still using mine. Anyway, that's not why I'm here. I'm looking for a student to bang the gong on Friday. I figured I'd start at the top, and work my way down, until I found someone willing to—"

3. D   He strode toward Stephen, then placed his big hands on both sides of Stephen's desk and leaned over. "Be in my office on Friday, at two minutes before three o'clock!" he ordered. "You will get one, and only one, swing of the mallet, so you better not miss! You must hit the very center of the gong, at exactly three o'clock. Not a second early! Not a second late!! There are no second chances!!!" Stephen's right leg was shaking.

4. D   The second thing on Dr. Pickle's desk was a handheld mirror. Dr. Pickle checked his beard at least five times per day, to make sure it was trimmed just right.

5. C   Sometime later, a car horn blared. It sounded like there was an angry driver right behind him. Dr. Pickle woke up.

6. C   "This is very interesting," he said aloud. Clearly, the face shifts to whoever stares at it, he realized.

7. A   There is a reason it is called a bust. It was made of bronze, and felt heavy in his hand. He flipped the mirror over, and slammed Sigmund Freud down on top of it. The face shattered.

Chapters 19 & 20

1. D   Louis kneeled and then patted Stephen on the back. "Keep at it, Stephen," he encouraged. "Every day you'll get a little stronger. In a month, I bet you'll be able to do five push-downs." "A month!" exclaimed Deedee. "Stephen doesn't have a month." "He has to bang the gong on Friday!" explained Ron.

2. A   "YOU!!!" he boomed, pointing at Dana. Dana had a mosquito bite on her ankle, however, and at that moment, she bent down to scratch it. Stephen sat behind Dana.

3. A   Stephen wished Louis hadn't mentioned dropping the mallet on his toe. Now that was all he could think about.

4. B   "It got all bent in my backpack," he explained, too tired to think about what he was saying. "Unbent really. I guess the nine-hundred-and-ninety-nine-page book was too heavy for it." He showed Mrs. Jewls his paper clip, now unbent into a crooked line. Mrs. Jewls put her hand to her mouth, horrified. "You bent your paper clip?" she gasped. "Unbent," said Jason.

5. C   Mrs. Jewls turned the dial on the padlock as she quietly said the combination to herself. "Twenty-four . . . seventeen . . . six." The lock opened.

6. D   "Don't lock me in there, Mrs. Jewls!" he pleaded. "I didn't do it on purpose. The book was too heavy!"

7. D   Jason looked again. The closet wasn't completely empty, after all. There, in the back corner, was a small cardboard box. Mrs. Jewls picked it up. A price tag stuck to its side read, "89¢." Mrs. Jewls opened the top flap and removed a paper clip.

Chapters 21 & 22

1. B   For lunch, Miss Mush made pepper-only pizza. Stephen ate his slice, but did not remember eating it. His only clue was that he was very thirsty and his tongue and lips burned.

2. B   "If you didn't want to do it, why'd you raise your hand?" asked Mac. "Everyone else had their hands raised," Stephen explained. "I mean, I guess I was excited about it at the time, but now . . ." "You have cold feet," said Mrs. Jewls. "Yes!" exclaimed Stephen.

3. A   Mrs. Jewls's class always had music on Friday afternoons. "I'm sorry, we don't have musical instruments today," she announced. "They were sent out to be cleaned, and we haven't gotten them back yet."

4. A   Dana loudly blew her nose. Ron twiddled his lips. Mac puffed out his cheek and popped it with a flick of a finger. Calvin and Bebe whistled. Joe stood on his head and sang "Jingle Bells."

5. C   "This is Stephen," said Louis. "You chose him to bang the gong today?" "Him? Why would I choose him?" "Because you're the best principal ever!!!" said Louis. "Well, yes, that's true," said Mr. Kidswatter. "I'll do my best, sir," said Stephen. "That's what

worries me," said the principal. Louis handed Stephen two cotton balls.

6. D   He swung with all his might . . . and missed! He didn't just miss the red dot. He missed the gong.

7. D   "He did it!" shouted Mac. "Yay, Stephen!" yelled Jenny. Everyone in Mrs. Jewls's class whooped and hollered.

Chapters 23 & 24

1. D   "But it wasn't my fault, Mrs. Jewls," Joy complained. "It's the Cloud of Doom. It made me change my answers!" The door swung open and Bebe walked in more than fifteen minutes late. "Bebe, you need to put your name on the board under DISCIPLINE," Mrs. Jewls told her. "Don't blame me," said Bebe. "I left my house on time. The Cloud of Doom slowed me down." "Oh. Okay, then," said Mrs. Jewls. Leslie screamed. Mrs. Jewls turned. "Paul pulled my pigtails!" she accused. "Both at the same time!" "Paul, what do you have to say for yourself?" demanded Mrs. Jewls. Paul shrugged. "Cloud-a-Doom?" he tried.

2. A   Terrence crumpled his test into a ball and brought it to the front of the room, where he dropped it in the trash. He stood there a moment, staring at the trash basket.

3. D   "Enough!" shouted Mrs. Jewls. "I get it. It's hard with that cloud hanging over us all the time. But you can't blame it for everything that goes wrong. You have to take responsibility. And that means working extra hard so things don't go wrong! So, I'm doubling all your homework." "That's not fair!" complained Benjamin.

4. A   Above them, the dark cloud continued to churn, as it turned itself inside out again and again. No one hardly noticed it anymore, but it continued to grow larger and more powerful every day.

5. A   The test would last three days. Each day would have several minor tests, and one Major Event. On day one, the Major Event was a spelling bee.

6. C   Joy did a lot better when she could write the words. She was a master of fudge-squiggles. If she didn't know the letter, she made a fudge-squiggle that could have been any number of letters. Mrs. Jewls always gave her the benefit of the doubt.

7. D   Ron gave it his best shot. "W-h-u-m-p-h." "I'm sorry, Ron," said Mrs. Jewls. "There are two m's in whummph." "I win!" Maurecia exclaimed. The class cheered. Ron felt cheated. If it's a made-up word, who gets to decide the number of m's?

Chapters 25 & 26

1. D   Deedee only got to six. Jumping rope wasn't easy for her, since one leg was shorter than the other.

2. D   Joy lay sprawled across the blacktop. Sixes and sevens always tripped her up. Still, she had broken one hundred, and set a new world record! Her classmates rushed up to her. "You're the best ever!" said Kathy. "True," Joy agreed.

3. C   In the end, Maurecia whummphraaaapped on an easy one, two plus three. She was probably just tired. She had been jumping for almost an hour and had earned 211 points.

4. B   The students were worn out before they started. They'd already had the science crawl, right and left handwriting, animal imitations, upside-down singing, and blindfolded smelling.

5. A   This was Deedee's special talent. Deedee was a pretty fast runner on flat ground, but she was even faster going up and down stairs.

6. C   Miss Mush asked the question on the fifteenth floor. "How many points on a fork?" Deedee formed a picture of a fork in her mind, but when she tried to count the points, they blurred. "Three?" she tried. "I'm so sorry, Deedee," said Miss Mush. She didn't have to go all the way back down to the bottom, just to the tenth.

7. D   Maurecia was still inside the school. Photographers were snapping her picture, and she was being questioned by newspaper reporters from all around the world. When she finally came outside, she was carrying a giant trophy.

Chapters 27 & 28

1. C   Mrs. Jewls sat on the floor, turning the pages until she got to the index. The kachooga booping continued, making it difficult for her to concentrate.

2. B   Suddenly, a loud BOOM shook the classroom. The lights went out. This time nobody screamed. They were too scared.

3. B   Paper clips were strewn all over the floor. Benjamin and Rondi started picking them up. "Leave them!" shouted Mrs. Jewls. Now they knew it was serious.

4. D   A door had opened, and there was a light coming from inside a classroom. A teacher stood in the doorway. "Quick. Come inside," she beckoned. "You'll be safe here." She had a long fingernail on her pinky.

5. D   "Who's Mary Bopkins?" asked Mrs. Jewls. "Was she famous?" "Why?" asked Miss Zarves. "Does your class only study famous people? Do you think famous people are more important than people who aren't famous?" "But there isn't enough time to study everyone," said Mrs. Jewls. "We don't play favorites in my class," said Miss Zarves.

6. C   Myron stared helplessly at his stack. "I can't even read this," he complained. "I think it's Chinese." "Well, yes, a lot of people were born in China," said Miss Zarves.

7. A   Myron pressed hard on the scissors and snipped it off. "That does feel better,"

said Miss Zarves. "Thank you, Myron." Myron held the fingernail up in the air. Except, he was no longer standing in the front of the classroom. He was standing on the stairs, and everyone else from Mrs. Jewls's class lay sprawled across the staircase.

Chapters 29 & 30

1. C   Between the twenty-sixth and twenty-seventh floors, the stairs were completely blocked off by Mr. Kidswatter's enormous desk. They all had fun climbing over it, including Mrs. Jewls.

2. D   Louis, the yard teacher, shoveled snow off the roof. Among other things, the cloud had dumped huge amounts of snow. The playground sparkled white.

3. D   Recess was three hours today. The kids had been sent out to play, while the teachers were stuck with cleaning up the mess made by the storm.

4. B   Some cooks considered things like taste, or perhaps nutrition, when preparing a meal. For rainbow stew, color was all that mattered.

5. A   Mr. Kidswatter's voice came over the speaker. "GOOD MORNING, STUDENTS. IT'S ANOTHER GREAT DAY HERE AT—" There was the sound of paper rustling. "—WAYSIDE SCHOOL. FOR LUNCH TODAY, MISS MUSH WILL BE SERVING RAINBOW STEW. IT WILL BE THE GREATEST LUNCH EVER!" Fifteen floors beneath them, Miss Mush felt her stomach tighten. She too heard Mr. Kidswatter's morning announcement. Now the pressure was on.

6. D   "How about oranges?" suggested Mr. Pepperadder. "Too obvious," said Miss Mush.

7. C   "Sorry, it was supposed to be a bit more colorful," explained Miss Mush. "I don't know what went wrong." Joy was next. "Sorry," Miss Mush said again as she handed a bowl to Joy. "Sorry, Ron," she said. "Sorry, Deedee. Sorry, Joe. Sorry, John. Sorry, sorry, sorry . . . ."

WAYSIDE SCHOOL BENEATH THE CLOUD OF DOOM

1판 1쇄   2023년 3월 14일
1판 2쇄   2024년 2월 12일

지은이 Louis Sachar
기획 이수영
책임편집 김지혜 명채린
콘텐츠제작및감수 롱테일 교육 연구소
저작권 명채린
디자인 이혜련
마케팅 두잉글 사업 본부

기획 김승규
펴낸이 이수영
펴낸곳 (주)롱테일북스
출판등록 제2015-000191호
주소 04033 서울특별시 마포구 양화로 113, 3층 (서교동, 순흥빌딩)
전자메일 help@ltinc.net

ISBN 979-11-91343-04-5 14740